AF592683

Muslim Education and Learning During the Muslim Rule in India

(13th and 14th Centuries)

Muslim Education and Learning During the Muslim Rule in India

(13th and 14th Centuries)

By

Dr. Aneesa Iqbal Sabir

RANDOM

RANDOM PUBLICATIONS

NEW DELHI (INDIA)

Muslim Education and Learning During the Muslim Rule in India

ISBN 978-93-5111-465-9
© Reserved

All Rights Reserved. No Part of this book may be reproduced in any manner without written permission.

Published in 2014 in India by

RANDOM PUBLICATIONS

4376-A/4B, Gali Murari Lal, Ansari Road
NewDelhi-110 002
Phone : +9111-43580356, 011-23289044
E-mail : sales@randompublications.com
info@randompublications.com

Reprinted 2026

Type Setting by : Shah Computer Graphics, Delhi-110094

Dedicated to my dear husband

Late Dr. Iqbal Sabir

Foreword

The book entitled: Muslim Education and Learning During the Muslim Rule in India (thirteenth and fourteenth century: by Dr. Aneesa Iqbal is among those rare pieces of research that have significantly contributed to the comprehensive understanding of Medieval Indian History. The book is absolutely fascinating work and deals with varied aspects of the subject such as evolution of Muslim education, their institutions, content, pedagogy, learning, education among the royalty, establishment of *madarsas* and royal patronage to scholars and their contribution to Medieval Education System. Dr. Aneesa Iqbal has defined the history of all these aspects very meticulously wherein multiple and new empirical pieces of evidence have been brought in to illustrate the issues involved in imparting education at various levels. The author has used her narrative talents in this book to give the reader a very useful and broad sense of history of education.

It shall be immensely useful to future researchers/scholars working on the subject. The discussion is very enlightening and she has recast the contours of Muslim Education and Learning during the Delhi Sultanate with force and wit.

I have great pleasure in spotting these words after reading this book. The author is a very brilliant teacher and an excellent researcher. She is really capable of handing any serious research in her field and is known for raising very important academic questions that are essential for evolving any fresh perspective in the field of Medieval Indian History.

(Professor Rattan Lal Hangloo)

Preface

The thirteenth and fourteenth century are considered a period of metamorphosis with several facets and alterations in politico-cultural as well as socio-economic domain in the context of Indian subcontinent. During these centuries the Sultanate developed its foothold in India and also underwent crucial changes in its basic patterns. Muslim education and learning of Medieval period in India especially the Delhi Sultanate phase is a rather unexplored field of study.

Muslim education was a part of the medieval Islamic concept and was infused with the religious warp and weft of that period. Religion and education was closely intermixed. Religious ideas were the dominating factor in the system of education and learning. The authoritative basis of the Quran was a dominating factor. Thus the basic idea in Muslim education was typically religious but it was not against the study of rational, metaphysical or practical subjects.

This book entitled "Muslim Education and Learning During the Muslim Rule in India (13th and 14th Centuries)" makes an attempt to study and analyse the development and progress in Muslim Education and Learning during the 13th and 14th centuries. My research on Muslim education started with the 16th century (Mughal period) during my M. Phil. Course from Mumbai University (1997-2000). This interesting topic was suggested by my M.Phil. supervisor, my revered teacher Prof. Ruby Maloni (present head of the Department of History,

Mumbai University). Consequently the study of Muslim Education and Learning during the Sultanate period became of utmost importance for me to have an indepth understanding of the Muslim Education and learning during the Muslim period in India. Thus I commenced my Ph.D. Course in 2005 from A.M.U on 'Muslim Education and Learning during the Delhi Sultanate' and submitted it in 2008 under the supervison of my revered teacher, Mrs. Azra Alavi, former Reader, Women's College, AMU. I am publishing my Ph.D. research work as a book of reference for the study of Muslim Education and Learning during the Sultanate period.

The thrust on this subject is not just confined to the effort of the Delhi Sultans for the patronization of learning but also the other agencies through which education was imparted. Also the significant role the Sufi 'Mashaikh' have played in the promulgation of Muslim Education and Learning has been observed and presented in this work. Being an academician I felt it my 'academic responsibility' to bring into focus and emphasize on this rather neglected subject of study.

This research work forms a part of the historiography of medieval Indian history, the Delhi Sultanate (13th and 14th centuries) to be specific. I have attempted to juxtapose as well as analyse some of the notions and ideas already viewed by eminent historians on the topic under review. While in this humble attempt, it is hoped that I have been able to present some new vision and fresh knowledge into the study of Muslim Education and Learning during the Delhi Sultanate.

It has been my endeavour to follow a systematic methodology and an analytical approach. The exigency of this subject encouraged me to make use of contemporary Persian Sources of both early medieval and later medieval period, modern works in English (on religion, history and literature). Travellers accounts and Travelogues, archeology and archeological reports, modern works in Urdu, Encyclopedias and dictionaries, articles in English and Urdu. In this work the *Malfuzat* and *Tazkiras* have especially been used as a vital source pertaining to the subject under review.

This book forms the authentic reference to the students studying B.A and M.A. course namely medieval Indian History.

Acknowledgement

First and foremost I want to thank the Almighty for being very kind and generous towards me. I feel deeply obliged towards my Supervisor, my revered teacher, Mrs. Azra Alavi, Former-Reader in the Women's College, Department of History AMU, whose constant encouragement has kept me going from the beginning of selecting the subject of research to its completion.

I would like to record my thanks to Prof. Shahabuddin Iraqi, former chairman, Department of History AMU, for granting me the departmental fellowship for the year 2005-2006.

I am grateful to Prof. Tariq Ahmed, Prof. B.L Bhadhani, Prof S.L.H. Moini, Prof. Ali Athar, Prof. Afzal Khan, Prof. Fatima Bilgrami, for acceding to my requests during my research work.

I am also grateful to Prof. Dr. Rattan Lal Hangloor, the vice chancellor of Kalyani University, West Bengal for writting a Foreword of this book, inspite of this busy schedule.

Special thanks are due to my friends Dr. Neeta. M. Khandpekar, Dr. Mrs. S. Chandni Bi, and Mrs. Durdana. Thanks are due to Hasan Imam bhai, and Bhabi.

I specially thank my M. Phil Supervisor, my revered teacher, Prof. Ruby Maloni, Head, Department of History, University of Mumbai for her consistent moral support and incessant encouragement because of which I was able to complete my work.

I wish to thank Prof. Deepak S. Gaikwad, Prof. Department of History, University of Pune, for his constant encouragement.

I also acknowledge the courtesy and kindness of the staff members of the Seminar Library of our Department, the staff of Maulana Azad Library, especially its Persian, Urdu and Manuscripts sections, and the seminar libraries of the Departments of Islamic Studies and Sunni Theology also deserve my thanks. Thanks are also due to Mr. Atul Mehra and his team (Random Publications) for their effort to publish my book.

I would be failing in my duty if I don't mention my heartful thanks towards my husband, Late. Dr. Iqbal Sabir, Asmat Bano (sister-in-law) and my children Ijaz and Aisha. My parents, sisters and brother have always been a source of inspiration, who have always emanated positive energy and pushed me towards more hardwork, I wish to express my deep sense of love, affection and gratitude towards them.

(Dr. Aneesa Iqbal Sabir)

Contents

Chapter-VI

Introduction

The Arab conquest of Sind and Punjab in AD 712-13 marks the genesis of the medieval age in India. It introduced new political and cultural institutions. Then Sultan Mahmud of Ghazna and his successors also remained confined to Sindh and Punjab from the eight to the close of the 12th century A.D. but the Ghurian conquest of north India led to far-reaching socio-cultural and eco-political changes in the subcontinent. It paved the way for the emergence of an independent Sultanate that gradually brought almost the whole of the subcontinent under its sway. The relevant evidence contained in contemporary sources of information about patterns of political behaviour of the individual Sultans, suggests that it often made a great impact on the social, economic, cultural life under the Delhi Sultanate. The policies of certain Sultans drastically had an effect on society and culture resulting in socio-cultural changes.

The extent of development and progress in education and learning is a prerequisite for understanding the spirit of the age. It serves as a barometer to measure the prosperity of any historical period. The acquisition of knowledge and learning, both of religious subjects and rational sciences is considered as an act of religious merit in Islam.[1] There are numerous Quranic verses which stress the importance of learning and the high 'place' accorded to the learned by God. The Prophet

(PBUH) of Islam had decreed knowledge to be obligatory upon every male and female.[2] Reflecting the central importance of 'Ilm' the Prophet had said *'maut al alim, maut al alam'* i.e., the death of a scholar is the death of the whole universe.

Islam provided an open educational system since 7th century A.D. Region, caste, sex, creed, age remain no bar in Islam for the acquisition of knowledge.[3] Thus there arose a need for educational institutions which became known as *Madarsas.* History testifies the fact that wherever the Muslims settled down they built mosques and started *Madarsas* there in. Since the beginning of the first century, A.H. Muslims whether in Arabian countries, Africa, Iran, Turkey, Central Asia or South Asia, paid great attention to promote Islamic education and learning. The initial establishment of *Madarsas* took place in the fourth century A.H. but the process of imparting religious education had already initiated during the Prophet's time.

The Turkish conquest of India was not just substitution of the ruling class but it led to crucial changes in various facets of life. The resultant rise of Urban centres from Lahore to Lakhnauti exhibited a new culture in the 11th century.[4] Debul, Uchh, Multan and Lahore emerged as centres of learning. The Delhi Sultans established large number of *Madarsas* such as *Muizzi, Nasiriya, Alai, Hauz Khas* etc. S.M. Jaffar writes 'The Muslim Kings of Medieval India opened Schools and Colleges and established libraries in the various parts of their dominions, and sought to supplement their educational achievements by extensive patronage of literary worth from whatever sources it was evinced'.[5]

The traditions of Muslim Education as they had developed under the Abbasids of Baghdad were the nucleus of the Muslim Education system in India.[6] They were transplanted in India by the literati and scholars of Muslim lands after the Mongols had overrun them. Within a century of its foundation the Sultanate of Delhi came to occupy an unrivalled position in the sphere of Muslim Education. Barani informs us that during Alauddin Khalji's reign Delhi was a rendezvous of the intellectual Islamic world comprising of scholars of eminence in their field of study such as Imam Ghazzali, Imam Razi, Imam Abu Yusuf and Muhammad Shibani.[7]

Iqtidar Husain Siddiqui opines that individual scholars took to the teaching profession in preference to the state service because they equated it with worship.[8] Thus other than the *Maktabs* and *Madarsas* there were other institutions through which education was imparted during the period under review. The individual centres were the most popular medium of imparting knowledge. The observatories and astrolabes functioned as a medium to provide knowledge in astronomy,[9] hospitals functioned as institutes for the provision of medical knowledge[10] and *Karkhanas*[11] functioned as agencies to provide technical knowledge and develop industrial skill and craftsmanship. Shihab-u'ddin-al-Umari states that 'there are 70 *bimaristans* called *Darul Shifa* in Delhi alone. Further, he states that about 12,000 *tabibs* (physicians) got stipends from the state in the Sultanate.'[12]

The *Madarsas* in Medieval India had hardly any fixed syllabus[13] the review of subjects taught in the *Madarsas*, individual centres of education and study of rational sciences discussed in this work reveals the trends and objectives of learning during the Sultanate period. There is great debate about the liberal atmosphere created by the *Madarsas* in the country. Since the advent of the Khaljis to power towards the close of the thirteenth century, opposition to the study of *Ilm-i-Maqul* (rational sciences) ended and rationalist scholars were patronized by the Sultans.[14]

Equally important in this work is the study of the role performed by the royal court. Progress of intellectual culture resulted from royal patronage to the men of learning and talent. The Indo-Persian literature produced under the patronage of Sultans and members of ruling elite does not serve as a source of information alone but provides us with images of the past rammed in language which are of great significance. The present study examines this literature critically inorder to study the intellectual climate in medieval India during the Delhi Sultanate. This culture continued to exercise its influence on the society during Mughal period as well.

Moreover, the female segment of society has also been discussed. Since women in the royal household enjoyed a privileged position and, sometimes, could influence the course of political events, it becomes important to analyze her role.[15] An attempt has been made to explore the position held and role performed by women in the Sultanate of Delhi during the thirteenth and fourteenth century. A contribution of the Sufi *Mashaikh* in creating a congenial environment in the field of

Muslim Education and Learning has been highlighted in this work. The study of Sufi literature of the fourteenth century reveals that even some of the learned Sufis were influenced by rationalist thinkers. Generally Sufis are blamed by the orthodoxy for popularizing unauthentic traditions *(Zaif ahadith)*. But Shaikh Nizamuddin Auliya and Shaikh Sharafuddin Yahya took a critical approach to verify the authority of the hadith.[16]

Objective of the Study

This book proposes to study the following aspects and questions:

1. After the establishment of the Muslim rule in India in the 12th century, was the indigenous system of education accepted or did the rulers introduce their own educational system in India?
2. The aims and objectives of Muslim education, whether education was restricted and related only to religion and religious themes, and if so why?
3. Inspite of the absence of a separate and specific administrative department of education, was considerable patronage given for this purpose?
4. Did only the elite class acquire education, whether education was open and accessible to all the people?
5. This book also proposes to study the institutions through which education was imparted, to know what was the position of the teacher, the subjects of study, the curriculum and the methods adopted for teaching and learning.
6. One of the aims is also to examine whether teaching was commercialized and were examinations conducted in a structured manner.
7. Another purpose is to understand whether education and learning during the period under review had a positive impact on the socio-cultural status of the Indian sub-continent.
8. Restructuring the information presented by historians on the basis of a systematic research procedure.
9. Presentation of the history of Muslim education as a prerequisite for historical studies and investigations.

10. Presentation of a select bibliography of both primary and secondary sources, travelers accounts, archeology and archeological report.

Research Design and Methodology

A combination of authentic primary sources and secondary sources has been utilized for this work. The whole spectrum of issues subjected to detailed research include evolution of Muslim Education, types of institutions for the dissemination of knowledge, trends and objectives of education, personal education and learning of the Sultans, patronization of scholars by the Sultans, establishment of *Madarsas* and the contribution of Sufis for the spread of education and learning.

The chapters are written on the basis of available source material collected from different libraries namely the Seminar library of Department of History, Department. of Islamic Studies, Department of Theology, Maulana Azad Library (Urdu and Persian Section), AMU.

Hence an attempt has been made to place this work in a historical framework using critical analysis, comparative analysis, diagnostic methods. Critical analysis of issues in this research has enabled the facts to speak for themselves. Thus this work is not just a narration of history of education but a thorough study of Muslim education and learning during the Sultanate period (specifically thirteenth and fourteenth century).

Review of Primary Sources:

(A) Persian Sources

I. Early Medieval Period:

The *Tarikh-i-Sindh* often called *Tarikh-i-Masumi*, a history of Sind from the Muhammedan conquest to its annexation by Akbar This source has been utilized to reflect the annexation of Sind by Muhammad Qasim and the first Arab conquest in India.[17]

The *Tarikh-i-Fakhrud Din Mubarakshahi*,[18] This source has been used in the present work for information on development of education and learning during Iltutmish's reign.

Due to the Mongol invasion, there was an endless influx of scholars, saints and literate, and they were in many cases, actively engaged in cultural activities, our historians have not bothered to discuss their role in the society and culture of the newly conquered country. Minhaj was in India when saints like Shaikh Mu'in-u'd-din Chishti, Shaikh Qutb-u'd-din Bakhtiar Kaki, Shaikh Hamid-u'd-din Sufi Nagauri and many others flourished but he makes absolutely no mention of any of them.

The *Tabaqat-i-Nasiri* of Minhajuddin Siraj Juzjani has also been used. In 1949 another *Tabaqat-i-Nasiri* was published by Abdul Haiy Habibi of Qalandar. Though incomplete, it is from the beginning to twenty first *tabaqah.*[19] This volume has been utilized in the present work which provides ample information on the personal education of the Sultans right from Qutb-u'd-din Aibek to Nasiruddin Mahmud and the patronage provided to scholars by them. Its English translation with informatory notes and comments by Major H.G. Raverty was published in 1881 but it begins from the seventh *Tabaqah.*[20] It has also been utilized to acquire information on the education of Sultans in the present work.

The *Lubab-al-Albab* authored by Sadid-al-Din M.b. Imam Sharaf-al-Din Abi Tahir Yahya b. Tahir b. Uthman al-Aufi al-Bukhari, contains notices of nearly 300 poets written probably in 1221-22 A.D. This source has been utilized to show the poets patronized by the early Sultans of Delhi.[21]

With Barani a significant break through takes place. He occasionally refers to Sufis, scholars and other celebrities. He starts with the Balbani era and finishes with sixth regnal year of Firoz Shah Tughlaq. Thus Ziauddin Barani's *Tarikh-i-Firoz Shahi* has been extensively utilized in the present work for describing in detail the personal education of Balban's sons, the education and learning of the Khalji and Tughlaq Sultans. Barani has mentioned some scholars of the period under review but has not given details of them but whatever information is available of the scholars and their contribution has been fully utilized. Details of the *Madarsas* during the Firozi period have also been discussed.[22]

The observatories were agencies through which experiments were conducted in the field of astronomy. The hospital played a double role of health centres where remedy and treatment was provided and also medical training and lectures on medicine were conducted.

To explain the importance of hospitals and observatories as agencies of education the facsimile edition of the manuscript of the *Sirat-i-Firoz Shahi* has been utilized.[23]

Shams Siraj Afif's *Tarikh-i-Firoz Shahi*[24], a life sketch of Firoz Shah Tughlaq (1351-88 A.D.) also has been utilized in the present work to describe the development in technical and mechanical education. *Karkhanas* were the foci of several aspects of non-agricultural commodity production. They also acted as the technical training ground for apprentice craftsman, and thus can be looked as a base for vocational training and technical education.

The *Futuhat-i-Firoz Shahi*, is a brief account by Firoz Shah of his own edicts and ordinances, the abuses and evil practices abolished by him, the buildings erected and the works of public utility carried out in his reign.[25] The *Futuhat-i-Firoz Shahi*[26] has been utilized to discuss the Sultans deep interest in the establishment of new *madarsas* and the renovation and repair of old ones.

The *Futuh-us-Salatin* is an epic poem on the rulers of India from Ghaznavides to the date of composition i.e. 1349-50 A.D. composed by Isami. Isami's conversations in his *Futuh-us-Salatin*[27] have also been utilized to especially discuss the development of learning during the Shamsi period.

Amir Khusrau's poetic works constitute a veritable source of information for the social and cultural history of medieval India. Thus some of the verses of Amir Khusrau have been utilized to describe some situations and to enhance information on the development and progress in Muslim education and learning.

The *Qiran-us-Sadain* (The conjunction of the two Auspicious stars') is the first long poem in *Mathnavi* form composed by Khusrau at the request of Kaiqobad. The *Qiran-u's-Sa'dain*[28] edited by Maulvi Muhammad Ismail Meruti and Syed Hasan Barani has been referred to discuss the generosity shown to Amir Khusrau.

The *'Hasht Bihisht'* (the light Paradises) the fifth and the last poem of the *Khamsa*, an initiation of Nizami's *Haft Paikar*, was completed in 701 A.H. and contains 3,350 couplets.[29] The Hasht Bihisht[30] edited by Sulaiman Arif has been used to describe the merits of scholars.

The *Dewal Rani Khizr Khan* also known as *'Ashiqa'* or *'Ishqujiya'* is the story of Khizr Khan and Dewal Rani. The *Dewal Rani Khizr Khan*[31] edited by Rashid Ahmad Ansari has been referred to describe the high popularity and status that Delhi enjoyed and had become equivalent to Bukhara.

The *Ijaz-i-Khusravi* or *Rasail-ul-Ijaz* is a voluminous prose work of Amir Khusrau. The second volume[32] of this source has been used to describe the intellectual calibre of scholars.

II. Later Medieval Period

Sources of the later medieval period such as Badayunis *Muntakhab-ul-Tawarikh*, Abdul Baqi Nahavandi's *Maa'athir-i-Rahimi*, Nizamuddin Ahmad's *Tabaqat-i-Akbari*, Ferishta's *Tarikh-i-Ferishta*, Yahya Sirhindi's *Tarikh-i-Mubarakshahi*, Gulam Azad Bilgrami's *Ma'athir-ul-Kiram* have also been referred, to describe the picture of Muslim education and learning during the Sultanate period.

The *Muntakhab-ut Tawarikh* often called *Tarikh-i-Badauni* is a history of India from the time of Subuktigin A.H. 367/997-8 to A.H. 1004/ 1595-96 A.D., the fortieth year of Akbar's reign, followed by short biographies of contemporary sheikhs, scholars and physicians.[33] The first and second volume of the *Muntakhab-ut-Tawarikh*[34] edited by Kabiruddin Ahmad Ali have been utilized for extracting information on scholars and poets of the Sultanate period.

The *Mathir-i-Rahimi* authored by Abd al-Baqi Nahavandi is a life sketch of Abd al-Rahim Khan-i-Khanam The first volume of *Maathir-i-Rahimi*[35] edited by M. Hidayat Husain has been utilized to discuss the number of *madarsas* during Firoz Shah Tughlaq's reign.

The *Tabaqat-i-Akbari* authored by Nizam-ud-din Ahmad written in 1592-93 during Akbar's reign is the earliest of the general histories of India and the basis of subsequent works like the *Muntakhab-ut-Tawarikh* and *Gulshan-i-Ibrahimi* The 1875[36] publication has been utilized in this work to discuss the existence of hospitals during Firoz Shah's reign.

The *Gulshan-i-Ibrahimi* usually called *Tarikh-i-Ferishta* by M. Qasim Hindu Shah Artarabadi Firishtah as he calls himself in the *Gulshan-i-Ibrahimi*, is a general history. The Lucknow edition of the *Tarikh-i-Ferishta*, Vol. I and II[37] have been utilized in this work to discuss the personal education of the Sultans and royal patronage provided by them to scholars and their deep interest in building *madarsas*.

Yahya b. Ahmad Sirhindi dedicated his *Tarikh-i-Mubarakshahi* to Muizz-al-din Abul Fath Mubarak Shah (of the Saiyid dynasty) The edition of M. Hidayat Husain[38] published by the Asiatic Society of Bengal has been referred to discuss the number of hospitals during Firoz Shah Tughlaq's reign.

The *Maathir-al-Kiram* authored by Mir Ghulam 'Ali' "Azad" Bilgrami was completed in 1752-53 A.D. The *Maathir al-Kiram* published from Agra has been referred to discuss the men of learning of the Sultanate period.[39]

III. Tazkiras

The *Akhbar-ul-Akhyar* is a famous *Tazkira* authored by Shaikh Abdul Haq Muhaddith Dehlavi (of. 1642) in 1590 A.D. It is the most complete and reliable biography of Indian Sufis of the four main orders -*Chishtis*, *Qadiris*, *Shattaris* and *Suhrawardis* which flourished between the thirteenth to sixteenth century.

The Delhi edition of the *Akhbar-ul-Akhyar*[40] published in 1332 A.H. has been extensively referred to in this work to discuss the scholars of the Sultanate period, their subjects of study and their genuine interest in the development of education and learning.

The *Siyar-ul-Auliya* by Mir Khurd is a biography of the lives of *Chishti* saints written in the reign of Firoz Shah Tughlaq (1357-88 A.D.) The *Siyar-ul-Auliya*[41] published from Delhi in 1885 A.D. has been referred to discuss subjects of study of the sufi scholars and their love for learning.

The *Tazkira-i-Ulama-i-Hind*,[42] is a description of *ulama* arranged in alphabetical order. It has been extensively utilized to discuss the subjects of study of the scholars and the structure of their scholarship.

The *Siyar-ul-Arifin* is a biography devoted to the lives of 14 *Chishti* saints completed in Humayun's reign.[43] The *Siyar-ul-Arifin*[44] has been referred to discuss the scholarship of some scholars of the Sultanate period.

IV. Malfuzat

The *Siraj-ul-Hidaya* is the famous collection of *Makhdum-i-Jahaniyan's malfuzat* compiled by Ahmad Barani The *Siraj-ul-Hidaya*[45] edited by Sajjad Husain has been utilized to discuss the subjects studied by *Makhdum Jahanian* and to describe his scholarly traits.

The *Fawaid-ul-Fuad* are the *malfuzat* (table talks) collected by Amir Hasan Sijzi. The *Fawaid-ul-Fuad* published from Nawal Kishore[46] has been referred to discuss the subjects studied by Shaikh Nizam-ud-din Auliya. Also the subjects discussed and the reference books studied during the period under review.

The *Khair-ul-Majalis* is a record of one hundred mystic gatherings of Shaikh Nasir-ud-din Chiragh-i-Delhi. The *Khair-ul-Majalis*[47] edited by K.A. Nizami has been referred to in this work to discuss the subjects of study and the books studied by scholars during the Sultanate period.

Review of Pre-existing Literature on Muslim Education and Learning

S.M. Jaffar's book *Education in Muslim India*[48] has discussed education of the complete medieval period i.e. the Sultanate and Mughal period both, in which emphasis has been laid on the personal education of the Sultans and the Mughal emperors but not much has been discussed on the patronage provided to scholars. The curriculum has been discussed very briefly and no attention has been paid to the subjects of study, the reference books for different subject and the immense amount of development in Muslim Education and learning. The syllabus has not been clearly discussed.

N.N. Law's '*Promotion of Learning in India* During Muhammadan Rule[49] (by Muhammadans) deals with the promotion of learning and not to the quality of learning, earnest efforts of the Muhammedan emperors, chiefs and private individuals of India to promote learning and diffuse education among the people of this country. Its more a dynastic history as Law writes 'The Present work is a history of such efforts and an attempt to show in a connected narrative that the long roll of Muslim rulers, emperors and invaders from Mahmud downwards were not altogether inattentive to the literary interests of the people, and that private individuals also were not quite inactive in this direction.'

Some modern scholars have also written in Urdu some information on Muslim education and learning. Syed Abdul Hayy in his *'Islami Ulum wa Funun Hindustan Mein*[50] has attempted to discuss the syllabus of the Sultanate period (infact 13-18 century A.D.) but which according to K.A. Nizami is incomplete and he gives another list of books in his *Hayat-i-Shaikh Abdul Haq Muhaddith.*[51] Gilani, Manazir Husain in his *Hindustan Mein Musalmanon ka Nizam Talim wa Tarbiyat* was the first to discuss the syllabus of the Sultanate period and gives some information of the same.[52]

The *Bazm-i-Mamluqia*[53] describes the personal education of the Sultan of the Slave dynasty starting from Qutubuddin Aibek to Kaiqobad (i.e. 1206-1290 A.D.). It contains a detailed description of the scholars patronized by these Sultans and detailed description on the propagation of Islam in India.

The *'Salatin-i-Dehli kay Mazhabi Rujhanat*[54] of K.A. Nizami discussed in detail the personal education of all the Sultans of the Slave, Khalji, Tughlaq and Lodi dynasty and the scholars patronized by them. It has been utilized in this work. But its a book in which the main theme is the religious leanings of the Delhi sultans.

The *Aab-i-Kauthar*[55] of Shaikh Muhammad Ikram discusses the dynastic history from the coming of Muslims till the Lodi period in which he has given brief information on the patronization of scholars by the Sultans and the eventual development in learning and literature.

The *Fuqaha-i-Hind*[56] is a description of *Fuqaha* (jurists) and *ulama* (scholars) from 622 A.D.-1397 A.D. It also discusses the religious leanings and intellectual stature of the Sultans of Delhi and the position of the jurists in the Sultanate.

Abdul Majid Salik's *Muslim Saqafat Hindustan Mein'*[57] covers the cultural history of the whole sub-continent from ancient time. The fourth chapter is devoted to *ulum wa funun* (science and arts). The first fasl of the fourth chapter is about *'ilm Aur Taalim ki sarparasti'* where a brief survey has been of the ruler's interest and patronization of education and learning from Mahmud Ghaznavi to Firuz Shah Tughlaq.

Abdul Hasanat Nadvi's *Hindustan ki Qadeem Islami Darsgahien,*[58] is a very informative work providing details about the centres of education and learning in India during the medieval period. The author sheds light on different *madarsas* in the sub-continent, activities of ulama and scholars and discusses the syllabus in the same way as Syed Abdul Hayy has discussed in his "*Islami Ulum wa Funun Hindustan Mein*'.

Said Ahmad Rafiq's '*Islami Nizam-i-Talim*[59] contains information about education and learning. The third chapter is entitled as "Educational developments during the time of Sultans of Delhi" in which brief information is provided on the subjects of study and whatever syllabus has been discussed is the same information, which has been given by Syed Abdul Hayy in '*Islami Ulum wa Funun Hindustan Mein*' and Abdul Hasanat Nadvi in '*Hindustan ki Qadeem Islami Darsgahein.*'

The publication of 2007 on education by Suresh .C. Ghosh entitled 'History of Education in India'[60] is divided into three parts. Part I discusses, Education in Ancient India, 3000 C – 1192 A.D., Part II discusses, Education in Medieval India, 1192 A.D. – 1757 A.D. Part III discusses Education in Modern India, 1757-1999. The initial part of Part II discusses my period of study i.e. Education in Sultanate period from pages 143-180 which serves the purpose of only being a narrative with no references and footnoting.

The hagiological literature plays a significant role in providing information on the political, economic, social, cultural scenario of any age. The hagiological literature comprising the *Malfuzat* and *Tazkira* of the Sultanate period is very informative as regards the social and cultural life of the period in review. The *Malfuzat* and *Takira* which provide a mine of information on the social and cultural life of the people have been completely ignored by many secondary sources. N.N. Law, S.M. Jaffar, and some Urdu writers such as Abdul Majid Salik, Abdul Hasanat Nadvi and Rafiq Said Ahmad, have completely avoided the use of *Malfuzat* and *Tazkira* as a source to provide information on Muslim eduction and learning.

This book entitled "*Muslim Education and Learning during the Delhi Sultanate (13th and 14th Centuries")* is different from other secondary works because I have fully and extensively made use of the *Malfuzat* and *Tazkira* as a primary source to acquire information on the scholars attitude, lifestyle, subjects of study, reference books and the resulting development in Muslim education and learning.

Thus, the *malfuzat* of the medieval saints have a great value in understanding an important segment of medieval society. *Malfuz* writing is the greatest literary invention of medieval India[61] which if properly utilized can give information on the medieval society. The *malfuzat* such as *Fawaid u'l Fu'ad* and the *Khair-u'l-Majalis* and the Tazkiras such as *Siyar-u'l-Auliya* and *Akbar-u'l-Akhyar* have been extensively utilized to create a proper picture of the scholars and Sufis and their contribution towards education and learning. Through the thorough study of the above mentioned *malfuzat* and *tazkiras* it has been possible to discuss some very crucial aspects of Muslim education and learning. With the help of these sources a detailed discussion of the curriculum, subjects of study, position of the teachers, relationship between the teacher and students, the method of teaching, the agencies for the provision of education has been possible.

Some modern works in Arabic such as the *Nuzhat-ul-Khawatir* have also been used to showcase the capabilities of the scholars and their contribution towards Muslim education and learning. As far as possible many Urdu and English modern works have been studied for this work.

References

1 *Azizuddin Husain, S.M. (ed.) Madrasa Education in India,* (11th to 21st Century) New Delhi,Kanishka Publishers, 2005, p. 1.

2 Bhargava Meena and Dutta Kalyani, *Women, Education and Politics,* New Delhi, OUP, 2005, p. 1.

3 Azizuddin Husain, S.M., Op. Cit. P. 2

4 Ibid. P. 2

5 Nizami, K.A. Development of the Muslim Educational System in Medieval India, Islamic Culture, Vol LXX, No. 4. Hyderabad, Oct. 1996, p. 27.

6 Jaffar, S.M. *Education in Muslim India,* Delhi. Idarah-i-Adabiyat-i-Delhi, 1936, p. 9.

7 Barani, Ziauddin, *Tarikh-i-Firozshahi,* ed. Sir Syed Ahmad Khan, Sir Syed Academy, AMU, 2005. pp. 353-354.

8 Siddiqui, Iqtidar Husain, *Delhi Sultanate–Urbanization and Social Change,* New Delhi, Viva-Book, 2009, p. 42.

9 Ibid, p. 126.

10 For details see, Siddiqui, Iqtidar Husain, *Composite Culture Under the Sultanate of Delhi*, New Delhi, Primus Book, 2012, pp. 49-57.
11 Jaffar S.M. Op.cit, p. 201-203.
12 Shah-a-buddin Al-Umari, *Masalik-ul-Absar-Fi-Mumalik-ul-Amsar*, eng. trans. by Otto Spies, Aligarh, Dept. of History, 1943, p. 116.
13 Jaffar, S.M, Op. Cit, pp. 21-22
14 Siddiqui, Iqtidar Husain, *Medieval India: Essays in Intellectual Thought and Culture*, New Delhi, Manohar Publishers, 2003, pp. 86-87.
15 *Composite culture under the Sultanate of Delhi*, Op.Cit, p. 151.
16 *Delhi Sultanate, Urbanization and Social Changes*, Op. cit, p. 148.
17. Syed, Muhammad Masum, *Tarikh-i-Masumi*, Bombay, Matba-i-Qayyama, 1938.
18. Fakhr Mudabbir, *Tarikh-i-Fakhr'd-Din Mubarakshah*, ed. E. Denison Ross, London, R.A.S. Forlong Fund.
19. Juzjani, Minhaj-i-Siraj, *Tabaqat-i-Nasiri*, Vol. I, ed. Habibi Abdul Haiy, Kabul, Historical Society of Afghanistan, 1963.
20. Raverty H.G., *Tabaqat-i-Nasiri*, Vol. I, New Delhi, Oriental Books Reprint Corporation, 1970.
21. Awfi, *Lubab-ul-Albab*, Isfahan, Ibn sina Kitab Khana, 1333 Shamsi.
22. *Tarikh-i-Firoz Shahi* is a history of the Sultans of Delhi from Balban to Firoz Shah's sixth regional year A.H. 758/1357 A.D. forming a continuation of the Tabaqat-i-Nasiri. See: Storey C.A. Vol. I, Part I, p. 507.
23. Anonymous, *Sirat-i-Firoz Shahi* (Fascimile edition), Patna, Khudabaksh Oriental Library, 1999.
24. Afif, Shams Siraj, *Tarikh-i-Firoz Shahi*, ed. M. Wilayat Husain, Calcutta, A.S.B., 1891.
25. Storey C.A., *Persial Literature*, Vol. I, Part I, London, Luzac & Company, 1970 p. 509.
26. Tughlaq, Firoz Shah, *Futuhat-i-Firoz Shahi* ed. Abdur Rashid, Aligarh, Department of History, 1954.
27. Isami, *Futuh-us-Salatin*, ed. Usha, A.S., Madras, University of Madras, 1948.
28. Amir Khusrau, *Qiran-us-sadain*, ed. By Maulvi Muhammad Ismail Meruti and Syed Hasan Barani, Aligarh, Institute Aligarh College Press, 1918.
29. Mirza, Mohammad Wahid, *The Life and Works of Amir Khusrau*, Delhi, Idarah-i-Adabyat-i-Delli, rep. 1974 p. 201.
30. Khusrau Amir, *Hasht Bihisht* ed. Sulaiman Arif, Aligarh, Institute Press, 1918.

31. Khusrau, Amir, *Dewal Rani Khizr Khan* (Ashiqah) ed. By Rashid Ahmad Ansari, Aligarh, Madrasat-ul-um, 1917.
32. Khusrau, Amir, *Ijaz-i-Khusrawi*, Vol. II, Lucknow, Nawal Kishore, 1868.
33. C.A. Storey, Vol. I, Part I, p. 439.
34. Badauni, Abdul Qadir, *Muntakhab-ut Tawarikh*, Vol. I, ed. Kabiruddin Ahmad Ali, Calcutta, A.S.B., 1868. Badauni, Abdul Qadir, Muntakhab-ut Tawarikh, Vol. II, ed. Kabiruddin Ahmad Ali, Calcutta, A.S.B., 1869.
35. Nahavandi, Abdul Baqi, Ma'*athir-i-Rahimi*, Vol. I, ed. M. Hidayat Husain, Calcutta, A.S.B., 1924.
36. Nizamuddin Ahmad, *Tabaqat-i-Akbari*, Lucknow, Nawal Kishore, 1875.
37. Ferishta, Muhammad Qasim, *Tarikh-i-Ferishta*, Vol. I & II, Lucknow, Newal Kishore, 1864-65.
38. Sirhindi, Yahya bin Ahmad bin Abdullah, *Tarikh-i-Mubarakshahi*, ed. Hidayat Husain, Calcutta, A.S.B., 1931.
39. Bilgrami, Ghulam Ali Azad, *Maathir-ul-Kiram*, Agra Mufid Am Press, 1910.
40. Dehlavi, Shaikh Abdul Haq Muhaddith, *Akhbar-ul-Akhyar*, Delhi, Matba-i-Mujtabai, 1332, A.H.
41. Mir Khurd, *Siyar-ul-Auliya*, Delhi, Matba-i-Muhitbb-i-Hind, 1302 A.H., 1885 A.D.
42. Rahman Ali, *Tazkira-ulama-i-Hind*, Lucknow, Nawal Kishore, 914.
43. Storey, C.A., Vol. I, Part II, p. 971.
44. Jamali, *Siyar-ul-Arifin*, Urdu translation by Ghulam Ahmad, Moradabad, 1319 A.H.
45. Sajjad Husain ed, *Siraj-ul-Hidaya*, Delhi, Indian Council of Historical Research, 1983.
46. Sijzi, Amir Hasan, *Fawaid-ul-Fuad*, Lucknow, Nawal Kishore, 1894.
47. Hamid Qalandar, *Khair-ul-Majalis*, ed. Nizami, K.A. Aligarh, Dept. of History, 1959.
48. Jaffar, SM., *Education in Muslim India*, Delhi, Idarah-i-Adabyat-i-Delhi, rept. 1972.
49. Law, N.N., *Promotion of Learning in India During Muhammadan Rule (by Muhammadans)*, Delhi, Idarah-i-Adabyat-i-Delhi, p. viii.
50. Syed, Abdul Hayy, *Islami Ulum wa Funun Hindustan mein*, Azamgarh, Darul Musannifin, 1969.
51. Nizami, K.A., *Hayat-i-Shaikh Abdul Haq Muhaddith Dehlavi*, Delhi, Nadwat-ul-Musannifin. 1953.

52. Gilani, Manazir Husain, *Hindustan Mein Musalmanon ka Nizam Talim wa Tarbiyat*, Delhi, Nadwat-ut-Musannifin, 1987.
53. Abdur Rehman, Syed Sabahuddin, *Bazm Mamluqia*, Azamgarh, Matba-i-Marif, 1959.
54. Nizami, K.A., *Salatin-i-Dehli kay Mazhabi Rujhanat* Delhi, Nadwat-ul-Musannifin, 1981.
55. Shaikh, M., Ikram, *Aab-i-Kauthar*, Delhi, Taj Company, 1987.
56. Bhatti, Muhammad Ishaq, *Fuqah-i-Hind*, Vol. I, Lahore, Idarah-i-Saqafat Islamia, 1974.
57. Salik, Abdul Majid, *Muslim Saqafat Hindustan Meini*, Lahore, Idarah-i-Saqafat-i-Islamia, n.d.
58. Nadvi, Abdul Hasanat, *Hindustan ki Qadeem Islami Darsgahein*, Azamgarh, Darul Musannifin, 1971.
59. Rafiq, Said Ahmad, *Islami Nizam-i-Talim*, Karachi, Idarah-i-Tasnif wa Talif, n.d.
60. Ghosh, Suresh, C., *History of Education in India*, New Delhi, Rawat Publications, 2007.
61. Nizami, K.A., *On History and Historians of Medieval India*, New Delhi, Munshiram Manohar Lal, 1983, p. 163.

Chapter-I

Evolution of Muslim Education

Islam ushered the advent of the age of enlightenment compared to the age of ignorance that preceded it. It has always laid great stress to the acquisition and extension of knowledge. The *Surah-i-Iqra*[1] the first revealed version of the *Quran*, opens with the injunction addressed to the Prophet (PBUH) to 'read'. There are numerous other Quranic verses, which stress the importance of learning and the high 'place' which those possessed of knowledge are accorded by God. The Prophet (PBUH) of Islam had decreed knowledge to be obligatory upon every male and female. *'Ilm'* – (knowledge) is the core of Islam. The ideal Muslim spends his life in pursuit of knowledge, as the Prophet suggested going to China to seek it. Reflecting the central importance of *Ilm* the Prophet had said '*mawt-al-alim, mawt-al-alam*" i.e. 'the death of a scholar is the death of the universe.'

Education and learning are deeply associated with Islam and Muslims. There are several Quranic verses and Prophetic traditions in this regard. The *Quran* exhorts Muslims to make continuous efforts to receive education. It also teaches them to invoke the almighty for the enhancement of their knowledge.

1 *Quran*, 96:1

وَقُل رَّبِّ زِدنِى عِلمًا[2]

"(And say, O' my Allah enhance my knowledge)"

The *Quran* and the *Hadith* are the fountainhead of all that is Islamic in whatever domain it might be.

It is a historical fact that wherever Muslims settled down they built mosques and started *madarsas* there in. Since the beginning of the first century A.H. Muslims, whether in Arabian countries, Africa, Iran, Turkey, Central Asia or South Asia, paid special attention to promote Islamic education and learning. Although historians and scholars are of the view that initial establishment of *madarsas* took place in the fourth century A.H. but infact the process of imparting religious education, had already been initiated during the Prophets time. The *Qaba mosque* (*masjid-i-Qaba*), *the House of Arqam* (*Dar-i-Arqam*) the Prophet's mosque (*masjid-i-Nabawi*) and its terrace (Suffah) were the best known places for imparting education and learning in those days.[3]

It was during the time of Prophet (PBUH) of Islam's immediate successors i.e. *Khulafa-i-Rashidin* that material prosperity and a keen and brisk intellectual activity went hand in hand; the Arab's

'Enthusiasm for learning was so great and universal that it seemed as if all the world from the Caliph down to the humblest citizen suddenly became students, or at least patrons of literature. In quest of knowledge, men travelled over three continents and returned home, like bees laden with honey, to impart the precious stores which they had accumulated to crowds of eager disciples, and to compile with incredible industry those works of encyclopedic range and erudition from which modern science, in the widest sense of the world, has desired for more than is generally supposed'.[4]

Within the first four centuries of the advent of Islam, there had

2 *Quran*, 20:114

3 For details see: Mubarakpuri, Qazi Atahar, *Khair-ul-Quran ki Darsgahein Aur unka Nizam-i-Talim-wa-Tarbiyat*, (Shaikhul Hind Academy, Dar-ul-ulum), Deoband, 1995, pp.23-50.

4 Nicholson, R.A. *Literary History of the Arabs,* England, Cambridge University Press, 1930, p.281.

developed throughout the Islamic world Muslim scholarship of a high order, in traditional (*Manqulat*) as well as rational (*Maqulaat*) sciences, so much so that the Muslim literati which flourished at such centres of learning as Mecca, Madina, Baghdad, Basra, Kufa, Damascus Constantinople, Cairo, Granada, Cordova, Isfahan, Shiraz, Tabrez, Herat, Nishapur, Samarqand etc0. have been considered pioneers who lighted the path of knowledge. It were these savants who not only saved the intellectual heritage of the ancient Greeks and Orientals from extinction, but also developed it further by their original contributions and were responsible for the dissemination of knowledge in every nook and corner of the world including Europe.

Early Methods of Education:

A sweeping survey of Muslim education shows that from the early days of Islam to the end of Umayyad period the main subjects of study continued to be the study of the holy *Quran*, the Prophet's traditions, the Arabic language, poetry, and mathematics. The method of teaching during those days was chiefly oral transmission of the lectures, direct from the teacher to his pupil. Emphasis was laid on the authencity of the transmitters. Only those schools were considered authorities who had received their education through a trustworthy chain of transmitters. While delivering lectures every teacher had to repeat the chain of authorities from whom he had received the particular information. The tree of these authorities was carefully preserved and transmitted from father to son. When in the Umayyad period the system of dictating lectures was introduced, mention of the authorities remained part and parcel of the compilations. Both methods, oral and dictation continued till the reign of the Abbasids when the well known legal schools, Hanafite School and Shafi'ite School were formed, and the practice of committing the lectures to paper prevailed over the oral system.

The development of Muslim theology began with the rise of the Abbasid dynasty. It was the golden period of Islamic learning. Among other subjects, theology reached the zenith of it's development. Great masters of theology flourished and founded schools of theology which are now known as the four Sunni schools or the four schools of Islamic jurisprudence – The *Hanafite*, the *Malikite, the Shafi'ite, and the Hanbalite.* Each founder of these schools has his own method of deducting the correctness of rituals and laws. For instance the chief instruments of Imam Abu Hanifah (699-766 A.D.) the founder of the *Hanafite* school, in establishing his system, was opinion (*rai*), and analogy (*qiyas*).[5] He believed in studying the actual circumstances and applying the Quranic spirit intelligently to solve any problem. Thus his school is considered "as the most tolerant school of Islam."[6]

Imam Malik b. Anas (715-795 A.D.) was the founder of the Malikite school. He did not place much importance to *Qiyas* (analogical reasoning). He was mainly guided by *Sunnah* and the *Ijma* (consensus).[7]

Imam Muhammad bin Idris Shafi'I (767-820 A.D.) founded the Shafi'i school. He adopted both the principle of *Ijma* and *Istadlal* (logical consclusions) of Imam Malik.[8]

The founder of the fourth school, Hanbali, was Imam Ahmad bin Hanbal (780-855 A.D.). He strictly followed the *hadith* and opposed the extension of *Ijma* and *Qiyas.*[9]

The sources utilized for building up the legal structure of Islam by these great jurists were – the *Quran*, the *Hadith*, the *Ijma* and *Qiyas.*[10]

Although all the four legal schools of thought are important, the *Hanafi* and *Shafi* school of thought are very significant from the point of view of the Sultanate period. These schools have played a significant role in the early stages of Muslim educational system of this period. The *Masalik-ul-Absar fi Mumalik-ul-Amsar* states that 'In Delhi, there are one thousand *madarsas* out of which one belongs to Shafites and

5 Nizami K.A. *Some Aspects of Religion and Politics in India during the thirteenth century*, Delhi, Idarah-i-Adabyat-i-Delli, 1974, p.36.

6 Hitti, Philips K. *History of Arabs*, London, Macmillan and Co. Ltd, 1970, pp.397-98.

7 Nizami, K.A., *Some Aspects of Religion and Politics during the thirteenth century*, Op.cit, p.36.

8 Shushtery, A.M.A., *Outlines of Islamic Culture*, Bangalore, University of Mysore, 1953, p.466.

9 Nizami, K.A., *Some Aspects of Religion and Politics during the thirteenth century*, Op.cit, p.37.

10 For details see: Shushtery, A.M.A., *Outlines of Islamic Culture*. Op.cit, pp.452-66.

the rest to Hanafites.'[11] It further states that 'The majority of the *amirs* and officers occupy themselves with *fiqh* and follow different schools of law, the people of India in general follow Abu Hanifa'.[12] These statements prove that maximum *madarsas* and educational institutions of the Sultanate period followed the Hanafi method of study. Moreover, all the Sultans of this period were Sunnis following the *Hanafi* law in their respective administrations. Thus, obviously the *madarsas* with Hanafi ideology functioned during the above period. Viewing the pivotal role the *Hanafi* schools have played in the medieval Muslim educational system of the Sultanate period, it deserves to be discussed in detail.

Hanafi-definition of Muslim Education:

The legal outlook of the Hanafi and Shafi'i schools is different; but the aim and object of education according to both schools is to understand the relation of man with God as revealed in the Holy *Quran*. This spirit has remained the chief source of all educational activities of the Muslims, although it has been approached by different ways and means. Imam Abu Hanifa says that "Education means understanding of what makes or mars a soul and learning something without putting it into actual practice is meaningless. One should therefore know how to distinguish between right and wrong in regard to both this world and the world hereafter and should choose the right conduct, so that his misguided intellect may not lead him astray and consequently Allah's wrath may fall upon him."[13] From this statement it appears that education according to Abu Hanifa means to teach a right way of thinking and living.

In the elementary stage of the Hanafite School other than the subjects which one requires daily in practical life such as the rudiments of devotional services (*aadat*) Prayer (*salat*) cleanliness (*tahara*) *zakat*, super property tax, law of marriage and inheritance etc—are as much compulsory subjects as contractual transaction for men dealing in trade

11 Shahabuddin Al-Umari, *Masalik-ul-Absar Fi Mumalik-ul-Amsar*, translated by Otto Spies, Aligarh, 1943, p.24.

12 Ibid, p.27.

13 Khan, Mohd. Abdul Mu'id, "The Muslim Theories of education during he Middle Age's", *Islamic Culture*, Vol XVIII, No:1, Hyderabad, Jan, 1944, p.421.

and commerce. Moreover, subjects like ethics, hygiene (medicine) and astrology as far as it is helpful in finding out the direction of the *Qiblah*,(*Ka'bah*) and timing of prayers are also recommended by the Hanafis.[14]

Both schools however agreed that the lectures should not be committed to paper unless they are fully understood and remembered. They also unanimously agreed that by education the students should intend to achieve pious conduct and look upto the Prophet (PBUH) for guidance in life. They should in no case use education as a means to gain worldly ambitions. They therefore made education a sacred duty equal in merit to devotional exercise.

Education Under the Holy Prophet:

One of the most significant event of world history is the rise and expansion of Islam. In 610 A.D. Prophet Mohammad (PBUH) began to preach a new faith in Arabia, a country in which flowed the currents of barbarism and superstition. The purpose of raising a Prophet in a nation is nothing but to teach mankind. The Prophet (PBUH) of Islam remarked, "I have been raised up as a teacher (*mu'allim*)"[15] The Holy *Quran* was revealed as an epitome of knowledge and wisdom. In his discourses the Holy Prophet explained the meaning and significance of the various verses of the Holy *Quran*. Education with Muslims thus began with the teaching of the Holy *Quran*. The Prophet (PBUH) trained a number of his companions in accordance with the teaching of the holy *Quran* and they were sent to various tribes in various places to educate the people in the basic doctrines of Islam. Islam thus became a dynamic educative movement.

The Prophet (PBUH) sent a teacher to Madinah even before he himself migrated to that place. Immediately after the Hijra inspite of enormous preoccupations in connection with defensive and precautionary measures, he found time to supervise the work of eradicating illiteracy from Madina. With this object in mind, Sa'id ibn-al A'as who was reputed

14 For details see: Ibid, pp.426-29.

15 Abdul Barr, *Ilm, Jami' bayan-ul Ilm wa Fazala,* Urdu Trans: by Malihabad, Abdur Razzaq, entitled as: *Al-Ilm wa-Al-Ulama*, Delhi, Nadwat-ul-Musannifin, 1953, p.47.

to write a good hand, was appointed to teach reading and writing to the people of Madina.[16]

There are general dicta of the Prophet (PBUH) regarding those who studied in mosque schools. He also enjoined upon people to learn *Fiqh* and *Quran* from their neighbour.[17] As the result of the personal efforts of the Prophet (PBUH) education in the Muslim Community spread far and wide.

Women also acquired education. The *Quran* has also enjoined upon the wives of the Prophet to teach others.[18] Even the slave girls were taught. A tradition says: "Who so possesses a slave-girl and teaches her well and trains her in the best manner and culture and then sets her free and marries her, he has a double reward (from his lord)."[19]

The exact course and syllabus in difficult to know. From the scanty material at our disposal we may conclude that there was no uniform curriculum followed everywhere. The teacher rather than the course was the main factor. Besides the study of the *Quran* and the *Sunnah*, the Prophet enjoined instruction in shooting (of arrows) swimming, mathematics, the rudiments of medicine, astronomy, genealogy and the practical phonetics necessary in reciting the *Quran*.

Education Under The Pious Caliphs (Khulafa-i-rashidin):

After the death of the Holy Prophet (PBUH) 10 A.H./ 632 A.D. the process of Revelation ceased. The Muslims therefore, had to obtain guidance from the Holy *Quran*, and the Traditions of the Holy Prophet. This boosted the process of development of education. During the period of the Pious Caliphs extensive conquests were made in the East and the West.

---

16 (Citing Abu Dawud), Al-Kattani, Al-Shaikh Abdul Haiy, *Nizam-Al- Hukumat-Al-Nabawiyah Al-Taratib Al-Idariyah*, Vol.1, Beirut (Pub. Hasan Jata) n.d., p.48; Hamidullah M., 'Educational System in the time of the Prophet, *Islamic Culture*, Vol. 13, No. 1, Hyderabad, 1939, p. 53.

17 Ibid, p.49.

18 *Quran* 33:34.

19 Syed, Mahmudunasir, *Islam and it's concepts and History*, New Delhi, Kitab Bhawan, 1983, p.393.

During the period of the Pious Caliphs, Kufa, Basra, Damascus, and Fustat emerged as great educational centres like Mecca and Madina. Taking the title '*Khilafat-ur-Rasul Allah*'[20] the successor of the Prophet (PBUH) of God, Hazrat Abu Bakr became the first Caliph of Islam in 632 A.D. The Prophet (PBUH) praising the purity of his life, had called him as *as-Siddiq*,[21] the veracious. Due to the continuous company of the Prophet he became apt in the Islamic sciences especially *Tafsir* (Exegesis) and *Hadith* (Traditions).[22]

The greatest contribution and achievement of Hazrat Abu Bakr's short period of Caliphate was that the collection of the Holy *Quran* was brought about[23] Caliph Abu Bakr, on the advice of Hazrat Umar ordered Zayb B. Thabit to compile a collection of the Quranic verses.[24] This was undoubtedly the greatest service to the cause of Islam—one book without the least variation for the whole Muslim world.

Hazrat Abu Bakr (ob.634 A.D.) nominated Hazrat Umar as his successor. The latter in turn, entrusted the task to a group of six senior companions of the Prophet (PBUH). They selected Hazrat Uthman as the third Pious Caliph, Hazrat Umar, the second pious Caliph was generally known as *Faruq* i.e. one who separates truth from falsehood. This title had been given to him by the Prophet (PBUH) after he embraced Islam.

When as a Caliph, Umar made education compulsory in Arabia, it was made so both for boys and girls. Women were also free to attend lectures, sermons and other similar functions.[25] It is significant to note

20 Martin, Richard C, *Encyclopedia of Islam and the Muslim world*, Vol.1, U.S.A. Macmillan Reference, 2004, p.70.

21 Hughes, Thomas Patrick, *A Dictionary of Islam*, Vol.1, New Delhi, Cosmo Publication, 2004, p.8.

22 Nadvi, Haji Muinuddin, *Khulafa-i-Rashidin* (being the first volume of *Siyar-us-Sahaba*), Azamgarh, Darul Musannifin, 1973, pp.71-72.

23 Muhammad Ali, *Early Caliphate*, Lahore, Ahmadiyya Anjuman-i-Isha'at-i-Islam, 1932, p.75.

24 Martin, Richard, C., Op.cit, p.7.

25 Muhammad Ali, Op.cit., p.186.

here that Hazrat Umar put teachers on the pay roll. He despatched the companions to distinct places for teaching the *Quran*.[26] He made great efforts for the publicity of the *Hadith* and encouraged the study of *Fiqh*.[27]

Hazrat Umar thus is treated by all Muslims as the greatest in early Islam after that of Prophet Muhammad, (PBUH) and considered a personification of all the virtues a Caliph ought to possess.

The third Caliph Hazrat Uthman was known amongst Muslims as *Zu'n-Nurain*, ("The Possessor of the Two Lights") because he married two of the Prophet's daughters, Ruqaiyah and Umm-i- Kulsum.[28] In the record of his services in the cause of Islam, one particular service must stand at the top. It was he who had copies made from the only authentic copy of the *Quran*, and had them sent to the big centres of the empire of Islam. So that it might serve as a reference edition and the local editions might be corrected accordingly. Thus Uthman is credited with establishing the canonical version of the *Qur'an* during his Caliphate.[29] This was an act of great far sightedness on his part. In an age when the printing machine had not yet been invented, no better arrangement could have been made to maintain the purity of the text of the *Quran*.

The fourth and the last pious Caliph, Hazrat Ali, being associated, from his very boyhood with the Prophet of Islam, got a long opportunity to be trained under him. He is said to have arranged the chapters in the order of revelation. A number of traditions regarding the *Tafsir* and interpretation of Quranic verses are attributed to him.[30]

In the preservation of *Hadith*, too he had a unique distinction. It was his deep knowledge of the *Quran* and *Hadith* which distinguished him so highly.[31] Hazrat Ali is also held as the source of Islamic mysticism

26 Numani, Shibli, *Al Farooq, The Life of Umar the Great*, translated by Maulana Zafar Ali Khan, New Delhi, Adam Publishers, 2003, pp.316-17.

27 Ibid, pp.319-20.

28 Hughes, Thomas Patrick, *A Dictionary of Islam*, Vol.II, New Delhi, Cosmo Publications 2004, p.673.

29 Martin, Richard, C., Vol.II, Op.cit, p.719.

30 Nadvi, Haji Muinuddin, Op.cit, pp.335-336.

31 Muhammad Ali, Op.cit, p.317.

(*Tasawwuf*). He is also reported to have introduced *Ilm-i- Nahv* (the science of Quranic syntax—Grammar).[32] His efforts gave rise to the liberal policy, and inspired all the classes with a desire for learning.

Education Under the Umayyads:

During the Umayyad period (661-749 A.D.), learned men especially physicians, came to Damascus, the capital. Except for Yazid all other Umayyad rulers were great patrons of literature and learning. It was a common saying in Damascus that 'under Walid, people talked of fine buildings, under Sulayman cookery and fair sex, while in the reign of Umar b. 'Abd-al-'Aziz the *Quran* and religion formed favourite topics of conversation.'[33]

The first thought of the Umayyads was to arabacize the non-Arab conquered races[34] and for this purpose they improved the Arabic script and adopted Arabic as the official language replacing Syrian, Coptic and Persian. This provided a sound basis for the study and interpretation of the *Quran* as well as for the collection of *Hadith* (Traditions of the Prophet).

During the Umayyad reign Basra and Kufa were the main centres of culture. The founder of Arabic grammar was a Basarite, a man called Abu-al-Aswad-al-Duali. The first Arabic dictionary was also compiled by a Basirite, al-Khalil-ibn-Ahmad. The founder of Muslim law (*fiqh*) also came from Basra. Among the earliest were Hasan-al-Basri and Shihab-al-Zuhri.[35] The Mutazalite movement also took it's birth in al-Basra.[36]

Kufa gave two famous names to the science of Islamic traditions (*Hadith*) Abdullah ibn Masud and Amir ibn Sharahil al Sha'bi. The latter was a great scholar who had Abu Hanifa, later the great Imam, as one of his pupils.[37]

---

32 For details, see: Nadvi, Haji Muinuddin, Op.cit, pp. 349-53.

33 Nicholson, R.A., Op.cit, p.203.

34 Ibid, p.201.

35 Sayyid, Fayyaz Mahmud, *A short History of Islam*, Pakistan, Oxford University Press, 1960, p.93.

36 Ibid, p.94.

37 Ibid, p.93.

Secular Arabic prose began during this period with the compilation of the early Arabic legends and the chronicles of the Islamic period, especially those dealing with the wars and conquests of early Muslims. Musa bin 'Uqba (d. 758) wrote a book of conquests, and Ibn Ishaq, a biography of the Prophet. Hammad ar- Rawyya, a famous anthologist, compiled thousands of ancient Arabic verses and poems.[38]

As regards scientific culture the age was no less important. The science of medicine reached pinnacle of perfection in Arabia under the Umayyads. During the seventh and eight centuries important medical works from Greece, Persia and India were translated into Arabic. The translator included Hunayn b. Ishaq, Thabit b. Qurrah, Qustah b. Lugah Ibn Muqaffa translated medical texts from Pahlavi into Arabic.[39]

The Umayyad dynasty, despite its tolerance of other religious communities, was predominantly an Arab organization. An anti-Umayyad movement was started by non-Arab Muslims especially the Muslims of Khurasan whose aim was to restore to the Caliphate the descendants of the Prophet, and to revitalize the traditions of Prophet Muhammad (PBUH) and his orthodox companions. This movement destroyed the power of the Umayyads, and put an end to their empire in 750 A.D.

Education and Learning Under the Abbasids:

After the collapse of the Umayyad dynasty in 750 A.D., the Abbasids—descendents of the Prophet's uncle rose to power under their first Caliph, Al-Saffah, and established their seat of government at Mesopotamia. In 762 A.D. Baghdad was chosen as the capital of the Abbasid Caliphate. Despite the political breakdown and insecurity in the tenth century, the progress in the material and cultural fields continued, and it was in this regard quite apt for the Swiss Orientalist Adam Mez to designate this period 'the Renaissance of Islam.'[40] It is not so much for it's conquests and military glory that the 'Abbasid Khilafat'

38 Najibullah, *Islamic Literature*, New York, Washington Square Press, INC, 1963, p.44.

39 Masudul Hasan, *History of Islam*, Vol. I, Delhi, Adam Publishers, 2002, p.673.

40 Bosworth, Clifford Edmund, *The Islamic Dynasties*, Edinburg, University Press, 1967, p.10.

is famous, as for it's achievements in peaceful pursuits such as commerce, arts, science and architecture.

Under the Abbasids the educational system was further enlarged and elaborated. On visiting Damascus in 1184 A.D. the Arab traveller Ibn Jubayr noticed that the writing practices of the pupils were not from the *Quran* but from secular poetry. Together with reading and penmanship the students were taught Arabic grammar, events from the life of the Prophet (PBUH), the elementary principles of arithmetic and poems. Throughout the entire curriculum, memory work was especially emphasized. Girls were welcome to all religious instructions. The children of the wealthy had private tutors i.e. *Muaddib* who instructed them in religion, literature and the art of versification.[41]

Besides the mosque, there were *maktabs*, which served as elementary schools. The education under the Abbasids was not only confined among children of primary schools but Al-Mamun founded the *Bayt-al-Hikmah* (House of Wisdom) where the higher branches of learning were also pursued.[42] The *Nizamiyah madarsa* founded in 1065-67 A.D. by Nizam-al-Mulk, the *vazir* of the Saljuk Sultan, Malik Shah was the greatest theological institution under the Abbasids.[43] Senior students studied Quranic exegesis, the science of apostolic tradition, jurisprudence, scholastic theology, lexicography, rhetoric and literature. Advanced scholars, engaged themselves in the study of astronomy, spherical geography, philosophy, geometry, music and medicine.

In the time of the second Abbasid Caliph, Al-Mansur, the task of translation of Greek learning into Arabic was taken seriously,[44] and the movement begun by him developed still more assiduously under Al-Mamun.[45] 'The actual process of transmission of the sciences of ancient civilization into Arabic is one of the most remarkable instances of cultural transmission in human history. It may be compared only with such other major process of translation and transmission as the

41 Hitti, Philip, K, Op.cit, pp.408-09.

42 Ibid, p.410.

43 Ahmad Aziz, *An Intellectual History of Islam in India*, Edinburg, T & A constable, 1969, pp. 569-70.

44 Thomas, Arnold and Gillaume Alfred, *The Legacy of Islam*, London, Oxford University Press, 1968, p.315.

45 Ibid, p.380.

rendering of Buddhist Sutras in Chinese, and Arabic works into Latin'[46] Due to this movement of translation Arabic became the most important scientific language of the world for many centuries and the ground was prepared for the rapid growth of Islamic sciences properly speaking.

Bartold is of the view that from the second half of the VIIIth century Christians formed the channel through which the Mussulmans began to learn the Greek sciences. The Mussulmans, thus could acquire Greek scholarship from their Christian co-citizens independently by Byzantium.[47]

George Sarton in his '*Introduction to the History of science*[48] remarks that Al-Mansur's age was memorable for the many translations from ancient oriental languages that were done under his benign patronage.

According to Hitti[49] medicine was treated among the foremost among the sciences which were translated.' Caliph Harun-al-Rashid and Al-Mamun. were deeply interested in literature and learning. Philby remarks; 'The treasures of the past were eagerly sought out in their obscure hiding places and the stored up knowledge of ancient Greece was replaced at the disposal of the world in Arabic translations of the works of her philosophers, astronomers, doctors, herbalists *et hoc genus omne*'.[50] Caliph Al-Mamun, from the beginning of his life, was an ardent lover of philosophy and free thought and was interested in the exact sciences as well. He ordered such books to be written as might refute "false notions" and this led to the development of scholastic theology.[51]

The Arabs also made their scientific contributions in chemistry, which they called al-Kimiya.[52] Abu Musa Jabir Ibn Hayyan al-Tusi al-

46 Sayyed, Hossein Nasr, *Islamic Science, An Illustrated, Study*, Westerhan, World of Islam Festival Publishing Company, Ltd., 1976. p.12.

47 Bartold, V.V., *Mussulman Culture*, trans. from Russian by Shahid Suhrawardy, Calcutta, University of Calcutta, 1934, p.14.

48 Sarton, George, *Introduction to the History of Sciences*, Vol.I, Baltimore, William and Wilkins Co., 1927, p.3.

49 Cf. Hitti, Philip, K, *History of Arabs*, Op.cit, pp.308-09.

50 Philby, H.S.T.J.B., *Harun-al-Rashid*, Edinburg, Peter Davies Ltd., 1933, p.60.

51 Samadi, S.B., "Literary and scientific development and the growth of Rationalism in the time of Al-Mamun", *Islamic culture*, Vol.30, No:2, Hyderabad, 1956, p.82

52 Sarton George, Vol. I, Op.cit, p.532; Khan, Muhammad A.R., A Survey of Muslim Contribution to Science and Culture, *Islamic Culture*, Vol. 16, No. 2, Hyderabad, 1942, p. 136.

Sufi who flourished mostly in Kufa nearabouts 776 A.D. came to be associated with this subject.

Biology[53] in it's modern sense had to wait till the invention of microscopes of high power, but rudimentary notions concerning the habitat, behaviour and classification of animals and plants were eagerly acquired and recorded by the Arabs even from the Umayyad days.

The Arabs also made better and more accurate devices for measuring time, clepsydras or water-clocks. The earliest reference to a clock is found in al-Jahiz's *Kitab-al-Hayawan* in the second half of the 9th century[54] The Arab Muslims invented the "mariner's compass" and voyaged to all parts of the world in search of knowledge or in pursuit of commerce which gave them inspiration to study geography. Ibn Khudelreh Jaihani, Al Masudi, Al Istakri, Ibn Haukal, Al Muqadassi and Idrisi are the most famous of Arab geographers.[55]

In the domain of history the Muslims also made great progress. Baladhuri, Hamadam, Masudi, Tabari and Ibn al Athir were the outstanding historians of the Abbasid period. Baladhuri's *'Futuh al Buldan'*[56] is written in admirable style and marks a distinct advancement of the historical spirit.

It was during the Abbasid period that the Muslims cultivated the science of jurisprudence which led to the establishment of four orthodox schools headed by Imam Abu Hanifa, Imam Malik, Imam Shafi'i, Imam Ahmad bin Hambal[57] which have been already discussed in the preceding pages.

With the gradual dismemberment of 'Abbasid Khilafat new dynasties rose to power in different parts of the Islamic world which continued

53 For details see: Ibid, pp.534-59.

54 Sarton George, *Introduction to the History of Science*, Vol.II, part II, Baltimore, William and Wilkins company, 1931, p.632.

55 Bhargava K.D. *A Survey of Islamic Culture and Institutions*, Allahabad, Kitab Mahal, 1960, p.234.

56 Nicholson, R.A.: Op.cit, p.349, Ahmad B Yahya-al-Baladhuri (892 A.D.) a Persian, wrote an account of the early Mohammedan conquests (*Kitab Futuhi 'l- Buldan*) edited by De Joeje, and an immense chronicle based on genealogical principles, *'The Book of the lineages of the nobles: (Kitabu Ansabi'l-Ashraf), of which two volumes are extant.*

57 For details, Nizami, K.A. *Some Aspects of Religion and Politics in India during the thirteenth century*, Op.cit, pp.36-37.

almost unabated the traditions of scientific inquiry and literary output established at Baghdad in it's golden prime. Some of the new dynasties rose such as the Tahirids (820-872 A.D.), Saffarids (862-903 A.D.) the Samanids (874-999 A.D.), the Buwayhids (945-1055 A.D.) and the Ghaznavids (962-1186 A.D.).[58]

The Ghazanavides who were an independent Sultanate of the Abbasid Caliphate later penetrated into India and established their rule there. So naturally the art, culture and tradition of education of the Abbasids was imported to India, and Delhi could start from the point Baghdad left.

But when the Ghaznavides entered India, it was not devoid of the wealth of knowledge. That's the reason why Amir Khusrau wrote in his *Nuh Sipihr*, no doubt, the learning of Rum is widely admired, and it is well known to the world. But India is not devoid of this wealth, logic, astrology, poetry and other branches of learning except *Fiqh* (Islamic Law) are found in India. As Fiqh is related to the religion of Islam (and it does not originally belong to this land) it is not found in India. He further wrote that the Brahmans of India have greater wealth of philosophical thought than what Rumi had revealed to the world. As nobody has tried to learn from the Brahmans, their learning has not been revealed (to the world)[59] When the Ghurides and Turks came to this land they spoke the Persian. When the Indian people came in contact with them they also acquired workable knowledge of Persian. Gradually the Persian language became the local language of people and the Islamic sciences developed in India.

Muslim Education In India:

In the first century of the Hijrah there began a new chapter of Indo-Arab relations. After their conquest of Persia, the Arabs turned their eyes towards India. With the possession of Makran and Baluchistan, the Muslim empire reached the frontiers of Sind. The fact that the North-Western sea-coast of India was a resort of powerful groups of pirates

58 Ibid, p.21.

59. Nath, R, and Gwaliari Faiyaz, India as seen by Amir Khusrau (in 1318 A.D.) being the English translation of Amir Khusrau Mathnavi the *Nuh Sipihr* also known as *Sultan Namah*, Jaipur, Historical Research Documentation Programe, 1981, p.54.

obliged the Arabs to look for means of protecting their trade. During the rule of Hazrat 'Umar, fleets of Arab ships were seen on the Indian coasts. The small port of Thanah (still existing today), a little above the place where modern Bombay is situated, was invaded in the year 15 A.H./636 A.D. by orders of the governor of Bharuch. Next Bharuch was raided. At about the same time an Arab named Mughirah invaded Daybal, a port in Sind situated near Thatta. A few years afterwards during Hazrat 'Uthman's Caliphate, a naval squadron came to see these ports and then went back. In 39 A.H./659-660 A.D. during the Caliphate of Hazrat Ali, an Arab chief was entrusted with a systematic supervision of the Sindhi ports, he was killed in 42 A.H./662-663 A.D. In 44 A.H./ 665 A.D. Amir Mu'awiyah appointed a chief named Mahlab to supervise the land frontiers of Sind. Later this became a permanent post.[60]

So far as, the beginning of Islamic education in the Indian Sub-Continent is concerned, we find evidence in the sources that the Muslims, who directly came from Arabia and settled down in the coastal areas in South India (Malabar and other parts of modern Kerala) established several mosques and *madarsas*, during the seventh century A.D. However the proper beginning of Muslim educational centres in India is said to have taken place during the eighth century A.D. It was after the invasion of the Arab general Muhammad bin Qasim in 711-12 A.D. that the first Muslim (Arab) rule was established in Sind. It lasted for a long time during which different cities emerged as centres of Islamic culture and civilization such as Debul, Mansura, Multan, Uchch etc. Special attention was paid to impart religious education in this connection. We are informed that several *madarsas* were also founded in the above mentioned cities.[61]

However, no considerable part of India ever belonged to the Caliphate. Soon after their conquest of Herat, the Arabs pushed to Kabul in 664 A.D. and thence descended to Multan but this

60 Nadvi, Syed Sulayman, "The early Relations between Arabia and India," *Islamic Culture*, Vol II, No:2, Hyderabad, 1932, p.174.

61 Nadvi, Syed Abu Zafar, *Tarikh-i-Sindh*, Azamgarh, Matb'a-i-Ma'arif, 1970, pp.369-78 also see; Mubarakpuri, Qazi Atahar, *Hindustan mein Arbon Ki Hukumatien*, Delhi, Nadvat-ul-Musannifin, 1967, pp.153-68, pp.251-53.

reconnaissance did not lead to continuous occupation. As we have already mentioned above, an advance from the South produced more permanent results. Practical expeditions by sea to the mouths of the Indus were frequent in the early days of Islam, and in 711 A.D., Muhammad Qasim, a nephew of Hajjaj, the celebrated governor of Basra,[62] conquered Sind from the coast as far as Multan, and although no attempt was made to enlarge this dominion, the province continued to be ruled by Arab governors for nearly two centuries.

In Stanley Lanepoole's opinion the conquest of Hindustan by Mohammedans however sprang not from Sind but from Afghanistan.[63]

Lanepoole writes that the early annexation of the Arabs of the mountainous country south of the Hindu Kush had been nominal and temporary, and Yakub-b. Layth the Safavid of Sijistan was the first to establish a settled Mohammedan government at Kabul. Here his dynasty was succeeded by governors appointed by the Samanids and it was Alptigin , one of the local governors of the Samanid, who laid the foundations at Ghazna of the first independent Muslim dynasty of Afghanistan.

Henceforth for two centuries Ghazna was the capital of a powerful dynasty to which it gave the name of Ghazanavids. The incursions of the Ghaznavids into India and other settlement at Lahore formed the true beginning of Muslim rule in Hindustan.[64] The Ghaznavid kingdom at Lahore prepared the way for Muhammad b. Sam, the Ghurid and

62 Syed, Muhammad Masum, *Tarikh-i-Masumi*, Bombay, Matba'-i-Qayyama, 1938, p.21.

63 Perhaps because the Arab conquest of Sindh under Muhammad bin Qasim did not provide the Arabs with a permanent foothold in India-most of the Arab principalities in Sindh were extinguished towards the end of the third century A.H. but one positive result was that it brought this country definitely within the orbit of Muslim political ambitions and prepared the ground for the later conquests by way of the North-Western Frontier.

64 Lanepoole, Stanley, *The Mohammedan Dynasties*, Delhi, Idarah-i-Adabyat-i-Delli, 1977, pp.283-84.

S.M. Jaffar is of the opinion that the Ghaznavids systematically encouraged education by opening schools and colleges and extending their patronage to learned persons at a time when no one in the west had yet evolved a regular system of educatin. Jaffar S.M., *Medieval India* under Muslim Kings *The Rise and Fall of Ghaznavids*, Delhi, IAD, 1972, p. 264.

his successors, the Sultans of Delhi who brought the whole of India under Muslim sway.

Thus so far as the beginning of Islamic educational centres (*madaris*) in Northern India is concerned, it took place during the conquests of the Turks. Sultan Mahmud of Ghazni who is held as a warrior and conqueror was a great patron of learning and held great regard for nobles and scholars. The renowned scholar and scientist Abu Raihan Alberuni (O.B. 1048 A.D.) was among his close associates.[65]

Subuktugin who was a great lover of learning advised his son Mahmud to conquer the hearts of the luminaries of his kingdom pointing out that his generosity in this sphere would immortalize his name.[66] A later writer and statesman of the Seljuks, the *Wazir*, Nizam- ul-Mulk, summed up the character of Mahmud as 'a just sovereign, a lover of learning, a man of generous nature and of pure faith.[67] Mahmud excelled in academic pursuits due to the tutorship of a leading Hanafi scholar "the father of Qazi Abu Nasr Sini and was trained in different branches of learning. He knew the *Quran* by heart and was familiar with Muslim Law and Tradition.[68] He is said to have been the author of a book *Tafrid-u'l-Furw* which was regarded as a standard work on Fiqh.[69]

The political side of his education was not neglected Subuktugin himself instructed him in the administrative skills and the principles of successful sovereignty and put them in the form of a *Pand Namah*.[70] The practical and military side of Mahmud's education came from accompanying his father into battle, and boyish exploits of his are recorded against the pagans of Ghur and against the Hindu Shahi Raja Jaipal at Langhan. No doubt Subuktugin passed on to him all his

65 Nazim, Muhammad, *The Life and Time of Mahmud of Ghazna*, New Delhi, Munshi Manoharlal, 1971, pp.127-28, also see Sachaw, Edward, *Alberuni's India*, Delhi, National Book Trust of India, 1993, p.12.

66 Ferishta, Muhammad Qasim, *Tarikh -i-Ferishta*, Vol. I, Lucknow, Nawal Kishore Press, 1864, p.21.

67 Powel Price, J.C, *A History of India*, London, Thomas Nelson & Sons Ltd. 1955, p.106

68 C.f. Bosworth, C.E. *The Ghaznavids, their Empire in Afghanistan and Eastern Iran, 994-1040* , Edinburg, University Press, 1963, p.129.

69 Nazim, Muhammad, Op.cit, pp.156-57.

70 Ibid, p.35.

distilled experience and skill.[71] Sultan Mahmud was a poet and scholar of some reputation. The Ghaznavid royal court was the only centre of Persian culture in the East. The poets born in Persia were attracted to Ghazni and Lahore, the Persian and Indian, seats of government. This means that the territory lying between the Persian towns and the Indian capital was all under the sway of Persian culture. Of the poets of Mahmud's court Unsuri, Asjadi,[72] Asadi, Farrukhi, Firdausi, Minuchihri, Ghaza'iri[73] were most prominent.

Lanepoole describes Mahmud's popularity and patronage of learning in these words, "If Mahmud is to Muslims for all times a model of God fearing king, zealous for the faith, his court had no less deservedly held a pattern of humane culture. Napolean imported the choicest works of art from the countries he subdued to adorn his Paris, Mahmud did better, he brought the artists and the poets themselves to illumine his court. From the cities of the Oxus and at the shores of the Caspian, from Persia and Khorasan, he pressed into his service the lights of oriental letters and compelled them, not unwillingly, to revolve about him like planets in his firmament of glory. The fall of Samanid dynasty, who had been noble patrons of literature, left many homeless scholars and poets who flocked with eagerness to new centre of learning."[74]

The Sultan was a great patron of learning and his royal *darbar* was the rendezvous of scholars from all parts of the Muslim world.[75]

According to Daulat Shah, there were four hundred poets in regular attendance at his court, presided over by the laureate Amir-ash-Shu'ara.[76] The Sultan was very generous to scholars and his liberality

71 Bosworth, C.E. Op.cit, p.129.

72 Awfi, Muhammad "*Lubab-ul-Albab*", Isfahan, Ibn-Sina Kitab Khana, 1333 Shamsi.

73 Abdul, Ghani, Muhammad *Pre-Mughal Persian in Hindustan*, Vol. I, New Delhi, Vintage Books, 1994, p.178.

74 Lanepoole, Stanley, *History of India*, New Delhi, Asian Education Services, 1987, p.31-48.

75 Barlhold, W, *Turkestan Down to Pre-Mongol Invasion*, London, Luzac Company Ltd, 1968, p.289. Barltold is of the view that Mahmud's patronage of learning was due to an ostentatious desire to convert his court into a cradle of culture and not to an innate love of learning is erroneous and illfounded. Mahmud might have been influenced by this ulterior motives, but in view of the fact that he was himself a scholar a poet and an author, it cannot be said that his love of learning was not genuine.

76 Abdul Ghani Muhammad, Op.cit, p.177, p.232

in this respect has rarely been surpassed. His meanest rewards were calculated in thousands of dinar[77] and later generations of poets cherished his memory chiefly as a giver of "elephant loads" of gold and silver.[78] His magnificent encouragement of sciences, art and literature was no less than his genius as a general and statesman. His munificence drew together perhaps the most splendid assemblage of literary genius including the poet Firdausi that any Asiatic capital has ever contained.[79] In Muhammad Habib's opinion 'Mahmud was the last of minor kings and the first of the great Turko-Persian Emperors. The inspiring motive of his life and the lives of his contemporaries was not Islam but the spirit of Persian Renaissance.[80]

From Baihaqi, we have a few details about the Islamic education which Mahmud gave to his own children. He had two of his sons Mas'ud and Muhammad and his younger brother Yusuf, who was only three years older than the two princes, educated together. Already by the age of fourteen Mas'ud had a good knowledge of *Adab* and was able to teach a few Al-Mutanabbi's odes and the Mu'allaqa (معلقہ) of Imru'l-Qais to another boy. Their tutor at this time was a eunuch, Raihan Khadim. Afterwards when Mahmud nominated Mas'ud to the governorship of Herat, Raihan Khadim accompanied him there as a tutor, with a strict commission to watch over Mas'ud's, moral welfare. In Saljuq times, Raihan Khadim would have been described as *Atabeg.*[81]

As Sultan Mas'ud was a competent Persian stylist. Not only did he fix his '*tauqi*' (توقیع), the royal signet put to documents, letters, patent and other public deeds) to the documents prepared by the *Diwan-i-Risalat,* he sometimes added sections in his own hand. Baihaqi retained in his possession many documents, drafts and notes by Mas'ud which he utilized in putting together his Mujalladat (مجلدات). From his

77 Ibid, p.232.

78 *Tarikh-i-Fakhruddin Mubarakshah,* p.52.

79 Elphinstone Monstruat, *History of India* , *The Hindu and Mohammedan period,* Allahabad, Kitabmahal Pub Ltd, 1966, p.290.

80 Habib Muhammad, *Sultan Mahmud of Ghaznin,* New Delhi, S. Chand and Co, 1967, p.63.

81 Bosworth C.E., Op.cit, pp.129-30

knowledge of *Adab*, Mas'ud was certainly able to read Arabic and apparently able to understand it when spoken.[82] Occasional expressions used by Mas'ud reveal his intellectual processes as thoroughly Islamic.

Sultan Ibrahim, (Masud's son) was also a great patron of literature and learning Abu Nasr Farsi known as *Adeeb* (an adept in Literature), who came from Persia to Lahore during Ibrahim's reign, founded at Lahore a University called Khanqah Abid Nasr or according to Awfi Khanqah Umeed[83] (خانقاہ عمید) which remained for centuries, under different designations the centre of Persian and Arabic cultures in the East. It imparted instruction in the various branches of Persian learning, besides those of Arabic, such as literature, rhetoric, philosophy, mysticism, commentary of the *Quran* and *Hadith*.

It is said that on his return after the conquest of Kanauj Sultan Mahmud founded the Jama Masjid and adjacent to it built a *madarsa* at Ghazni. He also established a library there and accumulated the most rarest books and manuscripts from different parts of his empire which Ferishta expresses in the following words:

"سلطان چون بفتح و فیروزی این سفر مراجعت نمود، تا در غزنی مسجد جامع بنیاد نهادند، واصل عمارت مسجد از سنگ مرمر در خام مربع و
مسدس و مثمن و مدور برآوردند بطرزیکه بیفندگان از متانت وطراحی آن متحیر شدند و بعد از اتمام عمارت بموجب حکم...... آن را
بانواع زینت و فروش وقندیل مزین ساختند که ظرفاے وقت آن مسجد را عروس فلک می گفتند و در جوارِ آن مسجد مدرسہ بنا نہادہ
وبنفائس کتب وغرائب نسخ موشح گردانیده وہان بسیار بر مسجد و مدرسہ وقف فرمود"

(When the Sultan returned after his grand victories, he laid the foundation of the '*Jami Mosque*' in Ghaznin. And the main building of the mosque was so beautifully built with marble blocks of different sizes—square, five sided, six sided etc., that whosoever looked at it, became amazed. And on the completion, it (the mosque) was so attractively adorned with various types of floors and lamps that people

82 Ibid, pp.129-30.

83 Awfi, Muhammad *Lubab-ul Albab*, Op.cit., p.80.

called it as the bride of Heaven. And adjacent to this mosque, a *madarsa* was established where a number of general and rare books were provided and available. A lot of property and wealth was endowed for this mosque and *madarsa*).

It may therefore be presumed that he might have made efforts to spread education in the regions conquered by him in India. The practice of opening *maktabs* and *madarsas* within the premises of the mosques was pioneered in India by Sultan Mahmud which later became a way of life. In other Islamic countries this practice was followed since the outbreak of Islam.

During Sultan Masud's reign many *Ulama* authored books and dedicated it to him, Qazi Abu Muhammad Nasiri wrote a book on *Fiqh* and called it *Fiqh-i-Masudi*, Abu Raihan Khwarazmi Munajjim who was an expert mathematician (*Riyazidan*) wrote the *Qanun-i- Masudi* and the reward he received for it has been described by Ferishta in the following words:-

"ابوریحان خوارزمی منجم کہ علامۂ وقت بود در ریاضیات نظیرے نہ داشتی قانون مسعودی در علم ریاضی بنام او نوشت و خیلے از نقد صلہ یافت"[85]

(Abu Raihan Khwarizmi Munajjim, who was a great scholar of his time, had no parallel in mathematics. He wrote *Qanun-i-Masudi* in mathematics with his name and received a lot in cash as reward).

This sultan established many *madarsas* during his regime about which Ferishta writes:-

"دراوایل سلطنت او در ممالک محروسہ چندان مدارس و مساجد بنیاد نہادند کہ زبان از تعداد آن عاجز و قاصر است"[86]

(In the beginning of his Sultanate, he founded so many *madarsas* and mosques in different regions under his rule that my tongue is unable to describe their number).

Completing one hundred and seventy five years of their rule in India, the Ghaznavids were replaced by the Ghurids in 552 A.H./1186 A.D.

84 *Tarikh-i-Ferishta, Vol. I, p.30.*
85 Ibid, p.44.
86 Ibid, p.44.

Administrative requirements of trained personnel, desire to increase cultural prestige among contemporary rulers, demands of Muslim religious life, patronage of religious classes, personal interest in education and learning, led the Sultans to establish *madarsas* and *maktabs* in their territory. Sultan Muizuddin Sam (Shahabuddin Ghuri) also evinced keen interest in the promotion of education and learning. Hasan Nizami in his *Taj-u'l Ma-asir* states that after the conquest of Ajmer in 587 A.H./ 1191 A.D. the Sultan paid special attention to the spread of religious education there. For this purpose, he is reported to have established several *madarsas* there.[87]

Shahabuddin Ghuri did not have sons but only a daughter and he took pleasure in educating Turkish slaves whom he afterwards made his viceroys. In 1206 A.D., a party of Ghakkars assassinated Muhammad Ghuri. His dynasty did not long survive him. His nephew Mahmud was proclaimed Sultan throughout the wide dominions conquered by his uncle, but the unity of the kingdom vanished with it's founder.

The Turkish slaves who had served as generals under Muhammad Ghuri assumed independent power. Qutb-u'd-din Aibek became the first of the Slave Sultan of Delhi, Nasir-u'd-din Qubacha ruled in Multan and Sind, and Yalduz governed Ghazna.[88]

Thus Qutb-u'd-din Aibek who was appointed by his master as the viceroy of Delhi, after his death in 1206 A.D. proclaimed himself sovereign of Hindustan and founded the first Muslim dynasty which exclusively ruled in India because before this Muslim India had been an outlying province of the kingdom of Ghazna. This dynasty, the first of five (Mamluk, Khalji, Tughlaq, Syed and Lodis) which preceded the Mughal conquest, is commonly known as the Slave dynasty or the rulers belonging to it as Mamluks. The education imparted to the generals Muhammad Ghuri comprised of training in work of governing along

87 Nizami, Hasan, *Taj-u'l-Ma'athir,* The History of India as told by it's own historians, edited by Elliot, H.M. Dowson John, Vol. II, Delhi, Low price publications rept 2001, p.215 also Husain, Yusuf, *Glimpses of Medieval Indian Culture,* Bombay, Asia Publishing House, 1957, p.70.

88 Lanepoole, Stanley, *Mohammedan Dynasties,* Op.cit, pp.294-95.

with literary instruction. Qutb- u'd-din Aibek also built many mosques which were not only centres of religious worship but also of education.[89]

Thuş it was after the foundation of the Delhi Sultanate in 1206 A.D. that the roots of Islamic Culture and civilization became strong in the Indian Sub-Continent. *Maktabs* and *Madarsas* were founded in Delhi and other cities and towns in large number. One special feature[90] of the new culture was that the Turks, who were already familiar with paper brought to India the practice of writing chronicles, based on the Islamic calendar, and henceforth the chronology of India becomes precise, so far as the facts recorded in the chronicles are concerned.

In this connection, mention may be made here of Al-Beruni's statement. He writes that the Hindus of South India grew slender trees like the date and coconut palms, the leaves of which were one yard in length and as broad as three fingers together which were called *tari* (tala or tar =Borassus fla-bellifornis) and used to write on them. In Central and Northern India people made use of the bark of the *tuz* tree. They take a piece one yard long and as broad as outstretched fingers of the hand and in order to make it hard and smooth, they oil and polish it and then they write on it. All the leaves are then bundled together wrapped up in a piece of cloth and fastened between two tablets of the same size such a book was called *puthi* (cf. pusta, pustaka).[91]

With the advent of the Delhi Sultanate education came to be organized there. With Mongol insurgence, many scholars flocked to Delhi from Central Asia and Iran, and the general level of learning rose considerably. The Mongol catastrophe in Central Asian lands threw large number of scholars, artisans, men of craft and culture into the country. The Sultans gave shelter and protection to them, and named many *muhallas* (localities), in Delhi after them.[92] They became "the

89 Keay, F.E. *Indian Education in Ancient and Later Times*, 2nd ed. London, Oxford University Press, 1938, rept, 1942, p.112.

90 Moreland, W.H., Chatterjee, Atul Chandra, *A Short History of India*, London, Longmans Green and Co., Ltd., 1944, p.144.

91 Sachau, Edward, C, *Alberunis's India*, Vol-I & 2, Delhi, Atlantic Publishers, rept, 1989, p.171.

92 *Tarikh-i-Ferishta*, Vol. I, p.75.

saviours of Muslim Culture."[93] The Mongol devastation in Central Asia thus became a blessing in disguise for the nascent Muslim state of India, particularly only for it's cultural efflorescence. Thus the traditions of Muslim education as they had developed under the Abbasids of Baghdad were the nucleus of the Muslim educational system in India.[94] They were transplanted in India by the literati and scholars of Muslim lands after the Mongols had overrun them. Within a century of it's foundation, the Sultanate of Delhi came to occupy an unrivalled place in the sphere of Muslim education.

By the middle of the thirteenth century the entire science and culture of the Islamic world was imported into India and Delhi became the greatest centre of Muslim learning in the East. Also during the 13th century the manufacture of paper had begun for it is mentioned by Amir Khusrau at the close of the century.[95] Moreover, by the middle of the 14th century, the material had become so cheap that the sweet sellers of Delhi were giving their products packed in paper to their customers.[96] In the fourteenth century also there was considerable amount of progress in education and learning which is proved by the fact that during the time of Sultan Muhammad bin Tughlaq there were about one thousand *Madarsas* in Delhi alone.[97]

93 Habibullah, A.B.M. *The Foundations of Muslim Rule in India*, Allahabad, Central Book Depot, 1976, p.137.

94 Nizami, K.A., Development of the Muslim Educational System in Medieval India, *Islamic Culture*, Vol. LXX, No.4, Hyderabad, Oct, 1996, p.27.

95. Amir Khusrau, *Qiran-us-Sa'dain*, ed. By Maulvi Muhammad Ismail Meruti and Syed Hasan Barni, Aligarh, Institute Aligarh College Press, 1918, pp. 117, 228-230.

96. Qalandar Hamid, *Khair-ul-Majalis*, ed. Nizami, K.A., Aligarh, Institute of Historical Research, Aligarh Muslim University, 1959, p. 203.

97 Zaki, Muhammad, *The Arab Accounts of India During the fourteenth century*, Delhi, Idarah-i-Adabiyat-i-Delhi, 1981, p.69.

Chapter-II

Institutions of Muslim Education

After the establishment of the Delhi Sultanate, all varieties of cultural activities including education received encouragement. A new chapter in Islamic education in the country started with coming of the Sultanate. The Delhi Sultans themselves were lovers of education and learning and the royal court warmly received all who came from abroad in search of patronage.

During the Sultanate period there were separate institutions for imparting primary, secondary and higher education. There was no uniformity and the system differed from place to place. However, to some extent they were identical in their functions. Primary education for young boys and girls was imparted in *Maktabs*. These were generally attached to mosques and were run by the local people. Higher education was imparted in the *Madarsas*. There were *Khanqahs* which were also run by pious Muslims. In these *Khanqahs,* students usually received secondary education in accordance with Islamic law and theology. It has been already discussed in the previous chapter that the faith in Islam is favourable to the pursuit of knowledge and education was held in high esteem. Through these institutions the Muslims, fulfilled their aim of spreading education far and wide which was considered a sacred duty.

Aim and Objects of Muslim Education:

Muslim education imparted during the period under review, was not exactly the same as today. In those days, the chief aim of education was the purification of the soul, and it was regarded as "preparation for life and life after death"[1] Great attention was paid to each and every student in the educational institutions and no attempt was made at standardized mass production. The aim of receiving education was mainly religious and moral training. Shaikh Abdul Haq Muhaddith, in his famous work entitled *Akhbar- ul-Akhyar*, has recorded an interesting conversation among the students which throws ample light on the aims and objects of their studies. 'Once the students were having a conversation among themselves and were asking each other about the aim and object of their studies. Some of them pretended and insincerely asserted that they were pursuing their studies to get an insight into divine mysteries, while others were truthful and straight forward and said that the object of their pursuing knowledge was to have some worldly gain in future. When they asked me about my opinion, I said that my purpose in pursuing knowledge was to acquaint myself with the views of men of erudition and wisdom of the past, know their intuitive method of resolving intellectual difficulties and realising the reality."[2]

Significance of 'ILM' (Knowledge):

The significance of *'Ilm'* is evident from the views of different scholars and Sufis of the Sultanate period. Shaikh Nasiruddin Chiragh's views about knowledge (*Ilm*), as found in *Khair-ul-Majalis*, reveal his emphasis on combining knowledge with action and precept with example, said he-

"مقصود از علم عمل است، علم حسن لعفسہ نیست"

---

1 Jaffar, S.M., *Some Cultural Aspects of Muslim Rule in India*, Peshawar, S. Mohd. Sadiq, 1939, p.79.

2 Quoted by Husain Yusuf, *Glimpses of Medieval Indian Culture*, Bombay, Asia Publishing House, 1957, p.81.

"Purpose of knowledge is action, it is not beauty in itself",[3]

Shaikh Nizamuddin Auliya's concept of *'Ilm'* (knowledge) was very high and it transcended all material considerations. He considered it a noble endeavour, an end in itself, which could not be made a means of earning bread. One day a student came to see him and in course of conversation said that he often went around the court so that he could have affluent circumstances in life. The Shaikh did not like his purpose of acquiring knowledge. Similarly the Shaikh did not like poetic talent to be wasted in writing panegyrics.[4] He cited in his assembly a remark of Shaikh Jalal-u'd-din Tabrizi that the ambition of *ulama* is confined to getting either the job of a teacher, or a *Qazi* or a *Sadr-i-Jahan* "They aspire for nothing higher, but the *darwesh's* have many stages of development.[5] The Shaikh once quoted Caliph Umar bin 'Abdul Aziz that when a man acquires knowledge he becomes respectable in the eyes of the people, but when he acts upon it he becomes a dear one of God.[6] He spoke in his assembly about persons whose salvation was due to their devotion of learning.[7] With the instinct and temperament of a real and dedicated scholar, he used to say that a scholars pleasure in solving an academic problem was greater than that of a king in ruling over a territory.[8] He repeatedly emphasized that one should be an *'alim'* with the qualities of a *darwesh* ingrained in him. He referred to three such scholar saints of this type whom he had the privilege to meet, Maulana Shihabuddin, Maulana Ahmad Hafiz and Maulana Ahmad Kaitheli.[9] Again and again he told his audience that *'ilm'* (learning) without a heart full of cosmic emotion was vain and fruitless.[10]

---

3 Qalandar Hamid, *Khair-ul-Majalis*, ed. Nizami, K.A., Aligarh, Institute of Historical Research, Aligarh Muslim University 1959, p.253.

4 Sijzi, Amir Hasan, *Fawaid-ul-Fu'ad*, Lucknow, Newal Kishore, 1894, p.182.

5 Ibid, p.237.

6 Mir Khurd, *Siyar-ul-Auliya*, Delhi, Matba-i-Muhibb-i-Hind, 1302 A.H., (1885 A.D.) p.534.

7 Ibid, pp.534-35.

8 Ibid, p.535

9 Ibid, p.536

10 Ibid, p.539

Types of Muslim Educational Institutions:

The centres in which the Islamic sciences have been taught over the ages have been an integral aspect of Islamic civilization. From the beginning the mosque was at once the religious and social centre of the Islamic community as well as the centre for learning. To this day Quranic schools where the (fountainhead) of all Islamic sciences the *Quran*, is taught are connected with the local mosques in various quarters of Muslim cities.[11]Three main institutions which played a key role in imparting knowledge to students were the *Maktab*, *Madarsa*, *Khanqah*.

Maktab:

The *Maktab* is a type of beginners or primary school. It provides a common educational basis for all who attend it. Since basic education (*Tarbiyat*) was usually imbued with a religious spirit, and it's professed goal was to produce a true believer, much of it was closely connected with the mosque, whose officials also provided further instruction. The *Quran* was studied in all the *Maktabs*, with stress laid on memorizing and absolute accuracy. Some calligraphy and a smattering of arithmetic were taught in some *Maktabs* in Turkey and Iran where Islamic history and fragments of Persian poetry (of Sadi and Hafiz) were included from the thirteenth century. The *Maktab's* curriculum laid a basic foundation for further study.[12]

Madarsa:

A *Madarsa*, is an Islamic college, literally a "place of instruction in religious law. In Medieval usage the term referred to an institution providing intermediate and advanced instruction in Islamic law and related subjects. As a rule the medieval *Madarsa* served male students who were past the elementary level and who intended to acquire credentials as *ulama*, religious scholars. A typical Islamic *Madarsa* contained rooms for students, a prayer hall, and classrooms for one or more professors, literary and sanitary facilities. It was usually attached

11 Seyyed, Hossein Nasr, Op.cit, p.14.

12 For details, see: Brills, E.J., *The Encyclopedia of Islam*, Vol.V, Leiden, the International Union of Academics, 1979, pp.567-68.

to a mosque, and large mosque compliances, but it appeared as a separate institution in about the eleventh century and evolved from the informal schools that operated in mosques or teacher's home. It was a dominant form of higher learning.

A *Madarsa* was legally a *waqf*, a charitable endowment. The founder would donate property, from whose proceeds the *Madarsa* was built and maintained. The founder's instruction governed such matters as the legal school to which the professor would belong. The *Madarsa* education was intended to teach the students how to deduce religious law from authoritative Islamic text. The students who went through the whole course were qualified to be judges and religious scholars, but some students dropped out earlier, becoming mosque *imams* or pursuing secular careers with the added prestige of religious education. The method of instruction was scholastic and dialectical involving, intense debate about the interpretation and difficulties of standard text books. Usually students committed *Quran* by rote and a fair amount of Arabic students studied Arabic, logic and the core subjects of Islamic religious sciences- *Fiqh* (Islamic Jurisprudence), Quranic interpretation, and the *hadith* (traditions of the Prophet). Better students went on to study *Usul-i-Fiqh* (Principles of jurisprudence) along with theology, philosophy mathematics, astronomy and sometimes medicine.[13]

But the *Madarsas* were not the only institutions through which higher learning was imparted. During the Islamic period of Indian history the *Madarsas* were generally considered more popular and important centres of higher learning.

Khanqah:

The '*Khanqah*[14] is a composite word of Persian origin meaning a building usually reserved for Muslim mystics belonging to a *darwesh* order. It was a centre of worship as well as of teaching and evangelism. Shaikh AbuSa'id Abul Khair (ob.1048 A.D.) drew up a code of ten rules

13 Richard, M. Martin, Encyclopedia of Islam and the Muslim World, Vol.2, U.S.A., Macmillan Reference, 2004, pp.418-19.

14 For details see: Nizami K.A., *Studies in Medieval Indian History and Culture*, Allahabad, Kitab Mahal, 1966, pp.80-96.

for the people in the Khanqahs.[15] Since they were institutions meant both for leading the communal life (rooms for prayer, corporate sessions) and also for sheltering individual mystics, often in significant numbers. All *Khanqahs* contained both type of accommodations (and frequently too various annexes and dependent buildings permitting self sufficiency). However there was a great gulf between the sumptuous buildings founded under official patronage and the *Khanqahs.*[16] Early in the 14th century a traveller informed Shihabuddin-al- Umari in Damascus, "In Delhi and it's surroundings are *Khanqah* and hospices numbering two thousand.[17]

Institutions For Provision of Higher Learning:

There is no doubt that the Muslim rulers took interest in the establishment and construction of *Madarsas*. This trend initiated, blossomed, developed and enlarged with the success of the Sultanate. In this the personal interest and popularity of the Sultans has played a vital role. Despite the large number of *Madarsas* and government's interest to improve their standard, the main role in providing specialization in higher learning or attaining knowledge in a particular subject was played either by individual centres of education or personal *majlis* of the *ulama*. Moreover, libraries, academic assemblies *Khanqahs* and observatories also participated for the development of education and the promotion of learning.

Following are the Various Institutions Through Which Higher Learning Was Imparted:

1. Individual Centres of Education.
2. Academic Assemblies.
3. Sufi's Assemblies
4. Observatories for the study of Sciences.
5. Hospitals – for the study of Medicine.

---

15 Nicholson, R.A., *Islamic Mysticism*, New Delhi, Aryan Book, 2002, p.46.

16 For details, see: Brill, E.J., *The Encyclopedia of Islam*, Vol.IV, Leiden, the International Union of Academics, 1978, pp.1025-1026.

17 Shahabuddin Al Umari, *Masalik-ul-Absar-fi-Mumalik-ul-Amsar*, Eng. Translation: Otto Spies, Aligarh, Department of History, 1943,p.24

6. Centres for Technical and Vocational Education.
7. Personal Study and Research.

1. Individual Centres Of Education

The significance of the individual centres of education for higher learning can be realized by glancing at the details of the educational live's of the nobles and *ulamas.* Here we find less information on their study through the *Madarsas* but rather we find mention of the teachers. Similarly in the case of those *ulama* who were busy imparting knowledge and learning we rarely find information on them teaching in any particular *Madarsa.* Rather there is evidence of, and more stress is laid on the fact that they were experts in teaching a particular book or a particular subject, particular composition or compilation or those places are mentioned where they used to teach. So far as the *Madarsas* and educational centres are concerned, teaching of the subjects in vogue was maintained upto a common level which may be supposed to be upto the standard of *maulvi.*[18] From this we can infer that more than the *Madarsas* the teachers of specialized subjects and their individual centres were more popular than the *Madarsas* for higher learning.

Further for specialization in any particular subject, an individual had to approach the teacher who had expertise in that subject or to attend his private classes. Here sometimes the scholar joined the group which was already taking lessons from a teacher in a particular subject, which was a more popular and famous method followed not only in India but also the other Muslim countries of the world during the period under review. For example, Maulana Alauddin Inderpati was a *Hafiz-i-Quran* and such an excellent teacher of Quranic teaching that many associates of Shaikh Nizamuddin Auliya memorized the *Quran* from him. Mir Khurd and his two uncles were also his students.[19] The historians and *Tazkira* writers have narrated that sometimes in order to attain scholarship and knowledge in a particular subject, students had to go to specific places and sometimes had to travel to foreign

18 For details of the above discussion we can study the famous *tazkiras* of the *ulama* and Sufis such as the *Siyar-ul-Auliya, Muntakhab-ut-Tawarikh* and the *Akhbar-ul-Akhyar.*

19 *Siyar-ul-Auliya,* Op.cit, p.316.

countries also. Specifying this trend of acquiring education Bilgrami writes in his *Ma'asir-u'l-Kiram*.

"طلبۂ علم خیل خیل از شہری بہ شہری می روند و ہر جا موافقت دست دہد بہ تحصیل مشغول می شوند"[20]

"Seekers of knowledge went in large number, from city to city and every where they engaged themselves in receiving learning according to their choice."

One of the *alims* (*ulama*) of the Sultanate period Maulana Qasim Dehlavi (Jalaluddin Qasim) studied *Hidaya*, *Bazdawi*, *Kashshaf*, and *Masabih*.[21] That means he acquired the knowledge of *Fiqh*, *Usul-i-Fiqh*, *Tafsir* and *Hadith*. Similarly another *alim* of this period, Abu Hafs Umr bin Ishaq Ghaznawi, other than the above books he also studied the *'Awarif-ul- Ma'arif*.[22] Moreover, some of the *ulama* studied *Lughat*, *Ma'ani*, and some others were interested in the rational sciences.[23] The famous Sufi Shaikh, Nasiruddin Chiragh of Delhi studied *Hidaya* from Maulana Abdul Karim Sherwani and Maulana Fakhruddin Hanswi. He took lessons on *Usul-i-Fiqh* from Maulana Muin-u'd-din Kashani and for other books he studied under the guidance of Shaikh Shamsuddin Muhammad bin Yahya Awadhi.[24] There are more evidences of this pattern of acquiring education, for instance in the case of Nizamuddin Auliya (his mentor Shaikh) who acquired knowledge of *Fiqh* (Jurisprudence) and *Usul-i-Fiqh* (Principles of Jurisprudence) from Maulana Alauddin Usuli. He studied *Maqamat-i-Hariri* (Arabic *Adab*) from Maulana Shams-ul-Mulk and *Mashariq-ul-Anwar* (*Hadith*) from Maulana Kamal-u'd-din Zahid and turned towards Shaikh Fariduddin

---

20 Bilgrami, Gulam Ali Azad, *Ma'athir-ul-Kiram*, Agra, Mufid Aam Press, 1910, pp.221-22.

21 *Siyar-ul-Auliya*, Op.cit, pp.215-16, Allama Abdu'l-Hayy-b. Fakhru'ddin-al-Hasani, *Nuzhat-u'l-Khawatir*, Vol.2, Hyderabad, Osmania Oriental Publications Bureau, 1966, p.110.

22 *Nuzhat-u'l-Khawatir*, Vol.2, pp.92-93, Bhatti Muhammad Ishaq, *Fuqaha-i-Hind*, Vol.1, Lahore, Idara-i-Saqafat-i-Islamia, 1974, pp.273-76.

23 Badayuni, Abdul Qadir, *Muntakhab-u't Tawarikh*, Vol.3, ed. Maulvi Kabiruddin Ahmad Ali, Calcutta, Asiatic Society of Bengal, 1869, pp.23,67,77, Rahman, Ali, *Tazkira-i-ulama-i- Hind*, Lucknow, Nawal Kishore, 1914, p.62.

24 *Tazkira-i-ulama-i-Hind.*, Op.cit, p.338, *Fuqaha-i-Hind.*, Vol.1, Op.cit, pp.294-95.

Awadhi Shafi for the study of *Tafsir Kashaf* and for the study of *Awarif-ul-Ma'arif* (*Tasawwuf*) presented himself to Shaikh Fariduddin Ganj Shakar.[25] Thus this method of teaching and learning was not limited to any particular subject but in the case of different arts and sciences this same method was followed. For the study of *Tafsir, Hadith, Fiqh, Tasawwuf* and along with these, in the field of rational sciences also in order to obtain specialization, this method was adopted which is evident from details of the lives of the scholars of rational sciences.

It is important to mention here that the *ulama* of different parts of Hindustan in order to obtain benefits in different fields of arts and sciences would not only travel within the country but also travelled abroad to derive benefits from the teachers of different subjects from different countries. This trend was prevalent during the Sultanate period. Specifically we find many examples of this trend in relation to *Ilm Hadith.* The eminent Muhaddith of Sultanate period Shaikh Hasan bin Saghani Lahori, (ob. 1352 A.D.) after obtaining the customary basic education in vogue in Lahore, travelled to Ghaznin, Iraq, Hejaz, and in these places specially obtained benefit from the *ulama-i-Hadith.* He studied the famous book on *Hadith,* the *Mashariq-ul-Anwar* when he returned several times to Hindustan and stayed for long durations, but in his later stage of life he was in Baghdad and he died there.[26]Another *alim* of the same period Shaikh Muhammad bin Muhammad Saghani (ob.1378 A.D.) who was entitled *Ziauddin Al-Hindi,* obtained his knowledge of *Hadith* in Qahra (Cairo) and Hejaz. In Madina other than benefiting from other *ulama,* he studied the *Muwatta* (A collection of *Hadith* compiled by Imam Malik, the founder of the Maliki school of jurisprudence), from the illustrious *Muhaddith,* Shaikh Ali bin Qutub Mukram. After completing his education he started teaching in Madina, then in Mecca and he died at this pious place.[27] There were also such *ulama* and *fuzala* (scholars) who went to other Arab countries to acquire knowledge and learning from the *Muhaddith* there, but after accomplishing their

25 *Nuzhat-u'l-Khawatir,* Vol.2, Op,cit, p.123, *Fuqaha-i-Hind.,* Vol.1, pp.273-74.

26 *Tazkira-i-ulama-i-Hind,* Op.cit, p.48, Allama, Abdu'l Hayy, b. Fakhru'd-Din al- Hasani, *Nuzha't-u'l Khawatir,* Vol.1, Hyderabad, Osmania Oriental Publications Bureau, 1962, pp.137-41, *Barni,* Saeed Hasan, 'Imam Sughani', *Ma'arif,* Vol.24, 1929, pp.4-13.

27 *Nuzhat-u'l-Khawatir.,* Vol.2, Op.cit, p.139, *Fuqaha-i-Hind,* Vol.1, Op.cit, pp.285-86.

objective returned back to Hindustan and started *tadris* (teaching) and *tasnif* (compiling scholarly works) and became busy in it. For instance Shaikh Bahauddin Zakariya Multani, (ob. 1267 A.D.) stayed nearly for eight years in Baghdad, for five years in Hejaz, and benefitted from several *ulama* of *Hadith* there, amongst whom was the famous *Muhaddith* of Madina, Shaikh Kamal-u'd-din Muhammad Yamani.[28] Another scholar, Shaikh Muhammad bin Yusuf Ali-ul-Kirani Al- Hindi, the famous Indian *alim* of the fourteenth century, studied *Hadith* from the teachers in Mecca. Amongst the names of his *Hadith* teachers we come across Razi-ul-Tabari, Zain-ul-Tabari, Jamal-ul-Mukri and Shaikh Jalil Maliki.[29]

Other than *Hadith* in the fields of other arts and sciences too the foreign *Ulama* played a pivotal role. The Indian scholars always took their guidance for acquiring knowledge and learning. For instance for the study of *Tasawwuf*, Shaikh Abu Hafiz Umar bin Ishaq Ghaznavi (ob.1361 A.D.) after completing his study of *Fiqh* and other sciences in Delhi paid a visit to 'Kabah' at Mecca and the tomb of the Prophet (PBUH) at Madina. During his stay there he attended the lectures of different *Ulama* and heard the *Awarif-ul-Ma'arif* from Shaikh Khizr and Shaikh Rubat Sadda.[30] Similarly, the famous Suhrawardi Sufi and *alim* Makhdum Jahanian travelled to Hejaz and Egypt to complete his various stages of education. He studied the *Awarif-ul Ma'arif* from Afifuddin Abdulla Mutari, while his stay at Madina.[31] These are some examples of the scholars of the Sultanate period. From these we can infer that during the period under review, the trend was that for the study of specific subject one had to approach particular teachers to acquire higher learning. For specialization in a particular subject or field of study more than the *Madarsas*, the individual centres of scholars played a significant role.

28 *Nuzhat-u'l-Khawatir*, Vol.1, Op.cit, p.187, *Fuqaha-i-Hind*, Op.cit, pp.140-41.
29 *Nuzhat-u'l-Khawatir*, Vol.2, p.157, *Fuqaha-i-Hind*, Vol.1, Op.cit, p.300.
30 *Nuzhat-u'l-Khawatir*, Vol.2, Op.cit, pp.92-93.
31 Dehlavi, Shaikh Abdul Haq, Muhaddith, *Akhbar-ul-Akhyar*, Delhi, Matba-i-Mujtabai, 1332 A.H., pp.141-43, Sajjad Husain (ed.), *Siraj-ul-Hidaya* (Malfuzat of Syed Jalaluddin Makhdum Jahanian, Delhi, Indian Council of Historical Research, 1983,pp.4-5 (Introduction).

There are also instances of studying all subjects under one particular teacher. Maulana Qasim bin Umr Dehlavi Musannif, author of *Lataif-ul-Tafsir* studied from one particular teacher, Jalal-ud-din Dehlavi, *Tafsir, Hadith, Fiqh, Usul-i- Fiqh* etc. and completed his education under that teacher itself.[32] Shaikh Alauddin Al-Alandi (ob.1375 A.D.) studied all the prevalent subjects of the course from Shaikh Muinuddin Imrani but turned towards Nasiruddin Chiragh Dehlavi for the study of mystical sciences.[33] Similarly, Makhdum-i- Jahanian Syed Jalaluddin Bukhari of Uchch, from his initial to the last stage of education, studied all the books of the curriculum from Qazi Bahauddin Uchchi. But in the field of mysticism Afifuddin Abdullah Mutri was his teacher.[34] Perhaps one more reason for this kind of private teaching was that teaching was considered as means for the service to religion and to popularize learning and education. Thus generally in the circles of the *ulama* there persisted deep interest in the process of teaching and learning. Amongst them those who were well-off and financially stable would willingly and satisfactorily conduct this service to mankind and religion successfully. Secondly there were also such *ulama* who other than teaching were involved in other occupations but inspite of this: they would spare time to fulfill their duty of spreading knowledge. Thirdly there were such *ulama* who were patronized by the Sultans and nobles and in exchange for their service were paid cash or given land in the form of gifts.[35] We find thousands of *ulama* mentioned in the contemporary sources who spent almost their whole life to spread knowledge or most of their time was occupied in this activity. Infinite seekers of knowledge gained from them. Moreover several such teachers taught for more than half a century.[36]

During the Sultanate period the trend of spreading knowledge and teaching was so strong that many scholars possessing love of learning

---

32 *Siyar-ul-Auliya.*, Op.cit, p.215, pp.110-111, *Fuqaha-i-Hind,*, Vol.1, pp.270-71.

33 *Nuzhat-u'l-Khawatir,* Vol.2, p.77, *Fuqaha-i-Hind,* Vol.1, pp.242-43.

34 *Nuzhat-u'l-Khawatir,* Vol.2, p.18.

35 During the medieval period the terms used for cash payments were 'Vazifa' or Inam and for the grant of land 'Madad-i-Ma'ash was used. For details see: Abul Fazl, *Ain-i-Akbari,* Vol.1, ed., Sir Syed Khan, Aligarh, Sir Syed Academy, 2005, p.946.

36 *Ma'athir-ul-Kiram,* Op.cit, p.142.

and teaching inspite of their governmental, administrative and other duties and engagements would show keen interest in this work. For instance, Shaikh Farid-u'd-din Shafi Awadhi was the *Shaikh ul-Islam* during Alaudin Khalji's reign but along with this huge responsibility he would also regularly teach *Tafsir*.[37] One of the important officers in the administration of the Balbani era Khwaja Shams-u'l-Mulk also used to teach the students. He was specifically popular for the teaching of Arabic Literature.[38] The scholars who obtained stipends and gifts, were not particularly attached to any *Madarsa* or educational institution but instead according to their convenience or point of view would conduct this service at any place. Sometimes a *Masjid* or a teacher's own residence would become a *Madarsa*, or the royal darbar, or the Haveli of *Umra* or portico of any home. Teaching would be conducted, in some *Khanqah* or some building adjoining it. During the reign of Firoz Shah Tughlaq the distinguished *alim* and excellent teacher Maulana Najm-u'd-din Samarqandi conducted his classes in the royal palace i.e. Balaband Siri which in one way became his *Madarsa* where numerous people benefitted by acquiring knowledge.[39]

In brief, we can conclude that the *ulama* and scholars of the period under review were free from the bondage of teaching in any particular *Madarsa* or educational institution. Any place they wished to teach and initiated teaching, that place itself would start functioning as a *Madarsa*. All the seekers of knowledge would reach there and would benefit from them. People belonging to different occupations, categories and strata would participate in the lectures. These teachers or experts of subjects were not so famous as being attached to any *Madarsa* or educational institution. Rather they were known and recognized for their distinction and expertise in teaching a particular art or science.

37 *Siyar-ul-Auliya*, Op.cit, p.285, *Akhbar-ul-Akhyar*, Op.cit, p.93, *Tazkira-i-ulama-i-Hind*, Op.cit, p.86, p.146, *Nuzhat-u'l-Khawatir*, Vol.2, Op.cit, pp.105-08, p.143.

38 *Akhbar-ul-Akhyar*, Op.cit, p.78, *Tazkira-i-ulama-i-Hind*, Op.cit, p.240.

39 Barni, Ziauddin, *Tarikh-i-Firoz Shahi*, ed. Sir Syed Khan, Aligarh, Sir Syed Academy, 2005, p.565, *Nuzhat-u'l-Khawatir*, Vol.2, Op.cit, p.169, Nadvi, Abul Hasanat, *Hindustan Ki Qadeem Islami Darsgahien*, Azamgarh, Darul Musannifin, 1971, p.23.

Students participated in their lectures having the faith and confidence that the teacher was an expert in the respective subject. From the above discussion it is evident that the teacher's private or individual centre of education proved to be a stable and strong channel for imparting higher learning.

2. Academic Assemblies

For the purpose of higher learning other than the *Madarsas* and individual centres, the academic gatherings and literary assemblies also played a vital role which can not be neglected and underestimated. It is a generally known fact that the Delhi Sultans and some nobles of the Sultanate period also possessed a keen interest in the spread of arts and sciences and always sought and favoured the company of the learned. In this way the royal *darbar* served as a centre of the scholars and experts of a particular art or science. The scholars who participated in these assemblies were experts of Islamic sciences and rational sciences as well, scholars who enlightened the field of poetry and literature and experts in the rare field of fine arts. Here not only did the scholars get an opportunity to discuss the various issues and problems pertaining to a particular topic but also to present their point of view. Separate meetings were held for different arts and sciences. Discussion was held there in liberal atmosphere and the participant's academic and artistic efforts regarding the topics under discussion and their results were brought to light. Some of the Sultans would also participate in these academic assemblies. We find evidence that during the Sultanate period several times under the supervision of the royal administration for the discussions of several issues the *ulama* of the period were specially invited. Special meetings with the jurists and *'ulama* on emergent problems were convened. These special assemblies called *Mahzar* were conducted several times during the Sultanate period to find the collective opinion of the *ulama* on some controversial issues. For instance in the reign of Iltutmish and Muhammad Tughlaq, the *Mahzar* was called to discuss the issue of *sama* (mystic songs) in the light of *Shariah*.[40]

40 Isami, *Futuhus-Salatin*, ed. Usha, A.S., Madras, University of Madras, 1948, pp.118-19.

When Sidi Maula was accused of rebellion against Jalal-u'd-din Khalji, the Sultan took steps to settle the issue through the *Mahzar*.[41] During the reign of Firoz Shah Tughlaq of course, no meeting of the '*ulama*' were called in the form of *Mahzar*, but they were invited several times to discuss the issues like levying dues on irrigation—(*Haq-i Shurb*), which was not sanctioned by the *Shariat* and punishment to the leaders of heretics and apostates.[42] The details of the discussions of these academic assemblies are not available but whatever we know from the scattered material and stray references is very interesting and holds great significance. Other than the discussions and debates that took place under the supervision or in the presence of the Sultans and nobles the *ulama* themselves also conducted discussions and debates on *Tafsir*, *Fiqh*, *Poetry*, *Literature*, *Philosophy*, *Logic* or any other subject or topic of discussion. It can not be refuted that because of these discussion the trend for deep study and research emerged and for any problem, discussions based on evidences and reasons were sought after and these are the factors that are a prerequisite for attaining mastery and expertise in any field.

3. Sufi's Majlis

The *majlis* of the Sufis also played an important role as an instrument through which education was imparted to people. It can be deduced from the activities in the *Khanqahs* of the famous Sufis and the proceedings of their *majlis*, people could benefit in the field of education. Firstly in these *Khanqahs* education was imparted by teaching specific books and most of the books were generally related to *Tasawwuf* (mysticism) and *Tafsir* (Exegesis).[43] Secondly some Sufis who were amongst the *ulama* class and were interested in teaching, would spare some time to teach in the *Khanqah* or small rooms (*hujras*) attached to it, books of such subjects which they were fond of, and the members of

41 Sirhindi Yahya bin Ahmad, *Tarikh-i-Mubarak Shahi*, (ed.) M. Hidayat Husain, Calcutta, Asiatic Society Bengal, 1931, pp.65-67, *Akhbar-ul-Akhyar*, Op.cit, p.73.

42 (Afif), Shams Siraj, *Tarikh-i-Firozi Shahi*, (ed.) M. Wilayat Husain, Calcutta, Asiatic Society Bengal, 1891, pp.121-22, 129-30, 28-29, Firoz Shah Tughlaq, *Futuhat-i-Firoz Shahi*, (ed.) Abdul Rashid, Aligarh, Department of History, 1954, pp.7-9.

the *Khanqah* and the general public took advantage of this. Thirdly, sometimes the Quranic verses and the *hadith* were explained regarding the problem under discussion, sometimes the questions of the participants were answered with reference to the *Quran* and the *hadith* in the assemblies of great Sufis and *mashaikh*. Sometimes minute problems related to some Quranic verse or *Hadith* were also solved in these *majalis*.[44]

Moreover, some Sufis would be interested in narrating important *Fiqh* issues in front of their *muridin* (disciples), there were interrogative sessions and answers were given to the questions put forward by the audience. In this way these *majalis* served the purpose of providing important information about *Quran*, *Hadith*, *Fiqh* and proved to be an important medium for diffusion of knowledge. During the period under review the *majalis* of Shaikh Farid-u'd-din Ganj Shakar, Shaikh Bahauddin Zakariya Multani, Shaikh Nizamuddin Auliya, Shaikh Nasir-u'd-din Chiragh Dehlavi, Syed Jalal-u'd-din Bukhari Makhdum Jahanian, Khwaja Husain Nagauri were considered very significant. The *malfuzat* of the great Sufi's and *Tazkiras* one comes across important information and facts can be obtained and here it is important to present some example.

Shaikh Nizam-u'd-din Auliya's *murid*, Fakhruddin Zarradi, a contemporary of Muhammad bin Tughlaq was deeply interested in the teaching of *Fiqh*. After joining the Sufi fraternity spent most of his time in the *Khanqah* of Nizam-u'd-din Auliya. He was continuously involved in the process of teaching. He would daily after the *Chasht* (prayer performed between sunrise and meridian) prayers teach the '*Hidaya*' (a famous book of Hanafi Fiqh) in a building adjacent to the *Khanqah*. According to the author of *Siyar-ul-Auliya* a lot of people attended his lectures.[45] In the *majalis* of the Sufis incidentally the problems or queries of the books that were taught were solved and a very good example of this is found in the case of another *murid* of the same Shaikh. Once Shaikh Nizam-u'd-din asked one of his *murids*, Shaikh Shamsuddin

43 Nizami, K.A., *Some Aspects of Religion and Politics in India during the thirteenth century*, Delhi, Idarah-i-Adabyat-i-Delli, 1974, p.43.

44 *Fawaid-ul-Fu'ad*, Op.cit, pp.126-27, *Siraj-ul-Hidaya*, Op.cit., p.51,60,105,120,125.

45 *Siyar-ul-Auliya*, Op.cit, pp.278-79, *Fuqaha-i-Hind*, Vol.1, Op.cit, p.257.

Yahya Awadhi about the books he had studied and in reply he mentioned the '*Usul-i-Bazdawi*'. The Shaikh asked him several questions and in the end Maulana Shamsuddin put forward the difficulties or problems from this book which he could not comprehend. The Shaikh explained and elucidated in such a manner by which the Maulana was very impressed and his faith in the Shaikh became more firm.[46] Here it is important to mention the *Khilafat-Nama* which Shaikh Nizamuddin obtained from his *murshid* (mentor) Khwaja Fariduddin Ganj Shakar. In it was the *Ijazat Nama* (permission) to teach the '*Tamhidat-al-Muhtadi*' (authored by Abu Shakoor Salmi), a book on the principals of religion. This means he got the certificate that Shaikh Farid had taught him this book and now he could teach this book to others. The '*Ijazat Nama*' which was included in the *Khilafat Nama* is as follows:

"فان الشروع فی الاصول یوسع دعاء الشهود ویبصر لمن یکرع منها محارق الورد علی ان الطریق مخوف والعقبة کؤود. ونعم الکتاب فی هذا الفن تمهید المهتدی ابی شکور برد الله مضجعه وقد قرأ عندی الولد الرشید الامام النقی العالم الرضی نظام الملة والدین محمد بن احمد زین الائمة والعلماء مفخر الاجلة والاتقیاء اعانه الله علی ابتغاء مرضاته واناله منتهی رحمته واعلیٰ درجاته سبقا بعد سبق من اوله الیٰ آخره قرأة تدبر وایقان وتیقظ واتقان مستجمع رعایة سمع و درایة جنان و کما حصل الوقوف علیٰ حسن استعداده کذالك وفور تهیاء واجزته ان یدرس فیه للمتعلمین۔ 47

"In the name of God, the Compassionate and the Merciful... He is the First and the Last, the Appearance and the Reality. Whomsoever God elevates, none can degrade and whomsoever god degrades no one can elevate. None can hide what he wants to reveal ... May God bless Muhammad and his followers, his Companions and other saintly persons... After His praise I declare that the study of the knowledge and principles of the Traditions... gives light to him who pours water on burnt places through its knowledge. This path is, in fact, perilous

---

46 *Akhbar-ul-Akhyar*, Op.cit, p.97.

47 *Siyar-ul-Auliya*, Op.cit, 127-28.

and full of hazards and difficult in view of results. In this branch of knowledge the best of book is the *Tamhid-u'l- Muhtadi* of Abu Shakoor Salimi... This book has been studied under me, lesson after lesson, from the beginning to the end, minutely, attentively, carefully and thoroughly, by the dutiful son, pious, the Imam of the age and blessed, Nizam-ul-Millat wa'd Din Muhammad son of Ahmad, who is an adornment of *imams* and scholars and the pride of the holy and the virtuous. May God bless him with the desire of submission to Him and be merciful to him and elevate his position... At the time of teaching him, I found him capable, able, meritorious, well-behaved and good mannered. I now permit him to teach this book to students, provided he avoids mistakes in teaching, writing and explaining it and utilizes his energy and knowledge in discussion, correcting the manuscripts and purification of the language. God is the real protector from errors of speech and a saviour from disruption and disease in religious work. This deed of permission was drawn during the month of Ramazan, on a Wednesday. May god extend the bounties of this blessed month. This document was drafted at the order of the Shaikh of the Shaikhs of the World , may God ever protect his honour and prestige, and was written by the humble slave of God, Ishaq son of Ali, a resident of Delhi, in the presence of the Shaikh of the Shaikhs of this world."[48]

In the *majalis* of the Sufis the most popular *Tafsir* that was taught and studied, and of which we find several evidences is the '*Tafsir Madarik*', authored by Hafizuddin Abdullah bin Ahmad Nafsi (ob.1310 A.D.). Especially amongst the Chishti circle this *Tafsir* had a stronghold. We find evidence that this *Tafsir* was taught by the Chishti *mashaikh*.

”این وظیفۂ تفسیر مدارک طریقۂ سلوک مشائخ ایشان است“[49]

"(This litany of the *Tafsir-i-Madarik* is the method of the way (suluk) of the saints of this order)."

48 Nizami K.A., *The Life and Times of Shaikh Nizam-u'd-din Auliya*, Delhi, Idarah-i-Adabyat-i-Delli, 1991, pp.187-188.

49 *Akhbar-ul-Akhyar*, Op.cit, p.186.

The Chishti Sufi Shaikh Husam-u'd-din Manakpuri (ob.1449 A.D.) would be busy in the study of the *Quran* and would try to understand it's meaning and always kept the *Tafsir Madarik* with him and if he found any difficulty in comprehending any verse of the *Quran* would consult it.[50] Similarly another famous Sufi Khwaja-Husain Nagauri (ob.1496 A.D.) along with preaching, was also busy in the dissemination of religious sciences. His daily routine included the teaching of '*Tafsir Madarik*' about which he was very particular.[51] Moreover during the Sultanate period the *Quranic* issues, it's meaning or comprehension or any point of view were discussed in the *Majlis*. The *Tafsir* books that were used for this purpose were the *Tafsir Kashshaf*, *Tafsir Razi*, *Tafsir Zahiri*, *Tafsir Nasiri*, *Tafsir Basara* and *Arais-ul Bayan*.[52] Other than these subjects it was essential to teach *Tasawwuf* (mysticism) in the *majlis*. During our period of study the *Awarif-ul-Ma'arif*, *Fusus-ul-Hikam*, *Kashf-ul-Mahjub* and *Qut- u'l-Qulub* were the famous books of mysticism taught in the Sufi *majalis*.[53]

4. Observatories

During the period under review other than the customary trend of education, in the field of science, research and experiments were conducted in observatories. The Sultan, other than taking efforts for the dissemination of religious education, also encouraged the learning of contemporary education. The Delhi Sultans patronized the rational and other sciences and gave rewards and gifts to the scholars who were involved in research and conducted experiments and especially established observatories and laboratories for research and training in the subjects of astronomy and medicine. From this aspect the reign of Alauddin Khalji and Firoz Shah Tughlaq is more famous. According to Barani during the reign of Alauddin Khalji, Hamiduddin Mutraz was an expert of astronomy and medicine, and was equal to the scholars of

50 Ibid, p.177.

51 Ibid, pp. 185-86.

52 *Khair-u'l-Majalis*, Op.cit, p.83, p.120, *Siraj-ul-Hidaya*, Op.cit., p.60, 125,126,145,163,164, Nizami, K.A., *Tarikh-i-Mashaikh-i-Chisht*, Vol.1, Delhi, Idarah-i-Adabyat-Delli, 1980, p.407,410,412.

53 *Khair-u'l-Majalis*, Op.cit, pp.23,58,155,178,249 *Akhbar-ul-Akhyar*, Op.cit, p.163, 195.

Greece in these fields.[54] Firoz Shah Tughlq under his supervision for the study, observation and conduct of experiments in the field of astronomy, established an excellent astrolabe and erected it on a *minaret* (tower) along with a sundial which functioned as a store house also. Here for the scholars of astronomy facilities were available for observation and research.[55] Both the astrolabe and sundial were also important aids in sea navigation, and by the thirteenth century the Chinese magnetic compass (floating needle) was in use on ships in the Indian seas.[56]

Firoz also established a unique astrolabe which was portable.[57] This Sultan's deep interest and love for the subject of astronomy is also evident by his getting a Sanskrit work on astronomy translated in Persian which became famous as '*Dalail-i-Firoz Shahi*'.[58] Thus we can infer that the observatories were established by the Sultans so that research and experiment could be conducted in the field of astronomy which led to immensive progress and development in this field.

5. Hospitals

In the field of medicine also hospitals were established and in these *Darul Shafas* (hospitals) of that period not only was treatment and remedy provided and available to the patients but also lectures were conducted for the students on different aspects of medicine and care was taken for the performance of experiments and for this purpose famous doctors were called. We find evidence about the doctors of that

54 *Tarikh-i-Firoz Shahi*, Op.cit, p.112.

55. Anonymous, *Sirat-i-Firoz Shahi*, Fascimile edition of the manuscript, Patna, Khudabaksh Oriental Library, 1999, pp.300-05.

56. The evidence has been exhaustively studied in an Urdu work, Sayyid Sulaiman Nadvi, *Arbon Ki Jahazrani*, Azamgarh, Darul Musannifin, 1935, pp. 148-152; Also Needham, Joseph,; *Science and Civilization in China*, IV(1), Cambridge, Cambridge University Press, 1962, pp. 247-248.

57 *Tarikh-i-Firoz Shahi* (Afif), Op.cit, p.370, Siddiqui Iqtedar Husain "Science and Scientific Instruments in the Sultanate of Delhi", Hamdard Islamicus, 17/3, Autumn, 1994, pp.11-12.

58 *Sirat-i-Firoz Shahi*, Op.cit, p.301, Badayuni, Abdul Qadir, *Muntakhab-ut-Tawarikh*, Vol.1, ed., M. Kabiruddin Ahmad Ali, Calcutta Asiatic Society of Bengal, 1868, p.249, Nizami, K.A. *Salatin Dehli Ke Mazhabi Rujhanat*, Delhi, Nadwat-ul-Musannifin, 1981, p.399.

period that other than their medical practice they would also impart medical knowledge to the students of medicine and worked as medical teachers and took it as a profession.[59] Especially during the Firozi period we find evidence that the hospitals (which were called *Darul Shafa*, *Bimaristan* or *Sahatkhana*) other than providing treatment and remedy for various ailments also functioned in the capacity of centres for providing training and knowledge in the field of medicine.[60] In *Afif's Tarikh-i-Firoz Shahi* there is mention of only one hospital but in the *Tarikh-i-Ferishta* the number of hospitals established by Firoz Shah Tughlaq is five[61] and in the *Tabaqat-i- Akbari* it is four[62]

Thus the hospitals other than being health service centres also played the role of an agency through which medical training and education could be imparted.

6. Centres For Technical and Vocational Education

For the information on technical and mechanical institutions for education and training during the period under review, we find scattered and dispersed references in the contemporary sources from which we can derive at some points. Firstly during that period there were many artists, artisans, and experts in different industries, skills and handicrafts available. Secondly, other than the things and materials used by the royalty, nobles and officers, different kinds of things, tools and weapons were produced and manufactured in the state. Thirdly, for the teaching and training of various arts and talents other than the private centres or household firms or home industries which provided domestic training, there were also workshops or centres of industrial training under the supervision of the administration called '*Karkhanas*'. These *Karkhanas* were specially established for manufacturing commodities for the use of the royal family, nobles and officers. In these under the supervision of expert artisans, craftsman, handicraft

59 *Tazkira-i-ulama-i-Hind*, Op.cit, pp.23,51.

60 *Tarikh-i-Firoz Shahi* (Afif), Op.cit, pp.355-59, *Sirat-i-Firoz Shahi*, Op.cit, pp.235-36, *Futuhat-i- Firoz Shahi*, Op.cit, pp.15-16, Salik, Abdul Majid, *Muslim Saqafat Hindustan mein*, Lahore, Idarah-Saqafat-i-Islamia, n.d., p.p.294.

61 *Tarikh-i-Ferishta*, Vol.1, Op.cit, p.151.

62 Nizamuddin Ahmad, *Tabaqat-i-Akbari*, Lucknow, Nawal Kishore, 1875. p.121.

workers, training was imparted by expert artisans through the system of apprenticeship. Under this system the trading class maintained their own schools for the instruction of their children or other people from which all took advantage and learnt the arts. This system of providing training in various skills and industry was prevalent in the villages and towns of the Sultanate and was free from various formalities.[63] Infact the *karkhanahs* of the royal household were, factories to manufacture articles needed at the court. During the reign of Muhammad bin Tughlaq elaborate arrangements were made for the manufacture of cloth. The Sultan distributed twenty thousand dresses annually. The manufacture of arms, engines of war, armour and other fighting equipment also received great care and attention.[64] There is detailed evidence available of the establishment of *Karkhana's* and centres for industrial training during the period of Firoz Shah Tughlaq. There was a special department specifically established only for the technical training and teaching of different arts and skills to the slaves during this period. Here it is clear that other than the religious teaching and training, the Sultan was deeply interested in providing industrial training and technical knowledge to his slaves. In the '*Karkhanas*' under the supervision of the skilled artisans and expert craftsmen training in different arts, crafts, skills were provided to the royal slaves. In this way according to Afif approximately 12,000 slaves became efficient artists and artisans.[65]

From this we can infer that different kinds of commodities were manufactured, such as the utensils for the purpose of eating and drinking, dresses and jewellery, carpets, items for decorative purpose, items given as presents and gifts on behalf of the Sultans, things for riding, instruments and appliances used for the purpose of hunting and wars, building, weapons and tools etc. were manufactured. Thus the home industries or household firms and *Karkhanas* functioned as agencies for providing technical and mechanical training.

---

63 Ray, Krishnalal, *Education in Medieval India*, Delhi, B.R. Publishing Corporation, 1984, pp.53-55.

64. Qureshi I.H., *The Administration of the Sultanate of Delhi*, Delhi, Oriental Books Reprint Cooperation, reprint, 1971, p. 70.

65 *Tarikh-i-Firoz Shahi* (Afif), Op.cit, p.270, For details, see: Banerjee, J.M., *History of Firoz Shah Tughlaq*, Delhi, Oriental Publishers, pp.183-84.

7. Personal Study and Research

The personal study of books also played a significant role in the process of teaching and learning. The teachers and scholars other than teaching and learning would also conduct personal research and study to enlarge and increase their knowledge of a particular subject or field. This trend was prevalent and its foundations were strong and firm during the Sultanate period. We have several evidences that inspite of the lack of facilities for printing and publication of books, there was no shortage of important books on particular topics and subjects. Other than borrowing books from each other for study the scholars also travelled to far off places in search of important books. Books for study and copies of their commentaries were made ready and generally people took keen interest in this work. The scholars themselves would make these copies ready for their personal use and also to gift them to their friends, teachers, and *Mashaikh*. One of the disciples of Shaikh Nizam-u'd-din Auliya, Rukn-u'd-din Chihmar, was very fond of calligraphy, he copied many books and presented it to his spiritual mentor. Amongst them were the copies of '*Tafsir-i-Kashshaf*' and '*Mufassal*'.[66] Another scholar, Maulana Zain-u'd-din Dehlavi presented a copy of '*Sahih Muslim*' to Shaikh Sharf-u'd-din Yahya Maneri.[67] During that period there were also such scholars who while copying particular books of different arts and sciences would also write the keys and marginal notes so that while studying or reading the scholar would not have to face the difficulty of separately referring to the key or commentary of a particular work.[68] Some scholars were so fast in writing books that they would copy hundreds of pages just within two or three days.[69] This was a discussion about the private or individual efforts for copying books. Other than this there was also a group or section that came into existence for making copies ready which adopted this work as a full time profession, they were called *Warraq* and *Nassakh*. They would keep investigating and kept information on the important books, as to where and which place they were available and in whose possession,

66 *Siyar-ul-Auliya*, Op.cit, p.327.

67 *Nuzhat-u'l-Khawatir*, Vol.2, Op.cit, p.44.

68 *Ma'athir-ul-Kiram*, Op.cit, pp.48, 225, 229.

69 *Ma'athir-ul-Kiram*, Op.cit, p.43, *Akhbar-ul-Akhyar*, Op.cit, p.250.

so that they could make copies ready for the scholars when the need arose. On their own also these professional copyists would copy important and popular books in demand and would keep selling them.[70] Other than the general *Warraq* and *Nassakh* there were also several expert copyists and calligraphists during that period. The Sultans and nobles along with the scholars and experts of arts and science would also encourage the calligraphists and would also patronize them in their *darbars*. It is obvious that a display of their talents would come forward in the form of compilations and writings of books which specially would be installed in the Royal Libraries. These libraries which were an important part of the educational activities of the administration also served as institutes for the spread of knowledge.[71] During the same period Delhi's famous Sufi Nizam-u'd-din Auliya had a huge library in his *Khanqah*. His *Khanqah* was in the town called Ghiyaspur in old Delhi and all scholars and seekers of knowledge benefited from it. Shaikh Abdul Haq Muhaddith Dehlavi writes in one place while describing the circumstances of Shaikh Siraj-u'd-din Uthman:-

''وبعد ازاں پیش مولانا رکن الدین کافیہ ومفصل وقدوری ومجمع البحرین تحقیق کردہ بعد ازنقل شیخ نظام الدین قس، سہ سال دیگر تعلیم کرد وبعضی کتب از کتب خانہ شیخ کہ وقف بود وجامہا وخلافت نامہ کہ از خدمت شیخ یافتہ بود با خود برد.'' 72

"Later he made a deep study of *Kafiyah,* the *Mufassal*, the *Quduri* and the *Majma-ul-Bahrain* under Maulana Ruknuddin, then for three years, he received higher knowledge from Shaikh Nizamuddin by benefiting from his library which was an endowment. And finally he took with him the robe and '*Khilafat Nama*' which he received from the Shaikh."

70 *Fawaid-ul-Fu'ad,* Op.cit, p.45, For details see: Gilani, Manazir Husain, *Hindustan mein Musalmanon Ka Nizam Ta'lim wa Tarbiyat*, Delhi, Nadwat-ul-Musannifin, 1987, pp.51-54.

71 Rafiq, Said Ahmad, *Islami Nizam-i-Ta'lim* , Karachi, Idarah-i-Tasnif wa Talif, n.d., pp.25,34..

72 *Akhbar-ul-Akhyar,* Op.cit, p.181.

Libraries were a part of the royal expeditions. The Delhi Sultan always carried important books in the form of small libraries in their war expeditions. Other than the Sultans and nobles the scholars also possessed private libraries and had their private collection of books.[73] The use of paper is likely to have facilitated the copying of books and book trade. It also enabled large collections of books to be accumulated by individuals. Kings and nobles had extensive libraries. Some such libraries, at least, were made available for scholars use for eg, Firoz Tughlaq deposited a large number of books on astronomy and astrolabes in the royal library (*Kitab- khana-i-khas*) and desired that these be made available to all those who wished to make use of them.[74] It is very surprising that we have many details about the personal accomplishments of the Sultans which prove them as great patrons of education but there is less information available about the presence of libraries. For instance we know that during Muhammad Tughlaq's reign there were about one thousand *Madarsas* but not a word is mentioned about the existence of libraries, the reason is perhaps that during that period the libraries were usually inside the *maktabs*, *madarsa* and *khanqahs*. Collecting rare and important books was a matter of habit and due to the love of learning. One can make a slight estimate of the large number of copies of books on different subjects and topics of that period. A glance at the large libraries of Hindustan, Pakistan and Great Britain and taking a look at the collection of manuscripts which were related to Hindustan of that period. This is a slight estimate. In these institutions only those manuscripts have reached which after the decline of the Sultanate came in the custody of the government and those books of private libraries belonging to families of scholars which the later generations did not care, with the passing of time have gone waste of which no estimate can be formed. Due to the absence of printing press sometimes shortage of books was faced by the people.

During the period under review, availability of books on different subjects like arts and sciences particularly *Tafsir*, *Hadith*, *Fiqh* and the important sources is evident from the sources and references mentioned in the presently available books which were compiled during that period.

73 *Akhbar-ul-Akhyar*, Op.cit pp.87, 250, *Ma'athir-ul-Kiram*, Op.cit, p.265.

74. *Sirat-i-Firoz Shahi*, Op.Cit, p. 320.

In the compilations and compositions not one or two but hundreds of, not only names of books but paragraphs and passages from other sources are to be found but the books are missing. For instance the compilation of the *Fatawa-i-Tatarkhania* (which is in several volumes), writing of this took place under the supervision of a committee of scholars. This committee was ordered that the points of differences between the jurists on different issues should be pointed out and the opinions of the jurists should be collected.[75]

The same method was used for the compilation of '*Tafsir Tatarkhania*' The method that was followed was that all points related to the exegesis of every verse and to reach to the depth of every issue the opinion of the senior scholars of *Tafsir* was taken into account and every point of difference or a difference of opinion was discussed and written by providing proves of the experts of *Tafsir* and evidence was mentioned for every point.[76] Other than the books on *Tafsir* and *Fiqh* there was no lack of books on *Hadith* during the Sultanate period. The writers and scholars of that period have in their works not only mentioned the six collections of *Hadith* but also references of other books of *Hadith* are to be found and are available in their works.[77] In the History books of that period apart from the references and mention of *Tafsir*, *Fiqh*, and *Hadith* we find paragraphs and evidences of old books related to subjects such as history, medicine, logic, philosophy etc. Thus we can infer that the non availability of these books imposed minor difficulties but this was not such a problem that it could become an obstacle for the personal study and research of scholars.

From the above discussion we can deduce that during the period under review the *Madarsas*, were not the only centres to provide education but there were various other agencies or channels through which education could be imparted. Generally the individual centres of scholars were the most commonly used channel for obtaining education

75. *Tarikh-i-Firoz Shahi* (Afif), Op.cit, p.392, Nadvi, Riyasat Ali, 'Kuch Fuqaha-i-Tatar Khaani ke bare main', *Ma'arif* 59/3, March, 1947, pp.165-80.

76 *Tarikh-i-Firoz Shahi* (Afif), Op.cit, p.392.

77 *Nuzhat-u'l-Khawatir*, Vol.2, Op.cit, p.44, for details see: *Fuqaha-i-Hind,* Vol.1, Op.cit, pp.280, 285, Khan, Muhammad Ijaz, "Timuri Ahd Se Pehle Hindustan Mein Ilm Hadith Ka Rivaj", *Ma'arif,* Vol. 24, 40, October 1929, pp.250-52.

and they were popular for the study of some or the other subject. That is why the scholars would turn towards these private institutions. However to attain specialization in a particular subject one had to approach the teachers and scholars of that subject and thus they benefitted from them. The observatories, astrolabes functioned as a medium to provide knowledge in astronomy, hospitals functioned as institutes for the provision of medical knowledge, and *karkhanas* functioned as a medium to provide technical knowledge and develop industrial skill and craftsmanship. Moreover rarely one will come across a scholar who has obtained all his knowledge and completed his studies under one particular teacher or one particular *Madarsa*, or individual centre. Instead in order to specialize in any particular science or art, be it traditional (*Manqulat*) or rational (*Ma'qulat*) one had to attend lectures and gain from various different centres for learning and only then this kind of scholarship was possible.

Chapter - III

Syllabus of Muslim Education and Learning

The syllabus or curriculum has always occupied an important position in the arrangement of teaching at *maktabs* and *madarsas* and other centres of learning. The curriculum infact plays an effective role in attaining the objective of education as well as for the development of the educational life of the students and for the embellishment of their aptitude. Secondly on behalf of the curriculum we can derive at the inclination of the Muslims, their contemplative attitude and ruminative leanings towards education. That is why if the syllabus of the educational institution is presumed to be a barometer to measure the deep regard and educational preferences, it won't be wrong. Education has always been an important source for the efflorescence and progress of the culture and civilization of communities. In order to attain this objective, the curriculum has to be effective and advantageous. It is generally presumed that the educational curriculum the Muslim period was a collaboration of the rational (*Ma'qulat*) and traditional (*Manqulat*) sciences and it included subjects of both the fields of study. In this context it will be appropriate to investigate and study, whether was there a fixed syllabus? Were there stages of study? Was there any time bound consideration and was a particular subject studied at one particular time? Some modern scholars have discussed about the stages of education. Let us first examine these.

Stages of Education:

While discussing the syllabus the first question that comes to one's mind is whether there were stages of education and what were they and what was the basis of this division or bifurcation? From the material available in the contemporary sources we can infer that like nowadays during the Sultanate period there was no division or fixation of groups and there was no limitation or building of standards (*Darjat*). During that period the teaching and learning depended upon the books of study and if at all a division of various stages of education is possible then it can be done on the basis of teaching of subjects alone. Many modern scholars like Rafiq Saeed Ahmad, have according to present system divided the stages of education into three i.e. primary, secondary and higher learning.[1] But there is no evidence of these stages of education in the contemporary sources, for instance, Barani in his *Tarikh-i-Firoz Shahi* has not mentioned a word about these stages of education.

When the Muslims arrived in India the method they adopted for the provision of education is that according to the custom the reading of the *Quran* was taught first. The teacher who taught to read the *Quran* was generally called a '*Muqri*'. The *Fawaid-u'l-Fu'ad* testifies that the person from whom Shaikh Nizam-u'd-din studied reading the *Quran* in his childhood was a Hindu slave called Shadi Muqri. He was an experienced and able teacher who knew how to teach the *Quran* and develop in boys a liking for memorizing it.[2] Shaikh Nizamuddin studied one verse from him and due to that *barqat* remembered the whole *Quran*. Shadi himself knew the *Quran* by heart and could recite it according to it's seven methods of recitation.[3] His life represented a strange pattern

1 For details of education during the Islamic period refer to, Rafiq, Saeed Ahmad, *Islami Nizam Ta'alim* Idarah-i-Tasnif wa Talif n.d., pp.55-56 and pp.264-74.

2 *Fawaid-ul-Fu'ad*, Op.cit, p.154.

3 *Siyar-ul-Auliya*, Op.cit, pp.110-11.

of living in those days, Shadi was originally the slave of a Hindu. Perhaps he secured emancipation in later life and became the pupil of a great scholar of Lahore, Khwaja Muqri. It was generally believed that whosoever received elementary instructions in the *Quran* from him eventually succeeded in commiting the Holy Book to memory.

After the *Quran* it is obvious that some Persian books were taught, for instance, Mir Khurd writes about Shaikh Nizamuddin Auliya:

"والده در مکتب فرستاد، کلام اللہ بخواند وتمام کرد وکتابہا خواند گرفت۔"[4]

"His mother sent him to the *maktab* where he read and completed the *Quran* and learnt to read books."

'*Kitabaha*' means the Persian books which were generally taught in the *maktabs* of that period since that was the language of administration and had become the language of the Muslims.

It is evident that an elementary knowledge of Arabic was also imparted so that an individual could understand the meaning of the verses of the holy *Quran* and was in a position to translate the famous *Hadith* (traditions). That's why the writers of that period made considerable use of Arabic also in their compilations and compositions. Perhaps this is the stage which the modern scholars call primary stage.

After this, in the next stage Arabic and Islamic sciences were taught which consisted of two stages. Mir Khurd writes that Nizam-u'd-din Auliya after completing *Ilm Fiqh, Usul-i-Fiqh* started with the books of the stage of *Fazl*'[5] which testifies that there was a stage of '*Fazl*'. In the different books of that period and the *tazkiras* of the *Ulama* and Sufis we find the usage of the term '*Ilm Fazl*'.[6] In other books another word used for *Fazl*' is '*Muntahiyana*'[7] and this is the stage which is interpreted as the stage of higher learning. Of the stage prior to this stage we do not find specific information in the books but in view of the term '*Fazl*'

4 Ibid, p.110.

5 *Siyar-ul-Auliya*,Op.cit, pp.100-101.

6 Ibid, p.111.

7 *Muntakhab-ut Tawarikh*, Vol.1 p.324, *Muntakhab-ut, Tawarikh*, Vol.3, p.67.

modern scholars have given the name *'Ilm Zaroori* or 'Compulsory Education' to the previous stage because whatever was studied before *'Ilm Fazl'* is presumed to be compulsory stage of education and who completed this stage was called a *Danishmand* (scholar).[8] That means any individual who did not go through this stage could not be called a *'Danishmand'*[9] or *'Maulvi'*. Maulana Siraj-u'd-din Uthman (Akhi Siraj) came from Bengal with just a book and paper and no other things to Delhi and after entering into the *Khanqah* of Nizam-u'd-din Auliya he became busy serving the people and hence did not get an opportunity to educate himself. When Shaikh Nizam- u'd-din desired to send his disciples to Bengal naturally he thought of Maulana Sirajuddin Uthman, also he desired to give the *Khilafatnama* to him since he belonged to this place but when he realized that the Maulana had not even completed the stage of *'Danishmandi'* he said:

"اول درجہ دریں کار علم ست"[10]

('Firstly the knowledge of this stage is very essential.')

Maulana Fakhruddin Zarradi was present in the *majlis* and he said that within six months he will make him (the *Maulana*) a *'Danishmand'* or (Maulvi).

درشش ماہ اوراد انشمند (مولوی) می کند[11]

Thus the study of this important stage of *'Danishmandi'* of Siraj Uthman was initiated. He started with the study of *Sarf* (Etymology) and it seems with *'Mizan'* the initial Arabic study was initiated, infact whatever is taught in *Sarf* i.e. the benefits of *gardan* (conjugation), *Ta'alil* (changing one of the weak letters to another) *qawa'id* (rules or principles of grammar) etc. were memorized by him. Maulana Fakhruddin Zarradi

8 *Siyar-ul-Auliya*, Op.cit, p.298, *Akhbar-ul-Akhyar*, Op.cit, p.67, pp.80-81, 98-99, 144,150.

9 For details see Latif 'Muslim Intelligentsia (*Danishmand*) As Portrayed in the Sufic Literature of the 14th Century.

10 *Siyar-ul-Auliya*, Op.cit, p.298.

11 Ibid.

wrote a book for Maulana Sirajuddin and called it *'Tasrif-i-Uthmani'*. Other than *Sarf* and *Nahv* (syntax) he studied *'Kafya'* and *'Mufussal'* and in *Fiqh*, *Quduri* and *'Majma-u'l-Bahrain'* from Maulana Ruknuddin Inderpati.[12] Thus in the compulsory stage i.e. *danishmandi* we can presume that *Sarf*, *Nahv* and *Fiqh* were taught.

Mir Khurd informs us that Shaikh Nizamuddin Auliya studied *Hidaya*, *Bazdawi*, *Kashshaf*, *Mashariq* and *Masabih* from Maulana Jamaluddin.[13] Probably these were the subjects taught in the *'Ilm Fazl'* stage. The *Tafsir 'Kashshaf'*[14] and the *'Tafsir Madarik'*[15] *Mashariq-ul-Anwar*, *Masabih* were commonly used books on religious sciences. Other than *Nahv* (Etymology) and *Sarf* (syntax), *Adab* (Literature) *Maani-o-Bayan* (Rhetoric and figures of speech) etc were also taught. In *M'aqulat* the study was limited to *'Qutbi'* *'Sharh Sahaif'*[16] Here it is important to mention that amongst the modern scholars the first person to discuss the syllabus in detail was Maulana Manazir Husain Gilani.

Making a survey of the prevalent syllabus of education in Medieval India, it also seems appropriate to explain that the fixation of subjects and the limitation of the discussion related to these subjects are important elements of the syllabus. In order to bring them into practice the clear division of different stages of education and fixation of classes and period of education are required. All these things are missing in the medieval educational system. In this context for the arrangement and organization of education the usage of the term *'Nisab-T'alim'* or *'syllabus of education'* perhaps is not very appropriate because there is no proper evidence to prove that there ever existed any committee or administrative body or any meeting of the *'ulama'* who decided and fixed the course of studies (curriculum or syllabus) for each stage of education and based on this syllabus the process of imparting education functioned in the *madarsas* or other individual centres of education.

---

12 Ibid, p.299.

13 Ibid, p.207.

14 Ibid, p.317.

15 *Akhbar-ul-Akhyar*, Op.cit, p.186.

16 For details see: Gilani, Manazir Husain, Vol.1, Op.cit, pp.196-200.

The '*Khanqah*'[17] as an institution was different from a *madarsa in* many ways. The *Khanqah* unlike the *Madarsa* was a mystic organization. It was always a residential institution the aim of which was to inculcate the spirit of community living among the mystics and learning about their moral and spiritual upliftment. The inmates followed strict discipline and believed in simple living. It was sometimes run by *futuh* (gift) and sometimes *waqf* (endownment).

The '*Khanqah*' organization differed from *silsilah* to *silsilah*. The *chishti* silsilah for instance was against having any relation or involvement with the government. It believed in a simple and humble living and close contact with common man but the *suhrawardi* silsilah did not eshchew politics and possessed an aristocratic atmosphere.

The *Qut al-Qulub*, the *Ihya-ul-'ulum* and its' translation, the '*Awarif*, the *Kashf al-Mahjub*, the *Sharh-i-Ta'arruf*, the *Risalah-i-Qushairi*, the *Mirshad al-'Ibad*, the *Maktubat-i-'Ain-al-Qudat* and the *Lawa'ih* and the *Lawami* of Qazi Hamid al-Din Nagauri, and *Fawa'id u'd-Fu'ad* of Amir Hasan had gained great popularity among mystic circles. People inquired from booksellers about books of devotion and mysticism.[18]

It is also apparent that inspite of the presence of several *Madarsas* and *Khanqahs* for imparting higher learning there also existed the private or individual centres of education where the teachers of a particular subject of their interest and choice gave lectures and students and seekers of knowledge according to their liking and leaning would attend these classes. In this way there is no evidence of any division of education into stages and no specific time table as such, no limitation of fixation of specific period of time, no limitation of the duration of study or the limitation of learning in a *madarsa* only or any geographical limitation as such. It is but obvious that under such circumstances it was not possible to fix a particular curriculum of studies but instead for the purpose of teaching and learning, certain books were selected related to each subject of study. Thus in the discussion of the medieval age it would be more appropriate to use the term "instruction of subjects or books" rather than curriculum or syllabus of education.

17 For details see: Nizami, K.A. *Studies in Medieval Indian History and Culture*, Op.cit, pp.80-96

18 *Tarikh-i-Firoz Shahi*, Op.cit, pp.343-345.

Review of Subjects Taught in the Madarsas, Individual and Private Centres of Education:

While studying the educational system or the teaching process of the period under review one is confronted with an important question i.e. which were the subjects taught in the *madarsas* and the individual centres of learning of the Sultanate period? There is no doubt that in the contemporary sources there are several evidences to show the construction and renovation of the *Madarsas*, the people responsible for building the *Madarsas*, for the arrangement, management and administration of these *madarsas*, the Sultanat's gifts, donations and provision of scholarships and stipends to the teachers and students, lot of information related to this is available. But there is less information available on the teaching and instruction during various stages and it's curriculum. That too the material is available in a dispersed form, in the *tazkiras* of the *ulama*, *Fuzala*, sufis, poets and not in a proper form.

By analyzing this material, the picture that emerges from it, we can surmise that in the traditional sciences (*Manqulat*) the subjects taught in stages of higher learning were *Tafsir* (Exegesis), *Hadith* (Traditions of the Prophet), *Fiqh* (Muslim Jurisprudence), *Usul-i-Fiqh* (Principles of Jurisprudence), *Adab* (Literature), *Ulum-i-Ma'ani* (Rhetoric) and *Tasawwuf* (Sufism) and the subjects of rational sciences (*Ma'qulat*) were *Mantiq* (Logic) *Phalsafa* (Philosophy), *Hayat* (Astronomy), *Ilm-i-Kalaam* (Scholasticism), *Riyazi* (Mathematics), *Kimiya* (Chemistry), *Tibb* (Medicine).

But due to the shortage of availability of material it is difficult to claim that all the above subjects were taught in all the *madarsas* and private educational institutions of that period. However, it can be claimed about the Firoz Shahi *Madarsa*, it can be claimed that the following subjects were taught:

(1). *Fiqh* (Jurisprudence)
(2). *Qir'at* (method of recitation of the Qur'an)
(3). *Usul-i-Kalam* (Principles of scholasticism)
(4). *Usul-i-Fiqh* (Principles of Jurisprudence)
(5). *Tafsir* (Exegesis)
(6). *Ahadis* (Traditions of the Prophet)

(7). *Ma'ani-o-Bayan* (Rhetoric)
(8). *Nahv-o-Sarf* (Syntax)
(9). *Ilm-i-Nazar* (Science of observation)
(10). *Ilm-i-Riyaazi* (Mathematics)
(11). *Tabi'i* (Physical sciences)
(12). *Illahi* (Theology)
(13). *Ilm-i-Tibb* (Medicine)
(14). *Tahrir-o-Khatt* (Calligraphy).[19]

From the contemporary sources of the Sultanate period, it is evident that an individual scholar studying at a time all the subjects would attain specialization in all of them at one period of time. There are only few subjects (such as *Tafsir*, *Hadith*, *Fiqh*, *Nahv-o-Sarf*, Language and Literature etc.) or books related to them were generally studied and commonly used by the *ulama*, *Fuzala* in the teaching process. While the studying of other subjects and to attain specialization in them depended upon the personal interest and individual efforts of the scholars and intellectuals.

Study of the Rational Sciences:

During the thirteenth century A.D. we can deduce from the contemporary sources there were innumerable scholars who were experts or specialized in the different branches of rational (*Ma'qulat*) sciences. According to Barani during the reign of Sultan Alauddin Khalji there were distinguished scholars of rational sciences along with scholars of traditional sciences and they were such experts and par excellence in their field that it was difficult to find their equivalent in other countries of the world.[20]

During the period amongst the scholars who specialized in Astronomy, Logic, Philosophy and Medicine, Sharf-u'd-din Badr-u'd-din Damishqi, Sadruddin Dehlavi, Alim-u'd-din, Ziauddin Nakshabi, Aziz-u'd-din Badayuni were present.[21] During the period of Sultan Jalal-

19 *Sirat-i-Firoz Shahi*, Op.cit, p.142, *Tarikh-i-Firoz Shahi*, Op.cit, p.564.

20 *Tarikh-i-Firoz Shahi*, Op.cit, pp.352-53.

21 *Tarikh-i-Firoz Shahi*, Op.cit, pp.362-64, *Nuzhat-u'l-Khawatir*,Vol.2, Op.cit, pp.14-16, Law N.N., *Promotion of Learning in India During the Mohammedan Rule*, Delhi, Idarah-i- Adabyat-Delli, rept 1973, p.39.

u'd-din Khalji, Sad-u'd-din Dehlavi was such an expert of Logic and *Hikmat* that he became very famous and was given the title of '*Mantaqi*'.[22] In the Delhi Sultanate, Sultan Muhammad bin Tughlaq was famous for his deep interest and popularization of the rational sciences.[23] Amongst the famous scholars of the rational sciences during this Sultan's reign were Alim-u'd-din Izzuddin and Muin-u'd-din Imrani . Both made significant contributions by delivering instruction in the books of these subjects and Izz-u'd-din himself was one of the teachers of the Sultan.[24]

During the same period in the field of medicine the degree of activity was such that the author of *Masalik-ul-Absar fi-Mumalik-ul-Amsar* states that 12,000 physicians were related to the Sultan's *darbar*.[25] Moreover the reign of Sultan Firoz Shah Tughlaq was generally famous for the domination of the sciences of '*Fiqh*' but as regards the interest of the rational sciences and the instruction in these sciences and it's compositions were also actively carried out. In some of the *madarsas* of this period, logic, philosophy, scholasticism were included in the course, the evidence of which is available. During this time Jalal-u'd-din Rumi, Jalal-u'd-din Kirmani, Azduddin Khalid Khani, Abdul Aziz Dehlavi etc. and several other scholars were present who had a deep knowledge and understanding in subjects such as Philosophy, *Hikmat*, and Physical sciences. Jalaluddin Rumi was the pupil of Shaikh Qutbuddin Razi, the interpreter of *Shamsiyah*. Teaching was his special profession. The last mentioned two *ulama* translated some Sanskrit works of astronomy into Persian. It is the best proof of their depth in this field.[26] Moreover there was no shortage of scholars of medicine. The appearance of many hospitals during this period testifies to the keen interest of the Sultan

22 *Tarikh-i-Firoz Shahi*, Op.cit, p.198, *Nuzhat-u'l-Khawatir*,Vol.2, Op.cit, p.46.

23 *Tarikh-i-Firoz Shahi*, Op.cit, p.464, Nizami, K.A., *Salatin-i-Dehli Ke Mazhabi Rujhanat*, Delhi, Nadwat-ul-Musannifin, 1980, pp.327-29.

24 *Akhbar-ul-Akhyar*,Op.cit, p.114, *Tazkira-i-ulama-i-Hind*,Op.cit, pp.228-29, *Fuqaha-i- Hind*,, Vol.2, pp.304-05.

25 Otto Spies, Op.cit, p.32.

26 *Nuzhat-u'l-Khawatir*,Vol.2, Op.cit, pp.15,22,68, *Tabaqat-i-Akbari*, Vol.1, p.234.

in this field.[27] As already mentioned in the previous chapter these hospitals not only provided remedy and treatment of diseases but also functioned as institutions where lectures were imparted on medicine. That period about which it is thought that the study of rational sciences was limited to certain books only (i.e. *Qutbi* and *Sharh-Sahaif*) instead the experts of this science were engrossed in imparting instruction in these subjects and those scholars who were interested in specializing in the rational sciences they would turn towards them for personal study and would conduct research also. Shedding some light on this trend of the period under review Maulana Manazir Husain Gilani writes:

”دانشمندی یا ملائیت کے لئے جن علوم کا پڑھنا ضروری تھا ان کی تحصیل کے بعد اور کبھی اس کے ساتھ بھی بطور اختیاری مضامین کے اپنے اپنے رجحان و ذوق کے مطابق علوم (سائنس) فنون وصناعات (آرٹس) زبانوں (لنگویجز) میں سے جن چیزوں کے پڑھنے کی ضرورت تھی ان کے ماہرین سے عموماً لوگ پڑھتے تھے اور جن کے لئے صرف علمی مشق یا مطالعہ، مزاولت و ممارست کی حاجت تھی، لوگ اس میں مشغول ہو جاتے تھے۔“ [28]

“Sometimes during the course and generally after studying the subjects which were necessary for ‘*danishmandi*’ or *mullaiyat*, they, according to their learning and interest, studied science, arts, language, whatever was necessary, under the experts of these sciences. People were also engaged in getting knowledge which required exercise, reading and practice.”

From all this, we can derive at the conclusion whether it was the rational (*Ma’qulat*) science or the traditional (*Manqulat*) sciences, in every field taking benefit from the teachers of specific subjects in the higher learning was the prevalent trend and these teachers had their specific groups of students. Infact in any subject after attaining elementary knowledge of it, for the specialization in one particular subject or

27 Tughlaq, Firoz Shah, *Futuhat-i-Firoz Shahi*, Aligarh, Department of History, 1954, pp.15-16, *Tabaqat-i-Akbari*, Vol.1, Op.cit, p.121.

28 Gilani, Manazir Husain, Vol.1, Op.cit, p.232.

subjects the personal effort and hard work played a more effective role. Maulana Shibli describes this method of study in the following words:

''قدیم اصطلاح میں کالج ایک شخص کے وجود کا نام تھا۔ وہ جہاں بیٹھ جاتا تھا، اس کے گرد مستفیدوں کی جماعت کثیر جمع ہو جاتی تھی۔ اس کے فیض کا بادل ہر وقت برستا رہتا تھا۔ دن رات جس وقت جو کچھ بولتا تھا علمی لکچر ہوتا تھا۔ استادوں کا سلسلہ، شاگردوں کا سلسلہ در سلسلہ پھیلتا جاتا تھا، یہاں تک کہ چند کے بعد یہ ذی روح کالج یونی ورسٹی یا جامعہ اعظم بن جاتا تھا۔ آج کل لوگ کالج کی طرف منسوب ہوتے ہیں لیکن اس زمانہ میں شخص کی طرف منسوب ہوتے تھے..... آج کل کی یونیورسٹیاں یا کالج صرف بڑے بڑے شہروں میں قائم کئے جاسکتے ہیں لیکن اس وقت کے ذی روح کالج ہر قصبہ، ہر گاؤں اور ہر جھونپڑے میں قائم کئے جاسکتے تھے۔'' [29]

"In old terminology the college was supposed to be an existence of an individual; wherever he sat, the seekers of knowledge gathered around him. He inspired everyone anytime. Whatever he spoke, during day and night, was his lecture. The number of teachers and students continuously increased, and after sometime this individual scholar became an University in himself. Nowadays people are ascribed to colleges but in those days they were ascribed to individuals. The college and Universities in modern times are established only in big cities but at that time these individual scholars were available in every town and village".

Trends and Objectives of Learning:

Another significant aspect of the learning process during the period under discussion is that it was generally simple and practical. It appears that it's object was not only just to provide the treasure of knowledge regarding different arts and sciences but also to create in them a sense to reach that treasure. Thus for teaching and learning such books were

29 Numani, Shibli, *Maqalat-i-Shibli*, Vol.3, ed., Syed Suleman Nadvi, Azamgarh, Matba-i- Ma'arif, 1955, pp.102-03.

selected by which the scholars could get a practice of thinking, by mentally exercising their faculties of thinking and an opportunity to enhance their power of understanding. The objective was to develop such skills and capabilities that after completing the study of elementary subject, if a student desired to require expertise or specialization in a particular subject then he would not face any difficulty in carrying out further study and research and accomplish his goal. Thus much attention was paid to gain knowledge in subjects such as etymology, syntax, language and literature, rhetoric etc. and in these subjects abridged and abstruse books were liked and preferred by scholars. For *Tafsir*, *Fiqh*, *Usul-i-Fiqh* and *Adab*, systematically arranged books like *Kashshaf,Hidaya,Bazdawi*, *Maqamat-i-Hariri* were preferred.[30] From these the students developed the capability of thinking and understanding and the skill of grasping the subject matter reached a high scale. Moreover here, one must remember that during that period in the teaching process there was large scale increase in the books on *mantiq* (logic) and *Phalsafa* (Philosophy), one of the reasons for this perhaps was to attain the above mentioned objective of embellishing the skill of thinking and understanding. Similarly in the case of *Usul-i-Fiqh* (Principles of Jurisprudence) we can deduce that the way in which the legal problems were discussed, to derive at a proper conclusion and to emphasize on the use of reasons and evidences, we find the capability to enhance the power of understanding.

During the teaching and learning process of the Sultanate period we find evidence that some books which were complicated and difficult were read again and again which we come across while studying about the details of educational lives of several scholars and sufis, who went to the extent of studying some books forty times. For instance Mufti Jamal-u'd-din Dehlavi studied the '*Azadi*' (book on *Ilm Kalaam*) forty times[31] Some times the complete books were memorized but there is no evidence available to understand whether the objective was to strengthen the power of memorization or any other reason. Shaikh Nizam-u'd-din

30 Gilani, Manazir Husain, Vol.1, Op.cit, pp.298-99, 305.

31 *Muntakhab-ut Tawarikh*, Vol.3, Op.cit, p.77, *Tazkira-i-ulama-i-Hind*,Op.cit, pp.43-44.

Auliya had memorized forty chapters of the *Maqamat-i-Hariri*[32] Muhammad bin Tughlaq had memorized the *Hidaya* and according to *Akhbar-u'l-Akhyar* and *Siyar-ul-Auliya* amongst the contemporary scholars of his reign, Maulana Husam-u'd-din Multani also remembered the *Hidaya* completely.[33]

Selection of Books For Study:

The selection of books played an important role in the acquisition of knowledge. Generally it is known that during that period for the purpose of teaching and learning instead of fixing debates and discussion on the prevalent subjects of study, books related to them were selected for study. This selection of books for teaching infact was in accordance with the personal leanings of the *ulama*, *Fuzala* and teachers of that period and depended upon their approval. That is the reason in the selection of books we find differences based on time and place. Moreover in some circles of scholars and teachers many books were prescribed for one particular subject according to their personal interest and likings. We can infer that during the Sultanate period for the teaching of Tafsir, Zamakhshari's *Tafsir*, (*Kashshaf*) was the most popularly used *Tafsir* but in the Sufi circles the teachers used another *Tafsir 'Madarik-ul-Tanzil'* (author: Abul Barkat Abdullah Bin Ahmad-ul-Nafsi) we also find evidence that they referred to *Kashshaf* also. It has already been discussed that the *Tafsir Madarik* was the favourite *Tafsir* of Chishti Sufis. Shaikh Husamuddin Manikpuri always kept it with him and whenever he found any difficulty in understanding any verse then he would consult it. The *Tazkiras* and other contemporary sources do not give any reason for the popularity of the *'Tafsir Madarik'* as compared to other *Tafsirs*. From the other *Tafsirs* that were prevalent in Sufi circles during that period we can infer that they were written from Sufi point of view. In this context the *Tafsir 'Arais-ul-Abyan fi Haqaiq ul Quran'* (author Shaikh Abu Muhammad Riz Bahan bin Abi-ul-Nasr) was also included.[34] From the above examples we can

32 *Akhbar-ul-Akhyar*,Op.cit, p.55, *Siyar-ul-Auliya*, Op.cit, p.111.

33 Otto Spies, Op.cit, p.38, *Akhbar-ul-Akhyar*,Op.cit, p.89.

34 Muhammad Husain-ul-Zahabi, *Al Tafsir wa-al-Mufsiron*, Vol.3, Alqahra, Darul Kutub-ul- Hadisa, 1962-pp.56-58.

understand the role of the individual leanings and thoughtful inclinations for the selection of books.

During the first phase of the Islamic period due to emigration of central Asian *ulama* and jurists and the governmental administrative needs the 'Fiqh literature' was patronized to a great extent. Maulana Shibli is of the opinion that in the teaching process of that period, books authored by foreign scholars were only prescribed and used and after the initiation of the syllabus of 'Dars Nizami' the books authored by Indian scholars became prevalent.[35] This claim of Maulana Shibli is not correct because we find evidence in the sources that before the appearance of *Dars-i-Nizami* many books authored by Indian writers were included and used in the teaching process. For instance in the teaching of *Hadith, Mashariq-ul-Anwar.*[36] (author: Hasan bin Muhammad Sughani Lahori) (ob.1252 A.D.), in *Nahv, Irshad*[37] (author: Qazi Shihabuddin Daulatabadi) (ob.1225 A.D.) in *Sarf, Risala Asmania* (author Fakhruddin Zarradi (ob.1347 A.D.)[38] and in Hikmat, *Shamsi Bazigha*[39] (author: Mullah Muhammad Jaunpuri (ob.1652 A.D.) can be presented. Other than this the Indian scholars have also written commentaries and marginal notes on different sciences and arts. In the above context *Bazdawi, Madarik, Mashariq-ul-Anwar, Hidaya,* and *Waqaya, Fusul-ul-Hikam, Awarif-ul-Ma'arif, Aqaid Nasafi, Aqaid Azadiya, Mawaqif, Shamsiya, Tehzib-ul-Mantiq, Salam-ul-ulum, Shamsi Bazigha,* and *Hikmiya-ul-Aa'in,* many commentaries and marginal notes were formulated.[40] And these books had become an important aspect of the teaching process under review.

---

35 Numani, Shibli, *Maqalat-i-Shibli,* Vol.3, Op.cit, p.99.

36 *Tazkira-i-ulama-i-Hind,*Op.cit, p.275, *Fuqaha-i-Hind,* Vol.1, Op.cit, pp.96-97, 126,204-05,240,276, Sufi, G.M.D., *The Evolution of Curriculum,* Delhi, Idarah-i-Adabyat-i-Delli, 1977, p.17.

37 *Fuqaha-i-Hind,* Vol.1, Op.cit, p.240, Sufi, G.M.D., Op.cit, p.17.

38 *Akhbar-ul-Akhyar,*Op.cit, p.87.

39 *Tazkira-i-ulama-i-Hind,*Op.cit, p.221

40 Syed Abdul Hayy, *Islami ulum wa Funun Hindustan mien,* Azamgarh, Darul Musannifin 1969, pp.155-58, 215-17, 219-20, 241-42, 260-62, 322-324, 325, 326, 352-54, 358-59, 368-69.

Maulana Abdul Haiy has given the following syllabus for primary stage in which he has mentioned the names of reference books for each subject.[41]

Nahv	:	*Kafiya, Lub-al-Albab of Qazi Nasiruddin Baizawi*
Fiqh	:	*Hidayah.*
Usul-i-Fiqh	:	*Manar, Usul-i-Bazdawi.*
Tafsir	:	*Madarik, Kashshaf.*
Tasawwuf	:	*Awarif, Fusus-ul-Hikam.*
Hadith	:	*Mashariq-ul-Anwar and Misabih-Al-Sanch*
Adab	:	*Maqamat-i-Hariri*
Mantiq	:	*Shah-i-Shamimah*
Kalam	:	*Sharh-i-Sahaif, Tamhid Abu Shakur Salimi*

But according to K.A. Nizami this list is not complete and he has presented on the basis of the contemporary *Tazkiras* and *Malfuzat*, the following list of books which were included in the study of the period so that the general religious and academic leanings of that age may be understood correctly.

(1). *Qut-ul-Qulub*

(2). *Risalah Qushairi*

(3). *Ihya-ul-Ulum*

(4). *Maktubat-i-Ain-ul-Quzat.*

(5). *Mirsad-ul-Ibad*

(6). *Tafsir of Imam Nasiri*

(7). *Nawadir-ul-Usul of Maulana Alauddin Tirmizi.*

(8). *Ruh-ul-Arwah*

(9). *Maqsud-ul-Aqsa*

(10). *Asnad-i-Ulliyah of Shaikh Abdullah Tastari*

(11). *Kimiya-i-S'aadat.*

(12). *Tuhfat-ul-Shabab*

(13). *Tafsir-i-Madarik*

41 See: Risalah, *Al Nadwah*, February, 1909, pp.7-8.

(14). *Nahj-ul-Balagha*
(15). *Kanz-ul-Adab*
(16). *Tafsir-i-Haqaiq*
(17). *Fiqh-i-Ma'qul*
(18). *Akhbar-ul-Athmar.*
(19). *Misbah-Al-Diya*
(20). *Siyar-al-Muluk*
(21). *Ta'ruf*
(22). *Maktubat-i- Maulana Fakhruddin*
(23). *Quduri*
(24). *Majma-u'l-Bahrain*
(25). *Tazkirat-ul-Auliya*
(26). *Khamsa-i-Nizami.*[42]

From the above detailed discussion we can conclude that whatever was the course of study it depended upon the selection of books. The selection of books in the process of teaching was such that after their completion a student would develop the quality of grasping the meaning of the subject and the power of understanding the different sciences and arts enhanced. The subject of study included both the traditional sciences as well as the rational sciences. Due to the efforts of the scholars and teachers towards personal study and research there was massive growth and development in the field of education which played a crucial role in the cultural efflorescence of the Delhi Sultanate.

42 Nizami, K.A., *Hayat-i-Shaikh Abdul Haq Muhaddith Dehlavi*, Delhi, Nadwat-ul-Musaniffin, 1953, pp.26-27.

Chapter - IV

Education of Princes—Royal Education

The early Turkish Sultans of Delhi belonged to tribes and ethnic groups which did not possess well-established traditions of education or scholarship. Infact, some of these tribes were new converts to Islam and lacked proper knowledge about the basic ideals and principles of the religion. However, as years passed, due to the Mongol and Ghuzz invasions the scholars of 'Ajam thronged into India, resulting in the rapid growth of academic centres and influenced the Sultans to cultivate literary interests.

The Mongol cataclysm consequently created climate of intellectual fervour, as a result of this, education of princes almost always attracted the attention of the Sultans of Delhi, some of the Sultans personally took keen interest in the education of their sons, the future heirs to the throne of Delhi. They were perhaps fully conscious of the fact that success in life largely depended upon the training which one receives during his early years.

Paucity of relevant material makes it difficult to portray in detail the personal qualities, qualifications, daily life and routine of the Sultans. The *Fatawa-i-Jahandri* thus refers to the expectation of the people in this regard:-

"The essence of the king's recognition of his great blessing is that he realizes the value of time and does not waste his time, which is more precious than the time of any other person ....
After the performance of the necessary religious duties, he should devote himself only to administrative affairs and consider himself dedicated to public service. He should not throw away his precious life in the pursuit of pleasures. But the properly attending to public business is not possible unless the king strictly allocates his time, both day and night, and assigns a period to every business and during that allotted period, he does not leave that specific business to attend to some other work. So far as possible, he should attend exclusively to government business and not waste his precious life in frivolities, armours and useless things.[1]

Aibek (1206-10 A.D.) was purchased in his childhood as a slave by the Qazi of Nishapur, Fakhr-u'd-din 'Abd-ul-'Aziz Kufi, a descendent of Imam Abu Hanifa. He provided the same facilities of education including archery and riding to Aibek which he had arranged for his sons.[2] Aibek recited the *Quran* in such an impressive voice with clear intonations that he earned the epithet of *Quran Khwan.*[3] He became proficient in Persian and Arabic and also acquired some knowledge of science.[4] He was very fond of playing Chaughan (Medieval Polo) and often went to suburban areas in Lahore to play the game. He died in an accident while playing polo.[5]

His interest in learning after his accession and his patronage of the *'Ulama*, Jurists, *Qazis*, pious men and the reformers has been praised by the historians.[6] He raised the prestige of Lahore as a centre of learning.[7] Delhi during his reign attained such academic eminence that "out of it's ten (residents) nine were scholars and out of ten scholars, nine were expert in Quranic exegesis.[8]

1 Habib Muhammad & Dr. Khan, Mrs. Afsar Umar Salim, *The Political Theory of the Delhi Sultanate*, Delhi, Kitab Mahal, n.d., p.41.
2 *Tarikh-i-Ferishta*, Vol.I, Op.cit, p.60, *Tabaqat-i-Nasiri*, Vol.I, p.416.
3 *Tarikh-i-Fakhruddin Mubarakshah*, Op.cit, p.21.
4 *Tarikh-i-Ferishta*, Vol.I, Op.cit, p.60.
5 Raverty, H.G., Op.cit, pp.513-528.
6 *Tarikh-i-Fakhr-ud-din Mubarakshah*, Op.cit, p.35.
7 *Taj-u'l-Ma'athir* (in Elliot, H.M. and Dowson. J, Vol.2), p.237.
8 Ibid.

Because of his generous nature he earned the title of *'Lakh Baksh*'[9] and the later generations used this title *'Qutb-u'd-din*, for a generous person, a title used for a person conspicuous for generosity.[10] Dr. Habibullah correctly remarks that 'he combined the intrepidity of the Turk with the refined taste and generosity of the Persian.[11] As late as the seventeenth century talks of his generosity were circulating in distant Deccan, and Ferishta informs us that when people praised anybody for his extreme generosity they called him 'Aibek of the time.'[12] Abul Fazl, praised Aibek and sums up his assessment of his contribution in the words: 'He achieved things, good and great'.[13]

After the information gathered above we can safely conclude and believe in what N.N. Law has to say about Aibek's illustrious reign, says he, 'when he (Aibek) came to power in India Mohammedan learning was promoted by the establishment of hundreds of Mosques which like the churches of Medieval Europe were centres of both religion and learning.'[14] Thus religious instruction went hand in hand with secular learning.

Iltutmish (1210-35 A.D.) also was an outstanding figure of the Ghurid ruling Oligarchy, just, brave, pious and devoted. In intrepidity remarks Minhaj, "He turned out another impetuous 'Ali and in liberality, a second Hatim-i-tai.'[15]

During his early days in Bukhara and Baghdad he came into contact with eminent religious figures of the age.[16] He visited hospices of many Sufi Saints of these places. When he was young, he met Shaikh Shibab-u'd-din Suhrawardi, the famous saint of Suhrawardi *Silsilah* (spiritual mentor of Shaikh Sa'di) in Baghdad who had forecast a bright future

9 *Tabaqat-i-Nasiri*, Vol.I, Op.cit, p.490.

10 *Tabqat-i-Akbari*, Vol.1, Op.cit, pp.21-22, *Tarikh-i-Ferishta*, Vol.I, Op.cit, p.63.

11 Habibullah, A.B.M, Op.cit, p.76.

12 *Tarikh-i-Ferishta*, Vol.I, Op.cit, p.63.

13 Mohd Habib, Nizami, K.A. (ed.) *The Comprehensive History of India, The Delhi Sultanate*, Vol.V, New Delhi, Peoples Publishing House, 1970, p.206.

14 Law, N.N., Op.cit, p.19.

15 Raverty, H.G. Op.cit. p.598.

16 Nizami, K.A., *Salatin-i-Dehli kay Mazhabi Rujhanat*, Op.cit, 102-104, Nizami, K.A. *Studies in Medieval Indian History and Culture*, Op.cit, pp.15-18.

for him.[17] All contemporary and later writers have lauded Iltutmish's respectful attitude towards the *'ulama* and the religious scholars. Minhaj remarks about him: "The probability is that never was a sovereign of such exemplary faith, and of such kind heartedness and reverence towards recluses, devotees, divines and doctors of religion and law from the mother of creation ever enwrapped in the swaddling bonds of dominion."[18]

When Iltutmish was a governor of Badaon, the city was bustled with scholars from Baghdad, Nakshab, Muhmara, Ghaznin, Ghur and other places which had suffered due to the Ghuzz and Mongol invasions. The full details are not available, Iltutmish could not have remained ignorant about these refugee scholars of Badaon. Shaikh Nizam u'd-din Auliya used to narrate in his mystic gatherings incidents of his life in Badaon with great appreciation.[19] Although due to his political preoccupations he did not have much time for the encouragement of learning but we find proofs that he was liberal[20] and Delhi continued to be a resort of learned men during his reign. Minhaj has written that if Qutb-u'd-din was *Lak Baksh*, then Iltutmish was a step ahead, he was *Sad Lak Baksh*.'[21]

Iltutmish had a keen desire to educate his sons and daughter. He procured books from Baghdad for their instruction. He obtained books like the *Adab-us-Salatin* and *Ma'asir-us-Salatin*[22] which testifies that he was aware of the intellectual progress and development in the Islamic world. It was under his patronage that the *Adab-ul-Harb-wa- Shuja'at'* and *Tarikh-i-Fakhr-u'd-din Mubarakshah* were prepared by Fakhr-i-Mudabbir. Muwayyid Jajarmi dedicated the Persian translation of the *Ihya-u'l-Ulum* of Imam Ghazzali to him. He and his son Rukn-u'd-din Firoz got Imam Razi's *Sir-al-Maktum* translated into Persian. The Bibliotheque Nationale has several copies of this work.[23] We can infer

17 *Fawa'id-u'l-Fu'ad*, Op.cit, p.212.

18 Raverty, H.G., Op.cit, pp.600-601.

19 *Fawa'id-u'l-Fu'ad*, Op.cit, pp.211-212.

20 Raverty, H.G. Op.cit, p.598.

21 *Tabaqat-i-Nasiri*, Vol.I, Op.cit, p.440.

22 *Tarikh-i-Firoz Shahi*, Op.cit, pp.144-45.

23 Nizami, K.A., *Royalty in Medieval India*, New Delhi, Munshi Manoharlal, 1997, p.101.

from this that the Sultan was deeply interested in the intellectual heritage of Islam.

After the death of his eldest son, Iltutmish realized the incapability of his other sons and preferred to nominate his daughter Razia as the Sultan of Delhi but the nobles raised Rukn-u'd-din Firoz (1235-36 A.D.) to the throne. He was very handsome, possessing a gentle temperament and like his father was extremely generous.[24] But after his accession he gave himself to pleasure pursuits, resulting in the utter chaos and confusion of state affairs. Although court poets like Taj-u'd-din Reza have called him extirpator of infidelity, 'supporter of Islam and 'pillar of faith' which is very doubtful viewing his life style filled with fun and frolic which portrays that he was least interested in education and learning. Minhaj concludes his account of Rukn-u'd-din with these remarks:

"It is essential above all things, that sovereigns should have justice in order that their subjects should dwell in tranquility and repose, and that they possess beneficence so that their followers may be satisfied and contented, and revelry and merriment and companionship with the base and ignoble, becomes the means of an empire's ruin."[25] Perhaps Minhaj had Iltutmish in mind when he made these comments on the life pattern of his successor.

Iltutmish had the foresight to visualize that his daughter Razia (1236-40 A.D.) had the calibre and possessed more capability as compared to his sons to rule over the kingdom. Therefore he elevated her to the throne by appointing her incharge of the capital when he returned from the Gwalior expedition.[26] This step taken by Iltutmish was a very bold Turkish experiment.[27] Minhaj aptly remarks that "she was endowed with all the admirable attributes and qualities necessary for kings."[28] Ferishta records that she was well-versed in the *Quran* which she could read with correct pronunciation.[29] She was a patron of learned.[30] She

24 *Tabaqat-i-Nasiri*, Vol.I, Op.cit, p.454.
25 Raverly, H.G., Op.cit, p.637.
26 *Tarikh-i-Ferishta*, Vol.1, Op.cit, p.68.
27 Nizami, K.A., *Royalty in Medieval India*, Op.cit, p.59.
28 *Tabaqat-i-Nasiri*, Vol.I, Op.cit, p.457.
29 *Tarikh-i-Ferishta*, Vol.1, Op.cit., p.68.
30 Raverty, H.G., Op.cit, p.637.

proved herself better qualified to rule than her brothers that's why Iltutmish had nominated her as his successor. Her political phantasm as a ruler and her tackful management of all grave situations show that Iltutmish had not neglected her education and training. After knowing all the positive qualities of Razia from contemporary historians it is difficult to rely on the remarks of Isami who has miscast her and has used the following words for her.

"She came out of purdah suddenly, discarded her modesty and became jovial. One day, she put on male attire and cap and came out of the exalted place. Then she mounted on an elephant and went out publicly" . . . . A slave of Ethiopian race used to stand by her side when she mounted on her horse. With one hand he used to hold her arm and help her mount the horse firmly. That man had been a slave of Iltutmish and was named Yaqut". One is not surprised at this opinion of Isami about Razia because his views about women were such that he wrote "A woman is a sign of danger wherever she be since she is of devilish disposition . . . . A woman cannot acquit herself well as a ruler, for she is essentially deficient in intellect".[31]

The next two reigns of Mu'izz-u'd-din Bahram (1240-42 A.D.) and Ala-u'd-din Mas'ud (1242-46 A.D.) are educationally not important except for the patronage of Minhaj Siraj, the author of *Tabaqat-i-Nasiri* who in 1238 A.D. was appointed the principal of *Nasiriyah* College and superintendent of it's endowments.[32] Minhaj calls Muizz-ud-din Bahram *Khunkhar* (blood thirsty) and Isami condemns him on account of his immoral activities, malicious and savage-like nature.[33] Alau'd-din Mas'ud who succeeded Bahram, was of pleasant manners[34] before his accession but later he got involved in gratification and hunting. His successor, Nasir-u'd- din Mahmud (1246-66 A.D.), was a capable prince and had proved his administrative skills as a governor of Bahraich at the age of 16. But as he ascended the throne he withdrew himself

31 *Futuh-us-Salatin*, Op.cit, pp133-134, Mahdi Husain, *Futuh-us-Salatin*, (Eng. Trans.) Vol.2, Aligarh, Deptt. of History, A.M.U., 1976, pp.253-54.
32 *Tabaqat-i-Nasiri*, Vol..I, Op.cit, p.470, Raverty, H.G., Op.cit, p.667, Law, N.N., p.22
33 *Futuh-us-Salatin*, Op.cit, p.137.
34 *Tabaqat-i-Nasiri*, Vol.I, Op.cit, p.468.

completely from administration due to the crafty and devious designs of Balban[35] who wanted to keep him only as a puppet king.[36] He found escape and solace from this tyrannical situation in his prayers and penitences, just like Mahmud of Ghazni he earned his living by copying the *Quran* and did not take a single penny from the state treasury for his personal use.[37] According to Nizam-u'd-din Bakhshi he usually completed two copies of the *Quran* in a year.[38] Ibn Batuta saw a copy of the *Quran* calligraphed by Nasiruddin Mahmud in Qazi Kamal-u'd-din's hand and appreciated it's calligraphy.[39] Thomas is of the opinion that the inscription on the Kol Minar was written by the Sultan himself.[40]

Balban's life during the period of his commandership was one of merry making and drinking. But after his accession he completely gave up his convivial lifestyle.[41]

Balban (1266-1287 A.D.) was deeply interested in the education of his sons and possessed a keen desire to train them in the art of administration Bughra Khan thus recalled his father's interest in education.

چون من و برادر مهتر من مفردات لغت و نبستن پیش خطاط تمام کردیم اتابکان ما پیش سلطان عرضداشتند که بعد ازین شاهزادگان را از نحو وصرف وفقه چه تعلیم کنند و کدام استاد تعلیم کند فرمان در باب این چه نوع می شود فرمود که خطاط را جامه وانعام بدهند و معذرت کنند و پسران مرا مورخان دانا و دبیر پیشگان استاد کتاب آداب السلاطین وتالیف ماثر السلاطین که از بغداد بر خواجه زادگان ما پسران سلطان شمس الدین آورده بودند تعلیم کنند و بعد از من بهلوی پسران من پیران کار دیده و تجربه یافته که در علم تاریخ و احوال بزرگان ایشانرا مهارتی بود باشد باشند و خسان دون همت گداطبع را گرد گفتن پسران من ندهند علمی که ایشان دانند و ایشان آموزند پسران مرا در جهانبانی کار نیاید.....ما هر دو برادران کتاب آداب السلاطین را پیش خواجه تاج الدین بخاری که از ندمای شمس الدین بود تلمذ کرده ایم و من اوله و آخره در خدمت او گذاشتیم و چون کتاب تمام کردیم و در خدمت سلطان گذرانیدیم سلطان شمس الدین خواجه تاج الدین را.....دو دیه و یک لک جیتل انعام فرمود۔

35 See Nizami, K.A. *Studies in Medieval Indian History and Culture*, (article on 'Balban, the Regicide) Op.cit, pp.41-53

36 *Tarikh-i-Firoz Shahi*, Op.cit, p.26.

37 *Futuh-us-Salatin*, Op.cit, p.156.

38 *Tabaqat-i-Akbari*, Vol.I, Op.cit, p.37.

39 Ibn Batuta, *The Rehla of Ibn Batuta* , Translation &Commentary, (Mahdi Husain) Baroda Oriental Institute, 1976, p.35.

40 Thomas, E., pp.129-30, Nizami, K.A., *Salatin –i-Dehli Kay Mazhabi Rujhanat*, Op.cit, p.144.

41 *Tarikh-i-Firoz Shahi*, Op.cit, pp.45-46.

"When I and my brother had learnt word meaning and the calligraphists had taught writing, our tutors petitioned to the Sultan: what are the Shahzada's to be taught after this—etymology, grammar or jurisprudence? . . . . My father's order was as follows: "The calligraphist's be dismissed after being given dresses and *inams*. My son's are to be taught what wise historians and eminent *dabirs* have written. They are to be taught the books, *Adab-us-Salatin* . . . . and *Ma'asir-us-Salatin* which were brought from Baghdad for the sons of my master, Sultan Shams-ud-din. Hereafter only experienced secretaries (*dabirs*) who are well acquainted with history and the affairs of great men are to be in the company of my sons . . . . we two brothers read the *Adab-us-Salatin* . . . . from the beginning to the end from Khwaja Taj-u'd-din Bukhari, who was a courtier of Sultan Shams-ud-din. When we had finished the book we were presented before the Sultan who gave Khwaja Taj-u'd-din . . . . two villages and a lac of *jitals* in *inam*".[42]

Though both the sons were brought up under the strict supervision of their father, both developed into two diverse personalities with distinguishing habits. Prince Muhammad became an embodiment of good virtues and never indulged in vivacious activities. Bughra Khan took to a entirely different design and developed the habit of drinking. Balban rebuked him for his bad habits[43] but it went all down the drain. His habits spoilt to the extent that he even drank in the presence of his son, Kaiqubad.[44]

Balban was very respectful towards the Shari'at laws. According to Barani he never took any step and decision contrary to the Shariat laws.[45] From the above account we can conclude that Balban paid serious attention to the education of his sons in order to make them able Sultans.

Prince Muhammad, the eldest son of the Sultan was a very promising youth with charming talents. He exhibited great taste for literature and

42 *Tarikh-i-Firoz Shahi*, Op.cit, pp.144-45.

43 Ibid, pp.93-94.

44 Ibid, p.144.

45 Ibid, p.383.

learning. This prince with his distinct literary taste took the initiative in the formation of literary societies. The place chosen for the meeting of the members of the society was the king's palace.[46]

The status of the royal court in the literary world was kept at it's high level mainly through the patronage and literary tastes of Prince Muhammad. This court was visited by the most qualified and competent men of the time. His attendants used to read to him the *Shah Namah*, the *Diwan-i-Sanai*, the *Diwan-i-Khaqani* and the *Khamsah* of Shaikh Nizami.[47] At this time the esteem of Delhi was so great that it inspired a few verses of Amir Khusrau in which he declared with pride that Delhi could now successfully compete with Bukhara, the great University city of Central Asia which he expresses in the following words:-

خوشا هندوستان و رونقِ دین   شریعت را کمالِ عزّ و تمکین

ز علمِ با عمل دہلی بخارا   ز شاہان گشتہ اسلام آشکارا [48]

"(How great and fortunate India is, the religion (Islam) is happily flourishing here,

The *Shariah* is attaining the highest form of respect and popularity.

It is on account of the popularity of knowledge (*ilm*) and *ilm-i- ba-amal*(knowledge with action) that Delhi has become Bukhara;

It is due to the efforts of the Sultan's that Islam is becoming popular and prosperous day by day)."

The next Sultan, Kaiqubad, reigned for only two years, but during his short rule he reduced the high spirit of literary culture that had been introduced into the society of the day by Sultan Balban and his worthy son Prince Muhammad. Kaiqubad's rise to power marked a total deviation from the royal traditions zestfully built up by Balban.[49]

46 Law, N.N., Op.cit, p.24.

47 *Tarikh-i-Firoz Shahi*, Op.cit, pp.66-67.

48 Amir Khusrau, *Dewal Rani Khizr Khan (Ashiqah)* ed. By Rashid Ahmad Ansari, Aligarh, Madarsat-ul-um, 1917, p.46.

49 *Tarikh-i-Firoz Shahi*, Op.cit, p.128.

His upbringing took place under the strict supervision of Balban, he therefore had neither looked at any women nor had tasted wine.[50] However, after his accession to the throne he threw himself thoughtlessly into revelries. His new palace at Kilugarhi became abode of musicians, dancing girls, jokers and wits who met and rejoiced.[51] *Maliks*, *Amirs*, high officers and the city elite built houses in it's proximity and the entire area hummed with fun, frolic and merriment. In a fury to do away with any possible rival to the throne he killed Prince Muhammad's son Kai-Khusrau, an act which was condemned even by Bughra Khan. He did not offer his prayers regularly. Mosques were emptied and many bars were built.[52] Thus Kaiqubad's chaotic reign resulted in the moral degradation of the rich culture established by his grandfather Balban. With him also ended the Mamluk dynasty in India which contributed immensely and was the first dynasty which brought in cultural efflorescence to bring in an aesthetic culture.

The founder of the Khalji dynasty Jalal-u'd-din Khalji (1290-95 A.D.) was seventy years of age when he ascended the throne. He had neither the time nor fondness for literary or academic pursuits. Barani gave him the title of '*Sultan-al-Halim*'[53] because of his clemency and mild nature, in sharp contrast with both Balban and Ala-u'd-din Khalji. He sank headlong in merry making and wasted his time in either playing chess or listening to music. Barani informs us that there was a great moral decline of court etiquettes and the court musicians males as well as females portrayed a degrading picture of convivialism, Mehr Afroz and Nusrat Bibi were beauties par excellence and unique in their flattering attitude and courtesanship.[54]

However, in his *majlis* Amir Khusrau presented a fresh ghazal every day.[55] Some of the *nadims* of the Sultan like Taj-u'd-din Iraqi, Amir Khusrau, Muuwaid Jajarmi, Amir Arsalan Kulahi, Taj Khatib and others, were remarkable for their interest in history and literature.[56]

The Sultan was deeply interested in poetry and sometimes composed stray verses, even full ghazals.[57]

50 Ibid, p.128.
51 Ibid, p.130.
52 Ibid, p.130.
53 Ibid, p.174.
54 Ibid, pp.198-99
55 Ibid, p.200.
56. Ibid, p.199.
57 Ibid, p.197.

It may be presumed, Sultan Jalal-u'd-din Khalji was comparatively not as popular as the other Sultans of Delhi but during his reign the royal *Darbar* had become to some extent a centre of learning for the nobles and scholars in which jurists, historians, philosophers, logicians and all sundry participated.

Sultan Ala-u'd-din Khalji (1296-1315 A.D.) had no academic interests like Iltutmish or Balban but during his reign Delhi was the rendezvous of the intellectual Islamic world comprising of scholars of eminence in their field of study such as Imam Ghazzali, Imam Razi, Imam Abu Yusuf and Muhammad Shibani.[58]

N.N. Law is of the opinion that Alauddin Khalji was so uneducated that he could not read or write, in fact all modern works state that Alauddin Khalji was illiterate.'[59] Perhaps this statement is based on Barani's consistent repetition of the illiteracy of Sultan Ala-u'din which he expressed as follows.

بسیاری جہل و جہالت .....

('Very ignorant and illiterate')

"واو مردی بود کہ از علم خبر نداشت و با علما ہم نشست و بر خاست نکردہ بود و نامہ نوشتن و خواندن ندانستی ..."

('He was the man who had no knowledge of learning and did not keep the company of *ulama*, and he did not know even to read and write letters')[60]

"سلطان علاء الدین بادشاہی بود کہ خبر از علم نداشت ....."

('Sultan Alauddin was such a king who did not know about learning')[61]

"قاضی مغیث من اگرچہ علمی و کتابی نخواندہ ام"

58 Ibid, pp.353-54.
59 Law N.N., Op.cit, p.32; Kishori Saran Lal is of the opinion that "The Sultan was almost without literary education, like Akbar and Ranjit Singh after him, he confined by example the Tennysonian diction "that only those who cannot read can rule" Lal, S.K., *History of the Khaljis AD 1290-1320*, New Delhi, Munshiram Manoharlal, 1980, p. 271.
60 Ibid, p.262.
61 Ibid, p.289.

('Qazi Mughis! Though I am illiterate and have read no book whatsoever _ _ _ _ _ _ _'[62]

Barani is the only one to make such allegations. It is a well known fact that Barani had no access to the private sittings of the Sultan. Barani's uncle Ala-ul-Mulk was a favourite with the Sultan but Barani even disliked him and has not said a good word for him.

Stanley Lanepoole writes about Ala-u'd-din Khalji 'Temperance has been forced upon the people, and with, the example of the sober court, men of great learning and piety abounded. Such results testify to the greatness of a remarkable king'.[63]

According to Ferishta he was quite well versed in Persian, so much so that he could read even *Khat-i-Shikasta* (broken letter)[64] says he:-

''زیرا کہ پادشاہ خط وسواد مطلقا نداشت اما در آخر چون او خواندن نامہای منہیان بمرتبۂ سوادش روش شد کہ خطہای مغشوش را
بفراغت می خواند واز برکت آن بعضی کتب فارسی نیز خواندہ با مردم اہل فضل ہمزبان گشت''

"(Although the Emperor did not at all know the taste of reading and writing but in old age he could read the names of legal terms, and gradually he gained so much ability that he could easily read the broken letters, and due to its good fortune he could read some Persian books also and converse with the people of excellence, i.e. scholars)."

Another episode in the *Siyar-ur-Arifin* states that Alauddin *Khalji* was not an illiterate and could read, which is as follow:

قرا بیگ ترک، سلطان علاء الدین خلجی کا نہایت خاص (شخص) تھا.....اور حضرت شیخ کا مرید تھا۔ سلطان اس کو بھیجتا تھا اور جس شعر پر
حضرت شیخ کو وجد وحال آتا تھا، قرا بیگ اس کو لکھ لیتا تھا اور سلطان (علاء الدین) کو پہنچاتا.....سلطان المشائخ (نظام الدین اولیاء) کو
ان شعروں پر جو حکیم سنائی کے حدیقہ میں تحریر ہیں، بڑا وجد آتا تھا۔

شعر

بیش معنا جمال حالا افروز   در نمودے برو سپند بسوز
آں جمال تو حیست حسن تو   واں سپند تو چیست ہستی تو

قرا بیگ نے ان دونوں شعروں کو لکھ لیا اور سلطان علاء الدین کے پاس لے گیا۔ سلطان بار بار پڑھتا اور اپنی آنکھوں سے
لگاتا۔

62 Ibid, p.295.

63 Lanepoole, Stanley, *History of Medieval India*, Vol.3, New Delhi, Asian Educational Services, 1987, p.121.

64 *Tarikh-i-Ferishta*, Op.cit, p.110.

Qara Baig Turk was a very important associate of Sultan Alauddin and a *murid* (disciple) of Hazrat Shaikh. The Sultan would send him and on the couplet, the Hazrat would reach ecstasy, Qara Baig would write it and give it to the Sultan _ _ _ _ _ _ _ _ _ Sultan-ul- Mashaikh (Nizam-u'd-din Auliya) on these two couplets, which were from the *Hadiqah* of Hakim Sanai reached extreme ecstasy.

Couplet

"(How precious is your beauty; whosever looks at you feels complexed,

How illumined is your face and how inspiring is your beauty; The fact is every body thinks how great is your personality)."

Qara Baig wrote these two couplets and went to Sultan Alauddin. The Sultan would *read it again and again* and touched it to his eyes.[65]

But the *Tarikh-i-Ferishta* and the *Siyar-ur-Arifin* are not contemporary sources and belong to the later medieval period which may or may not be considered authentic.

Moreover, we are told by Barani that the most wonderful thing which people noticed during Sultan Ala-u'd-din's reign was the multitude of great men of all nationalities, scholars of every science and experts in every art gathered in the capital. Thus Delhi, due to the presence of these unrivalled men of great talents, became the envy of Baghdad, the rival of Cairo and the equal of Constantinople, the centres of civilized world.[66] Barani had named such scholars who flourished in Delhi and raised the academic structure of India in the contemporary world of Islam.[67] The age of Ala-u'd-din saw a unlimited assemblage of erudite and distinguished scholars and saints. He did not exhibit the same dedication to them as Balban had shown to the celebrities of his reign but was not all together indifferent to them. Also a very bold and intelligent step taken by Alauddin Khalji was that he reduced the

65 Hamid bin Fazl Allah Maulana Jamali, *Siyar-ur-Arifin,* Urdu translation by Mohammad AyyubQadri, Lahore, Urdu Science Academy, first ed., 1976, 2nd ed., 1989. p.99.

66 *Tarikh-i-Firoz Shahi,* Op.cit, p.341.

67 Ibid, 354

influence of *'Ulama*[68] who had become a power in politics in the earlier reign.[69]

Dr. Ghulam Sarwar Khan Niazi writes "Indeed it may be said that if consolidation of Muslim Rule was the work of Balban, Muslim India attained cultural maturity in the days of Sultan Ala-u'd-din Khalji."[70] The unusual respect that he enjoyed after his death was unique in the history of medieval India. People tied threads on his grave expecting fulfillment of their desires on account of the blessing of his soul.[71]

Thus viewing the immense development of learning and literature and cultural efflorescence during Alauddin Khalji's reign it may be presumed that he did not know to read and write but he was not ignorant and indifferent to the cultural and literary development of his period.

After Ala-u'd-din Khalji, Sultan Qutb-u'd-din Mubarak Khalji (1316-1320 A.D.) completely reversed the picture of Ala-u'd-din's court, except for the prohibitions which he continued.[72] He terminated all the regulations of his father. We do not have details about his education, only Ibn Batuta has referred to Qazi Zia-u'd-din, the Vakildar as his tutor in calligraphy.[73] Thus he set a very bad example for his subjects least bothered about the people limitlessly depraved, he threw himself heart and soul into all the wretchedness of immoral living, fun and frolic.

Barani observes, 'Mubarak khalji's four years and four months of rule were spent in merry making, enjoyment, wine drinking and pleasure pursuits.[74]

---

68 *Tarikh-i-Firoz Shahi*, Op.cit, p.296.

69 See, Nizami K.A., *Some Aspects of Religion and Politics in India during the thirteen century*, Delhi, Idarah-i-Adabyat-i-Delli, 1974, pp.171-73.

70 Niazi, Ghulam Sarwar Khan, *The Life and Works of Sultan Alauddin Khalji*, Lahore, Institute of Islamic Culture, 1990, p.122.

71 *Khair-u'l-Majalis*, Op.cit, pp.241-242.

72 *Tarikh-i-Firoz Shahi*, Op.cit, p.384.

73 Ibn Batuta, Op.cit, p.46,. Ibn Batuta informs us about Sultan Qutb-u'd-din bin Sultan Ala-u'd-din that one of the chief of the army and keeper of the palace key, Qazi Khan was his tutor.

74 *Tarikh-i-Firoz Shahi*, Op.cit, p.387.

Thus he became more famous for his bacchanalianism and his reign proved to be a period of retrogression in the cultural history of the Sultanate. A modern historian, Elphinstone also writes that 'In Delhi, Mubarak gave himself upto a course of the most degrading and odious debauchery.[75]

The Tughlaq Sultans were men of character and learning. The moral degradation that had crept in the rule of Kaiqubad, Jalal-u'd-din and Mubarak had not touched them. They uplifted the moral standard of society by encouraging the study of philosophy and jurisprudence and adopting public welfare projects.

Ghiyasuddin Tughlaq (1320-25 A.D.) the founder of the Tughlaq dynasty was a patron of learning and literature. 'God fearing, pious, abstemious, dutiful generous, unostentatious, liberal and free from prejudice, fanaticism and hatred of all kinds.[76] Barani describes him 'truly a king of good intentions and of divine nature'.[77] He gave Amir Khusrau the poet a pension, a thing which no one else had thought of doing.[78]

People found in Ghiyasuddin a reincarnation of Ala-u'd-din.[79] He was on good terms with the *'ulama* and *mashaikh* of his day.[80] He had an excellent character and chroniclers have praised his remarkable qualities. The welfare of the people was always his main concern.[81] He was very respectful towards the *Shariat* laws.[82]

Muhammad bin Tughlaq was gifted with equally admirable good character as his father. His vast learning and scholarship further added

---

75 Elphinstone, Monstruat, *The History of India, The Hindu and Mohammedan periods*, Allahabad, Kitab Mahal, 1966, p.344.

76 Agha, Mahdi Husain, *Tughlaq dynasty*, New Delhi, S.Chand & Co. Pvt. Ltd, 1976, p.472.

77 *Tarikh-i-Firoz Shahi*, Op.cit, p.429.

78 Powell Price J.C., A *History of India*, London, Thomas Nelson and sons Ltd., 1955, p.150.

79 *Tarikh-i-Firoz Shahi*, Op.cit, p.425, Nizami, K.A. *State and Culture in Medieval India*, Op.cit., p.111.

80 For details, see, *Salatin-i-Dehli Kay Mazhabi Rujhanat*, Op.cit, pp.314-21.

81 *Tarikh-i-Firoz Shahi*, p.443, *Tarikh-i-Mubarakshahi*, p.92.

82 Ibid, pp.441-43

good flavour to his charismatic personality. Scholars from distant Muslim lands Syria, Central Asia, Egypt etc. were impressed by his vast store of knowledge and erudition.

No Sultan in Medieval India has aroused so much discussion concerning his policies as Muhammad Tughlaq. He was undoubtedly the most capable man among the Sultans of the middle ages. He was endowed by nature with a astounding memory, a ascute and discerning intellect, and a tremendous capacity for assimilating knowledge of all kinds. His multifaceted personality and genius surprised all his contemporaries. A lover of fine arts, an accomplished poet, he was equally at home in logic, astronomy, mathematics, philosophy and the physical sciences.[83]

Ghiyas-u'd-din Tughlaq had appointed 'Azd-ud-din as the private tutor of Muhammad Tughlaq[84] who was later replaced by Qutlugh Khan.[85] Of all the Sultans of Delhi, Muhammad bin Tughlaq was perhaps the most knowledgeable and intellectually gifted ruler. He had committed to memory the *Quran* and *Hidayah.*[86] He possessed knowledge of both *manqul* (traditional) and *ma'aqul* (rational) sciences. He was well versed in logic, metaphysics, rhetoric and medicine.[87] He had immense knowledge of medicine and even prescribed medicines for different ailments. His knowledge of medicine had reached so far that in his discussions and debates with the most experienced doctors, it is proved that he outwitted them.[88]

From this we can infer that he was a brilliant conversationalist and in debate he could hold his own against the most eminent scientists and other people. He was good at drafting and a great calligraphist.[89] Occasionally he himself composed verses in Persian.[90] He was well acquainted with the *Sikandar Namah*, the *Abu Muslim Namah* and the *Tarikh-i-Mahmudi* and could easily quote from them.

---

83 Ibid, pp.443-44, *Tarikh-i-Ferishta*, Vol. I,, p.130.
84 Prasad, Ishwari, *History of Medieval India*, Allahabad, The Indian Press, 1966, p.265.
85 *Tarikh-i-Ferishta*, Vol. I, p.133.
86 *Tarikh-i-Firoz Shahi*, Op.cit, p.454, p.506.
87 Otto Spies, Op.cit, p.37.
89 Ibid, p.464.
90 Ibid, p.463.

He had taste for Sanskrit and used to associate with Hindu ascetics.[91] Besides, he was bestowed with a very retentive memory and remembered vividly many facts and details of historic significance. He possessed a moderate knowledge of Arabic, he understood it but could not speak it fluently. He had taste for Sanskrit and used to associate with Hindu ascetics.[92] Early contact with philosophers had made his mind intrusive and conjectural, chroniclers speak of his rationalistic approach and faith in the supremacy of reason.[93] He was well conversant with Greek philosophy and regular discussions with philosophers were held at his court. Barani particularly refers to the influence of the famous philosophers 'Ubaid, the poet, Najmi Intishar, and Maulana 'Alim-u'd-din who were responsible for the development of a skeptical, analytical and rational attitude in him.[94] He also became expert at archery, riding and in the use of Javelin and the sword.[95]

Muhammad Tughlaq was however interested in music and kept twelve hundred musicians in his service besides specially for the purpose of teaching music one thousand slave musicians.[96] His music gatherings were free from revelries and all sorts of immoral activities.[97]

Viewing his accomplishments, Agha Mahdi Husain writes about Muhammad bin Tughlaq "Intellectually he was far in advance of his age, a great scholar, well versed in almost every science, then known to Orientals."[98] Infact Muhammad bin Tughlaq is the only Sultan of Delhi whose intellectual achievements have been referred to by foreign scholars like Shihab-u'd-din al 'Umari, Al Qalqashandi, Ibn Hajar Asqalani, and others in glowing terms.

---

91 Ibid, p.463, Otto Spices, Op.cit, p.37 According to Shahabuddin Umari he had one thousand Arabic, Persian and Hindi poets, in his court, Ibid, p.32.

92 *Futuh-us-Salatin*, Op.cit, p.515. Isami calls him a *kafir* and urges a revolt against him. He censures him for siding with the Hindus and mixing privately with the jogis.

93 *Tarikh-i-Firoz Shahi*, Op.cit, p.464, Otto Spies, Op.cit, p.37.

94 Nizami, K.A., *Salatin Delhi Kay Mazhabi Rujhanat*, Op.cit, pp.327-28.

95 *Tarikh-i-Firoz Shahi*, Op.cit, p.464.

96 Otto Spies, Op.cit, p.32.

97 Ibid, p.52.

98 Agha, Mahdi Husain, *Tughlaq dynasty*, New Delhi, S.Chand & Co. Pvt. Ltd, 1976, p.482.

Muhammad bin Tughlaq was very punctilious in offering his obligatory prayers. He always got up on hearing the *azan* (call for prayer) and remained standing till it was over. After the morning prayers he spent some time in reciting religious formula (aurad).[99] He was very fond of men of learning and loved to associate with the *ulama*, the *Mashaik* (saints), the Sufis and philosophers. But influenced by Ibn Taimiya's ideology Muhammad Tughlaq's relations with the mystics became sour in later life. Ibn Taimiya (1263-1328 A.D.) and his school of thought aimed at the revival of Muslim political power by doing away with the dichotomy of religion and politics which they argued had deprived the state of the services of sincere and talented men. They condemned the mystic approach of eschewment of state services.[100]

With such intellectual calibre and achievements, Muhammad bin Tughlaq was head and shoulders above all his contemporaries. No doubt, therefore Barani considered him a 'wonder of creation.[101]

''سلطان محمد از اعجوبۂ آفرینش باری تعالیٰ در وجود آمدہ بود''

"(Sultan Muhammad Tughlaq had come into existence as a wonder of creation of God Almighty)."

Sultan Firoz Shah Tughlaq (1351-1388 A.D.) was deeply interested in the promotion of Islamic education and learning. N.N. Law writes "In the long list of preceding Mohammedan emperors there was none who tried so much for the diffusion of education among his subjects.[102]

Nothing is known about the early education of Firoz but the wide interest he took in *Fiqh* (Law) religion, theology, astronomy, medicine and natural sciences as revealed in the '*Sirat-i-Firoz Shahi*[103] and his composition and dictation of Futuhat-*i-Firoz Shahi*, it can be safely deduced that he was well educated and Ghiyas-u'd-din Tughlaq must

---

99 *Tarikh-i-Firoz Shahi*, Op.cit, p.506.

100 Nizami, K.A., *State and Culture in Medieval India*, Op.cit, p.112., *Oxford Journal of Indian History*, I, (1990), p.120.

101 Ibid, p.497.

102 Law, N.N., Op.cit, p.56.

103 For details see: *Sirat-i-Firoz Shahi*, Op.cit, pp.297-356.

have made good arrangements for his education as that of Muhammad Tughlaq. He was only twelve when Ghiyas-u'd-din died and after that Muhammad bin Tughlaq always kept Firoz in his company and explained to him all important state affairs. Ibn Batuta[104] opines that Malik Firoz was the closest chamberlain to the Sultan who used to dine with him—a rare privilege in the important dinners. Sometimes Muhammad Tughlaq took him in military expeditions also. Thus not only was he trained in the art of administration but also military operations.

Firoz Shah Tughlaq's intellectual level and learning was less compared to Muhammad Tughlaq, but he possessed a variety of literary interests. He was enthroned in Sindh by a group of religious men including Shaikh Nasir-u'd-din Chiragh. During the course of his journey from Sindh to Delhi he visited Shrines and *Khanqahs* of saints and gave stipends and endowments to *Khanqahs* which had suffered during the previous reign.[105] His political administration was of an entirely different nature. He abhorred from making any bold experiments like Muhammad bin Tughlaq. He entrusted the routine administrative responsibilities to his *Wazir* and directed his attention and energy to projects of public welfare and undertook several programmes of educational development.[106]

The contemporary Persian sources unanimously acclaim the greatness of Firoz Shah Tughlaq. He is styled as 'the most gentle, modest, gracious, benevolent, grateful, faithful, and firm believer in the tenets of Islam after Muhammad bin Sam.[107]

Firoz Shah Tughlaq had a religious bent of mind. He regularly performed the obligatory prayers in congregation, daily recited the *Quran*, was deeply interested in Islamic jurisprudence, he banned the use of silver and gold vessels in the court, regulated the visit of women to tombs and festivals and use of silken clothes etc. These actions taken

104 Ibn Batuta, Op.cit, pp.58,64.

105 *Tarikh-i-Firoz Shahi,* Op.cit, pp.538,539.

106 *Sirat-i-Firoz Shahi,* Op.cit, p.142.

107 *Tarikh-i-Firoz Shahi,* Op.cit, p.548.

by Firoz proved his deep interest in religion. But there was another side to his personality without which the picture will be incomplete. He was fond of wine, interested in astronomy, had faith in omens, auguries, amulets and charms and loved music. Azra Alavi rightly observes "Firoz Shah projects an image of his religious personality in the pages of *Futuhat* which is correct so far as it goes, but is not complete."[108]

Firoz Shah's keen personal interest gave further fillip to *tibb* (medicine). During his time it was included in the syllabus of the government colleges. He used to write prescriptions like Muhammad bin Tughlaq and prepared under his personal supervision, a comprehensive work on medicine entitled *Tibb-i-Firoz Shahi,*[109] dealing with diseases and their treatment. He was also interested in the veterinary science and discussed the diseases and treatment of animals in a brochure entitled *Shikar Nama-i-Firoz Shahi.*[110] His interest is astronomy outstripped all other Sultans. He not only got sanskrit works on astronomy translated into persian (like *Dala'il-i-Firoz Shahi*), but collected a whole library of books on astronomy.[111]

His passion for astronomy reached such a stage that hunting of different animals was decided according to astronomical calculations.[112] He also got the construction of astrolabes.[113]

Considerable development took place in the making of mechanical devices also.[114] Firoz Shah paid great attention to the education and training of his slaves.[115]

However, the successes of the first half of Firoz's reign were due to an able and loyal minister named Maqbul, a Brahman convert to Islam, who had practically governed the kingdom for more than twenty years.

---

108. Alavi, Azra, The *Futuhat-i-Firoz Shahi*, Delhi, Idarah-i-Adabyat-i-Delli, 1996, p.8.

109. *Sirat-i-Firoz Shahi*, Op.Cit, p. 53.

110 Nizami, K.A., *Royalty in Medieval India*, Op.cit, p.132.

111 *Sirat-i-Firoz Shahi*, Op.cit, p.301.

112 Ibid, pp.95-96

113 Ibid, p.302.

114 *Tarikh-i-Firoz Shahi*, (Afif), Op.cit, pp.255, 369-70.

115 Ibid, p.164.

In 1372, Maqbul died and two years later Firoz, now an old man, broke down after the death of his favourite son. His judgment failed, there arose ruthless vengeance, speculation in provinces, factions in the capital, treachery among ministers and when at last the old king died no one emerged to restore the kingdom. Six reigns are reckoned in the reign which followed, the provinces began to break away and then in 1398 A.D, a new enemy arrived assiduously before Delhi, where there was no power to offer effective resistance . This new enemy was Timur who sacked Delhi for several days.[116] He was successful in breaking the Turkish kingdom in India and leaving nothing in it's place.

From the above information on the personal education of the Sultans we can surmise that great care was taken to provide the best possible education to the Princes. Other than the theoretical subjects of study including religious as well as secular subjects, they were also trained in the military tactics and art of administration. It can be conjectured that the motive behind such a good arrangement for the provision of education to the princes was to imbibe in them such qualities of head and heart, suitable to the future heirs to the throne of Delhi.

116 Moreland, W.H., and Chaterjee, Atul Chandra, *A Short History of India*, London, Longmans Green and Company, 1944, pp.170-71.

Chapter-V

Establishment of the Madarsas and Royal Patronage to Scholars

Education during the Sultanate period in India, received great impetus from the sovereigns. They were patrons of learning and learned men and their enlightened patronage drew many of them to their courts. The aims of the educational policy of most of the Sultans was motivated by the noble principles that as far as possible from this world, their contributions to posterity must survive. For the attainment of this end, they liberally patronized learned scholars and men of talent irrespective of race, caste or creed and they established numerous educational institutions with rich endowments and other grants.

As soon as the Muslims arrived in India, they established settlements, which eventually developed into big towns, with the passage of time, these towns became the important centres of Islamic education and culture. Almost in all parts of the country mosques were constructed. Higher education was imparted in *Madarsas*, which were usually established in towns, and were the capital seat of a Muslim ruler or the head quarter of some subahdar or chief possessing religious importance (being a *dargah* or *khanqah* etc.) usually grew into famous educational centres. Muslim scholars and saints chose to reside in big cities which provided better job opportunities.

The *Madarsa* developed into a full-fledged University around eleven hundred years ago, in which a variety of subjects from religious law to astronomy were taught regularly. Some of the earliest Islamic educational Institutions dating from the period of genesis infact still survive, best examples being perhaps the *Qurawiyyin* in Fez, the *Zaytuniyyah* in Tunis and *Al-Azhar* in Cairo.[1] Coming back to the *madarsas* of the Sultanate period, the *Mu'izzi,* the *Nasiri* and the *Firozi Madarsas* of Delhi[2] are some of the famous institutions of higher learning which imparted knowledge in both, traditional (*Manqulat*) and the Rational sciences (*Ma'aqulat*).

The literary and cultural scenario derived it's hew and colour from the life and activities of the Sultans. Sometimes their endeavour to promote education led to the rise of *Madarsa* towns.[3] Barani believed that after prophethood, kingship was the most prestigious institution[4] and according to Fakhr-i-Mudabbir the raison de'etre for having a Sultan:

"People would devour each other if there was no Sultan."[5]

The court set the morals of cultured behaviour and stimulated literary activities of the people. A cultured court influenced the life of the people, determined their academic interests and conferred respectability and dignity on cultured behaviour. The *Ulama*, the mystics, the nobles and the elite with religious sentiments and a beneficent attitude no doubt contributed to the educational activity according to their resources, but the Sultans played a crucial role in speeding up this process by establishing *maktabs* and *Madarsas*, providing boarding and lodging facilities and granting stipends and allowances to both the teachers and the taught.

1 Sayyed, Hossein Nasr, Op.cit, p.19.

2. Chopra, P.M. (ed.), The Gazeteer of India, History and Culture, Vol.2, New Delhi, Ministry of Education and Social welfare, Govt. of India, 1973, p.430.

3. *Tarikh-i-Firoz Shahi,* Op.cit, p.563.

4. Ibid, p.27.

5. *Tarikh-i-Fakhr-u'd-din Mubarak Shah,* Op.cit, p.13.

Barani writes about the munificence and endowments of the Sultans:

"But as to the king's gifts to the leaders of the Saiyyeds, religious scholars, *shaikhs*, men of virtue or wisdom or skill, persons of merit, travellers, the helpless and the needy—his grants to schools and mystic houses (*khanqahs*) and his expenditures on all accessions where charity is recommended—the more there is of all this the greater will be the kings success in this world and his rewards in the next. In such matters there can be no question of excessive expenditure or lack of thrift. The precept that there can be no over expenditure in good works is based on this principle."[6]

With the fall of Baghdad, Islamic scholars migrated to Delhi and the Sultanate became the repository of Islamic learning in the East. The generosity of the Sultans attracted celebrities from distant lands. Since the Mongol invasion and the rise of the Delhi Sultanate took place almost at the same time, the literary and religious legacy of Islam which reached India was of a very high standard.

Although there were other institutions like *maktabs* and *khanqahs* through which education was imparted, the *Madarsas* played a significant role for this purpose. There was hardly any Sultan who was disinterested in this work. Almost all the Delhi Sultans took deep interest in promoting education and learning, constructing mosque and Madarsas and providing financial assistance to students, teachers, scholars, *Ulama*, *Mashaikh* and other seekers of knowledge.[7]

"در دار الملک دهلی علمای بودند که انچنان استادان که هر یکی علامه وقت ودر بخارا ودر سمرقند وبغداد ومصر وخوارزم ودمشق وتبریز وصفاهان وری وروم ودر ربع مسکون نباشند ودر هر علمی که فرض کنند از منقولات ومعقولات وتفسیر وفقه واصول فقه ومعقولات واصول دین ونحو ولفظ ولغت ومعانی وبدیع وبیان وکلام ومنطق ..... بعضی ازان استادان درفنون علم وکمالات علوم بدرجه غزالی ورازی رسیده بودند"

6 Habib Mohammed and Mrs. Khan, Afsar Umar Salim, Op.cit, p.18

7 Nadvi, Abul Hasnat, Op.cit, p.14.

The Mongol cataclysm had driven the intellectual elite of Muslim lands to Delhi. Barani writes "There were scholars in Delhi, each top-master in his subject, the like of whom could be found in Bukhara, Samarqand, Baghdad, Egypt, Khwarzm, Damascus, Tabriz, Ispahan, Ray, Rum (Constantinople) or anywhere in the inhabited globe. They could split hairs in any subject, traditional or rational, that one can think of eg. exegesis, law, jurisprudence, principles of theology, scholastic theology, grammar, lexicography, literary ingeminity, and logic . . . . . Some of these scholars had attained in learning the stature of Ghazzali and Razi.[8]

Sultan Qutb-ud-din (1206-1210 A.D.) the Sultan was himself an educated person held great regard for the *Ulama* and scholars, educated and trained under the guidance of Qazi Fakhruddin Kufi, the renowned scholar. The Sultan built several mosque, in the areas conquered by him, in which religious education was imparted. The eminent historian Fakhr-Mudabbir is of the view that mosques and *Madarsas* were established in many such cities and towns where before, there was no sign of Islam and Muslims.[9]

Delhi became a great centre of Islamic learning and sciences. Though we get scanty information of the establishment of *madarsas* during his reign but unfortunately neither their names are known nor has anything been mentioned about their status in any work. The only *Madarsa* of his reign of which there is evidence is the *Muizzi Madarsa* named after his royal master. Sultan Muizuddin Muhammad bin sam.[10]

Of the *Ulama* who enjoyed his benefaction, the names of Jamal Muhammad, Qazi Hamid-u'd-din Iftikar, Sadr-u'd-din Hasan Nizami, Fakhr-i-Mudabbir, Maulana Baha-u'd-din Ushi and Imam Sughani are particularly noteworthy.

Maulana Baha-u'd-din Ushi was a distinguished scholar and poet from Ush. Awfi calls him a fine speaker, a good writer, and famous poet. Though his verses are very beautiful but his prose also was very attractive. His scholarship was acknowledged by almost all the

8 *Tarikh-i-Firoz Shahi*, Op.cit, pp.352-53.
9 *Tarikh-i-Fakhr-u'd-din Mubarak Shah*,, Op.cit, p.26.
10 Fawaid-ul-Fu'ad, p.23.

contemporary *Ulama*.[11] Jamal Muhammad was a court poet of Qutb-u'd-din Aibek, according to Awfi he was well versed in the Islamic sciences and was highly respected in the circle of the *Ulama* and scholars. His famous work *Majlis Arai-i Shahabi* speaks about his deep scholarly insight. He composed verses both in Arabic and Persian.[12] Qutb-u'd-din Aibek was very affectionate towards him. Qazi Hamid-u'd-din Iftikhar was also a great scholar of Aibek's time. He was the latter's court poet as well. He was widely known in the Islamic lands for his erudition and learning and Awfi has highly praised him for the same.[13]

Sadr-u'd-din Hasan Nizami, another scholar was the author of the famous work Taj-u'l-Ma'athir[14] which was written on the instance of Aibek. Another noteworthy scholar of Aibek's time is Fakhruddin Mubarak Shah commonly known as Fakhr Mudabbir Ghaznawi who spent his whole life in India. His book *Silsilat-i-Ansab* is dedicated to Sultan Qutb-u'd-din Aibek. It contains in the beginning, the brief history of the Qutbi period which has been published, entitled as the *Tarikh-i-Fakhruddin Mubarak Shah*. Fakhr Mudabbir's another important work is the *Adab-ul-Harb-wa-Shuja'at* which is the finest work on the art of warfare in Persian language, dedicated to Iltutmish.[15]

Imam Sughani was also a great scholar of Aibek's time and had been appointed Qazi of Lahore but he declined the offer. His famous work *Mashariq-ul-Anwar*, collection of *Hadith*, has been held as an important scholarly achievement and was studied by scholars for centuries. Shaikh Nizam-u'd-din Auliya of Delhi used to highly praise

---

11 *Lubab-ul-Albab*, Op.cit, pp.161-62.

12 Ibid, p.117.

13 Ibid, pp. 172-73.

14 It's significance lies in the fact that it is the first work comprising the history of Qutb-u'd-din Aibek and Shams-u'd-din Iltutmish. It contains the events of twenty six years written in a stylish and symbolic manner. Hasan Nizami was a poet as well and has therefore quoted Arabic and Persian verses in the *Taj-u'l-Ma'athir*. For details see: Shaikh, M. Ikram, *Aab-i-Kauthar*, Delhi, Taj Company, 1987, 9.116.

15 Abdur Rehman, Syed Sabahuddin, *Bazm-i-Mamluqia*, Azamgarh, Matbai-Ma'arif, 1954, p.

this book of Sughani.[16] According to the Shaikh, Maulana Razi-u'd-din Sughani belonged to Badaun.[17]

Sultan Iltutmish (1210-1235 A.D.), successor of Qutb-u'd-din Aibek, built numerous Madarsas in Delhi.

There is an evidence in another place that Iltutmish like Qutbuddin Aibek built another *Madarsa* by the same name, i.e, *Muizzi Madarsa* in Badaun.[18] We further learn that a *Madarsa* was built by this monarch and this edifice fell into a dilapidated condition in the time of Sultan Firoz Tughlaq more than a century afterwards, and Firoz, with his characteristic liberality shown in educational matters, rebuilt the college and furnished it with sandalwood doors.[19] This was the *Nasiriya Madarsa* which Iltutmish, built after the death of his son, Shahzada Nasiruddin Mahmud in 1228 A.D.. In many books it is wrongly stated that this *Madarsa* was built in the name of Iltutmish's father.[20] Later Sultan Razia during her reign appointed Minhaj Siraj, the author of *Tabaqat-i-Nasiri*, as the principal of the *Nasiriya Madarsa* and superintendent of it's endowments.[21] During the same period Nasiruddin Qubacha (subahdar of Sindh) established his independent regime, which lasted for seventeen years i.e. (1210-27 A.D.). He conquered Uchch and through the patronization of education and learning made it a great centre of learning. In this place there was a famous and magnificent *madarsa* named 'Madarsa Firozi'. This is not known who was the founder of this *madarsa* and when was it built. But this much is known that it was existent during Nasiruddin Qubacha's reign. Although there is no evidence to prove that this *madarsa* was built by Nasiruddin Qubacha, but Minhaj informs us that the authority of the management and

16 *Fawa'id-ul-Fu'ad*, Op.cit, p.103.

17 Ibid, p.103.

18 Rafiq, Sai'd Ahmad, Op.cit, p.37. Bismil, M.M. Raziuddin, *Kanz-ut-tawarikh*, Badayun, Nizamin Press, 1907, pp. 47-48.

19 *Futuhat -i-Firoz Shahi*, Op.cit, p.13.

20 Syed, Abdul Hayy, *Hindustan Islami Ahd Mien*, Op.cit, pp.158-59.

21 Juzjani, Minhaj-i-Siraj, *Tabaqat-i-Nasiri*, Vol.I, ed. Habibi Abdul Hayy, Kabul, Historical Society of Afghanistan,1963, p.470, Raverty, H.G. *Tabaqat-i-Nasiri*, Eng. Trans., Vol. I, New Delhi, Oriental Books Reprint Corporation 1970, p.667, Law, N.N. Op.cit, p.22.

administration of this *Madarsa* was given to him in 1226 A.D. by Nasiruddin Qubacha himself which he expresses in the following words:

ودرین سال (یعنی اربع وعشرین وستمایة) درماه ذی الحجه مدرسهٔ فیروزاچه حوالهٔ این داعی شد [22]

Nasiruddin Qubacha also built a *Madarsa* in Multan for Maulana Qutb-u'd-din Kashaani and appointed him incharge of this *Madarsa*.[23]

Although some renowned scholars and writers had migrated to India in the reign of Sultan Qutb-u'd-din Aibek, yet their number increased to a great extent during Sultan Shamsuddin Iltutmish's period and one of the reasons for this was the invasion of Chingez Khan because of whose fear the *Ulama* and nobles of Turkistan (Central Asia), Iran and Afghanistan migrated to India which was an asylum for them. They reached there in large numbers. It is mentioned in the *Tabaqat-i-Nasiri* with regard to the Shamsi Period.

وازاول عهد دولت وطلوع صبح مملکت دراستجماع علمای بانام وسادات کرام وملوک وامرا وصدور وکبرا به حضرت دهلی که دار الملک هندوستان است ومرکز دائره اسلام ومحیط اوامر ونواهی شریعت وحوزهٔ دین محمدی وبیضهٔ ملت احمدی وقبة الاسلام مشارق گیتی صانها الله عن الانهاد احضر با السادات جمع آوردو این شهر بکثرت انعامات وتمول کرامات آن بادشاه دین دار محط رجال آفاق گشت۔

("And from the beginning of his state and since the rise of his kingdom he gave more than thousands and lakhs to *Ulama*, Syeds, nobles, religious employees and aged people. And people from different parts of the world have gathered in Delhi that is the capital of India, the centre of Islam, campus of the injunctions of the *Shariah*. And this city became very famous in the world because of this Sultan's generosity and kindness.")[24]

Iltutmish received scholars from Central Asian lands with warmth and affection. Sometimes he went miles to receive them.[26] It appears

22 *Tabaqat-i-Nasiri*,Vol. I, p.420.
23 Nadvi, Abul Hasnat, Op.cit, pp.37-44.
24 *Tabaqat-i-Nasiri*, Vol.I, Op.cit, pp.440-41.
25 For details see: Nizami, K.A., *Salatin-i-Dehli Kay Mazhabi Rujhanat*, Op.cit, p.113.
26 *Tarikh-i-Firoz Shahi*, Op.cit, pp.144-45.

from the *Tarikh-i-Firoz Shahi* of Zia-u'd-din Barani that he not only warmly received the *Ulama* but caused to bring rare books from outside the country to enrich the treasures of learning and literature of this country. Among these books the *Adab-us-Salatin* and *Ma'athir-us-Salatin* are especially mentioned.[26] He held the *Ulama* in high esteem.[28] Many of them were rewarded with robe (*khilat*) and gift (*inamat*). He appointed Maulana Minhaj as the *Qazi* (Judge), *Khatib* (Orator), *Imam* (Leader of prayers), *Muhtasib* (Censor of morals) of Gwalior.[28] It is because of his patronization of *Ulama*, Sufis and scholars that Delhi became a famous centre of the men of literary and scholarly excellence and intellect.[29]

Ziauddin Barani says that because of the presence of eminent *Ulama* and scholars, the court of Iltutmish had become like the court of Mahmud and Sanjar.[30] Among the *Ulama*, scholars and poets of Iltutmish's court Tajuddin Reza, Bahauddin Ali, Fakhr Mudabbir and Muwayyid Jajarmi occupied important position. Being of low strature Tajuddin was known as 'Reza' who held the position of *Dabir-ul- Mulk*. Though a renowned poet of his time[32] he was held as one of the best prose writers and scholars as well. Bahauddin Ali, one of the nobles of Iltutmish, was highly valued for his scholarship and learning.[32] As mentioned above, the famous historian, literary and scholarly figure and poet Fakhr Mudabbir during the last years of life, had been closely associated with the Sultan and also dedicated his work *Adab-ul-Harb-wa-Shujaat* to him. This book has been held as the masterpiece of Persian literature.[33] Muwayyid Jajarmi's great contribution in the field of learning in those days was the translation of the *Ihya-ul-ulum* which he translated

27 *Tabaqat-i-Nasiri*, Vol.I, pp.440-41, *Fawa'id-u'l-Fu'ad*, Op.cit, p.213.

28 Ibid, p. 449.

29 Ibid, pp.440-41.

30 *Tarikh-i-Firoz Shahi*, Op.cit, p.27.

31 For his poetic achievements see: Abdur Rehman Syed Sabahuddin, *Bazm-i-Mamluqia*, Israt, 100-29.

32 *Tabaqat –i-Nasiri*, Op. cit. p171.

33 See: Shirani Mahmud, Adab-u'l-Harb-wa Shujaat, *Oriental College Magazine*, August, 1939.

on the instruction of the Sultan.[34] Other poets and scholars of his reign Amir Ruhani, Nasiri, Shihab Muhmara, deserve special mention.

Iltutmish was by nature and association, a man of mystic temperament.[35] He was on the best of terms with the saints of the Chishti and Suhrawardi *silsilahs*.[36] He was also among the favourites of Shaikh Muinuddin of Ajmer.[37] Shaikh Nizamuddin Auliya has also mentioned Iltutmish with great reverence.[38] He had also benefitted from the company of Shaikh Jalaluddin Tabrezi, Shaikh Bahauddin Zakariya of Multan, Shaikh Hamiduddin Nagauri etc.[39] Among the Sufi writers, Shaikh Hamiduddin Sufi Nagauri Sawali, a *Khalifa* of Khwaja Muinuddin Ajmeri and whose letters are very famous, is perhaps the first example in the art of letter writing (*fan-i-insha*). He wrote other works also one of them is *Usul-i-Tariqah*. Shaikh Abdul Haq Muhaddith Dehlavi in his *Akhbar-ul-Akhyar*[40] has highly appreciated this work. His *Malfuzat Saroor-us-Sudur*[41] are also available. Another Sufi scholar of that time was Qazi Hamiduddin Nagauri who was a *murid* (disciple) of Shaikh Shahabuddin Suhrawardi but having reached Delhi he had become faithful to Khwaja Qutbuddin Bakhtiar Kaki and is buried in the feet of the latters grave. He was very fond of *sama* (mystical songs) and during the reign of Shamsuddin Iltutmish had obtained the letter of permission to hear it, inspite of the opposition of *Ulama*. He wrote several books of these *Tawali'-ul-Shumus*[42] is very famous. Divine names have been defined in this work in the language of *tasawwuf* and *tariqat*-(Sufism and spiritual path). Another brochure *Ishqujah* which contains the

34 See: Urdu Magazine, Urdu, January, 1943, p.95.

35 See: Nizami, K.A., Iltutmish, the mystic, *Islamic Culture*, 1946, pp.165-80.

36 Nizami, K.A., *Salatin-i-Dehli Kay Mazhabi Rujhanat*, Op.cit pp.114-27.

37 *Siyar-u'l-Auliya*, Op.cit, p.63.

38 See: *Fawa'id-u'l-Fu'ad*, Op.cit, pp.119,211,212.

39 See: Jamali, *Siyar-u'l-Arifin*, Urdu translation by Ghulam Ahmad, Moradabad, 1319 A.H., pp.31-37.

40 *Akhbar-ul-Akhyar*, Op.cit, p.31.

41 For details see: Nizami, K.A., *Studies on Medieval Indian History and Culture* (article on 'The *Saroor-us-Sadur*—A fourteenth century Malfuz), Op.cit, pp.97-101.

42 *Akhbar-ul-Akhyar*, Op.cit, p.37.

subjects of Divine Love-(*Ishq-i-Ilahi*), has been published.[43] As many of these personalities were scholars of a high stature and were renowned for their teaching and methods of imparting education, Sultan Iltutmish established *madarsas* in Delhi so that the people in the city particularly students may fully benefit from them.[44]

Highlighting the merits of Shamsi period Isami says:

بسی کاسبان خراسان زمین بسی نقشبندان اقلیم چین

بسی عالمان بخارا نژاد بسے زاہد و عابد از ہر بلاد

حکیمان یونان، طبیبان روم بسے اہل دانش ز ہر مرز و بوم

در آں شہر فرخندہ جمع آورند چو پروانہ بر نور شمع آمدند

یکے کعبۂ ہفت اقلیم شد

دیارش ہمہ دار اسلیم شد

"Sometimes the experts of the regions of Khurasan; sometimes the Naqshbandis of the country of China.

Sometimes the Ulama and scholars originating from Bukhara; sometimes the devotees and worshippers of every city.

The philosophers from Greece and the physicians from Rum; sometimes the intellectuals from every territory.

All of them have gathered in this fortunate city; like the butterflies which come near the light of candle.

It (Delhi) became the Kaba of all seven regions (of the world); his (Iltutmish's) house (Delhi) became completely the house of protection.[45]"

43 Shaikh M. Ikram, Op.cit, p.123.

44 *Futuhat-i-Firoz Shahi*, Op.cit, p.13.

45 *Futuh-us-Salatin*, Op.cit, pp.114-15.

Sultan Iltutmish was succeeded by his son, Ruknuddin Firoz Shah. He too was deeply interested in poetry, learning and academic activities. Though he hardly ruled for seven months, his period is mentioned in the contemporary sources of history as full of literary and scholarly activities. During his governorship of Badaun on account of his close association with Ain-ul-Mulk who was his wazir in those days, had developed deep interest in different sciences and literature.[46] The earlier mentioned Tajuddin Reza was his court poet also.[47] The other court poet of the Sultan was Maulana Shihabuddin who belonged to a scholarly family of Badaun, who was well versed in Arabic and Persian too.[48] According to Amir Khusrau, Maulana Shihabudin was not only a high class poet but also a great alim and scholar of his time. It was because of his immense knowledge in philosophy and strong hold in wisdom that he was called the *Buqrat-i- waqt* (Hippocrates of the time) and *Aflatun-i-Zamana* (Plato of his age). He was an expert of theology (*Ilahiyat*) physics (*tabi'yat*), mathematics—(*riyaziyat*) and rational and traditional sciences—(*ma'qulat* and *manqulat*). Highlighting Shihabuddin's academic virtues and scholarly as well as literary insight, Amir Khusrau says in his mathnawi '*Hasht Bihisht*'.[49]

حکمتش داد از بس افزونی ملک بقراطی و فلاطونی

در الٰہی فنش نہ در حد کس حد او ہم الہ داند و بس

در طبیعی شناختہ بتمام راز مولودِ عنصر و اجرام

در ریاضی بیک صریر قلم باز کردست گوش جذر اصم

عقلیش از قیاس عقل بروں نقلیش از مقام نقل فزوں

"His wisdom gave the country an atmosphere in which flourished scholars like Socrates and Hippocrates.

46 *Tabaqat-i-Nasiri*,Vol.I, Op.cit, p.454.

47 *Tarikh-i-Ferishta*, Vol.I, Op.cit, p.67.

48 *Muntakhab-u't-Tawarikh*, Vol.I, p.70.

49 Amir Khusrau, *Hasht Bihisht*, ed. S. Sulaiman Arif, Aligarh, Institute Press, 1918, p.226.

In theology his knowledge is limitless and it is so wide that only God knows his depth.

In medicine also he is so deeply well versed that he knows the secrets of birth and end of life.

In mathematics his grip is so strong that he can solve any difficult problem in seconds.

He had complete command over almost all the rational sciences and similarly in the field of traditional sciences there is nobody equal to him."

Moreover, the *Ijaz-u-Khusrau* also contains two letters of its author Amir Khusrau addressed to Maulana Shihabuddin. One of these is in Arabic whereas the other is in Persian. Khusrau addresses the Maulana as *Imam*.[50]

This title indicates that Maulana Shihabuddin was *imam* (leader) of the *Ulama* and scholars of his time, Khusrau has highly praised him in his *Ghurrat-i-Kamal* also.[51] It seems that Amir Khusrau had benefited from Maulana Shihabuddin in the field of poetry. Another renowned poet of this age, Fakhr-ul-Mulk Amid Tolki always held him as his teacher[52] and, similarly Maulana Ziauddin Bakhshi, famous scholar as well as the author of the *Silk-ul-Suluk* and *Tuti Nama* also was his pupil.[53] The author of *Majma-ul-Fusaha* has very beautifully described Maulana Shihabuddin's scholarly excellence. He says:

وے از حکماء، فضلاء و شعراء مقرر مشہور معروف زمان خود محسوب می شده، طبع عالی و ذہن متعالی داشتہ

"(He was one of the leading philosophers, scholars, poets and orators of his time. He bore high moral character and intelligence)".

He further writes:

50 Amir Khusrau, *Ijaz-i-Khusrawi*, Vol.2, Lucknow, Nawal Kishore, 1868,pp.168.172.

51 *Nuzhat-u'l-Khawatir*, Vol.I, p.143.

52 *Muntakhab-u't-Tawarikh*, Vol.I, p.70.

53 *Akhbar-u'l-Akhyar*, Op.cit, p.106.

درزمان سلطان رکن الدین فیروز بن سلطان شمس الدین ایلتتمش سرآمد فاضل عہد بود

"(He was a renowned scholar during the time of Sultan Ruknuddin Firoz bin Shamsuddin Iltutmish)".

Paying his tribute to Maulana Shihabuddin, the famous intellectual and literary figure of the eighteenth century Sirajuddin Ali Khan Arzu says:

وی ازشعرائے بزرگ ہندوستان است

"(He is one of the great poets of India)"[55]

Sultan Razia 1236-1240 A.D. was an educated and talented lady and was not ignorant of politics and administration. That she was in complete sympathy with the stimulation of education is brought home to us by the existence of the *Muizzi Madarsa* which was in a flourishing state during her reign.[56] This *Madarsa* was located in Delhi and was so rich and magnificent that it was once attacked by the *Karamathians* in 1238 A.D., who were under the impression that it was the *Jami-Masjid*.[57]

It was after the death of Ruknuddin Firoz that, Razia, the daughter of Shamsuddin Iltutmish became the Sultan of Delhi. We get little information about her academic calibre in most of sources. However, Minhaj Siraj Juzjani, the author of the *Tabaqat-i-Nasiri* writes that she was a patron of learning. He himself acknowledges Razia's favours and generosity extended towards him. The *Nasiriyah Madarsa*[58] established by Iltutmish was in a flourishing state and acted as an important centre of Islamic education and learning during her rule. Among the poets, *Ulama* and scholars of her time Nasiruddin Aitmar Balarami and Amir Imam Nasiri held significant place.[59]

54 Abdur Rehman, Syed Sabahuddin, Op.cit, p.159.

55 Ibid.

56 Syed, Abdul Hayy, Op.cit, pp.154-55

57 *Tabaqat-i-Nasiri*, Vol.I, p.461, Raverty, Op.cit.646. Jaffar, S.M., *Education in Muslim India*, Delhi, Idarah-i-Adabyat-i-Delli, 1972, p.41.

58 *Tabaqat-i-Nasiri*, Vol.I, p.470.

59 Ibid, p.461.

Razia was succeeded by her brother Muizuddin Bahram Shah who ruled over the Sultanate of Delhi for about two years i.e. from 1240-1242 A.D. We hardly find any details of his patronization of learning and scholars. However, Minhaj Siraj, who himself was very close to this Sultan and had been appointed the *Qazi* of the Sultanate by him, refers to Shaikh Ayyub Turkmani[62] and Qazi Jalaluddin Kashani[61] but as mentioned above, no detail has been provided by him.

Though Muizuddin Bahram Shah's successor, Alauddin Masud Shah remained the Sultan of Delhi for about four years i.e. 1242-1246 A.D. yet all the contemporary sources are silent regarding his interest and endeavours in the field of education and learning. According to Minhaj Siraj the Sultan certainly showed favours to Maulana Jalaluddin Kashani by giving him a robe of honour, and sending him as his ambassador to Lakhnauti.[62]

Sultan Iltutmish's eldest son's name was Nasiruddin Mahmud who passed away in his father's life time. But when his youngest son was born Iltutmish named him Nasiruddin Mahmud and took special care for his education and training.[63] Minhaj has highly praised Nasiruddin Mahmud's moral virtues, piety, spirituality, honesty, generosity, impartiality, tolerance, patience and endurance.[64] His personal life was very simple and transparent. He never took a penny from the royal treasury for his personal expenses. As he was a high class calligraphists, he used to transcribe the copies of the Holy *Quran* and passed his days by spending what he earned through this means—the calligraphy of the *Quran*.[65]

Sultan Nasir-u'd-din Mahmud (1246-66 A.D.) was also a lover of learning. It is evident that during both's reign (i.e. Sultan Razia and

60 Ibid, p.466.

61. Ibid, p. 464.

62 Ibid, p.470.

63 Ibid, p.472.

64 Ibid, pp.472-75, For details see: the verses of the two *qasidas* composed by Minhaj Siraj in praise of this Sultan Nasiruddin Mahmud.

65 *Tarikh-i-Firoz Shahi*, Op.cit, p.26, *Siyar-u'l-Auliya*, Op.cit, p.581.

Nasir-u'd-din Mahmud) Minhaj Siraj was incharge of the Madarsa Nasiriyah[66] which he expresses in the following words:-

184

”روز پنجشنبہ ہفدھم ماہ صفر، بتربیت الغ خان معظم خان، مدرسہ ناصریہ باتولیت او قاف آن، وفضاء کالپور
وتذکیرات مسجد جامع جملہ بدین داعی، قرار قدیم مقرر شد، وداعی را اسپ وستام وتشریفی فرمود کہ ہیچ [یک]
67 از ابناء جنس، مثل آن نیافتہ بودند“

S.M. Jaffar is of the view that there is another *madarsa* in Jallandhar during the Nasiriyah period where Nasiruddin Mahmud's commander in chief, Balban and his friends performed the *Id-ul-Azha* prayers while returning from an expedition.[68] This information is based on Raverty's[69] english translation of the *Tabaqat-i-Nasiri* but there is no evidence of this in the Persian version of the *Tabaqat-i- Nasiri* to prove this.

Sultan Nasiruddin Mahmud was friendly and always associated with *ulama*, Sufis, pious people. Ferishta says:

صلحاء علماء را دوست داشتے

(He was friendly to *Ulama* and pious people).[70] He shared cordial relations with Minhaj Siraj, the author of *Tabaqat-i-Nasiri.* The latter accompanied Nasiruddin in his different journeys and expeditions.[71]

Minhaj was held among the famous scholars of the time. Shaikh Abdul Haqq Muhaddith Dehlavi says:

صاحب طبقات ناصری بزرگ بود از فاضل روزگار

(The author of the *Tabaqat-i-Nasiri* was among the renowned scholars of his time).[72]

---

66 Nadvi, Abul Hasnat, Op.cit, p.21.
67 *Tabaqat-i-Nasiri*, Vol.I, pp.470-71.
68 Jaffar, S.M., Op.cit, p.41.
69 Raverty, Op.cit, pp.678-679.
70 *Tarikh-i-Ferishta*, Vol.I, p.71.
71 For details see: *Tabaqat-i-Nasiri*, Vol.I, Op.cit, pp.478-97.
72 *Akhbar-u'l-Akhyar*, Op.cit, p.47.

As mentioned above, he dedicated his *Tabaqat-i-Nasiri* to Sultan Nasiruddin Mahmud and it is named after him. The Sultan always praised Minhaj Siraj's academic virtues. When the work was presented to Sultan Nasiruddin he gave a robe of honour, an annual stipend of ten thousand *Jital* and other gifts and at that moment he gave his shawl to Minhaj.[73] The noteworthy *Ulama* and scholars of his reign were Qazi Shamsuddin Bahraichi, Shaikh Jamaluddin Bistami etc. Qazi Shamsuddin Bahraichi was an old friend of the Sultan, who often took his advice in different matters[74] Shaikh Jamaluddin Bistami, was the *Shaikh-ul-Islam* of the Sultanate.[75]

Moreover, the above mentioned Qazi Jalaluddin Kashani and Maulana Qutbuddin also remained close to the Sultan.[76] Similarly among the poets of Nasiruddin Mahmud's reign, Amid Sanami held a significant place.[77]

Sultan Ghiyasuddin Balban (1266-1287 A.D.) patronized learning lavishly and spend immense amount of money from the state treasury for the promotion of education and learning and ordered his officers that they should not leave any opportunity to patronize and value learning.[78]

It was in 664 A.H./1266 A.D. that Nasiruddin Mahmud, on his death was succeeded by his deputy *naib-i-Sultanat* (i.e. prime minister) Ulugh Khan, who was also father in law of the Sultan. He ascended the throne of Delhi with the name and title of Ghiyasuddin Balban.

---

73 *Tabaqat-i-Nasiri*, Vol.I, p.452, It may be mentioned here that consisting of twenty three *Tabaqat* (sections), this work contains the historical events right from the beginning of the world to 1261 A.D. i.e. the sixteenth year of Nasiruddin Mahmud's reign. *Tabaqat* 11 and 17 to 23 supply the information of Ghazni and Ghori Sultan and from Qutb-u'd-din Aibek to Nasiruddin Mahmud. These chapters (tabaqats) have been jointly edited by Nassaw Lees, Maulvi Khadim Husain and Maulvi Abdul Haiy. This edition entitled the *Tabaqat-i-Nasiri* was published from Calcutta in 1864 by the Asiatic society of Bengal, see Storey, C.A., *Persian Literature*, Vol.I, part.I, London, Luzac and Company, 1970, p.69.

74 Ibid, p.487.

75 Ibid, p.490.

76 Ibid, p.483.

77 For his *Qasaid* see: *Muntakhab-u't-Tawarikh*, Vol.I, pp.96-127.

78 *Tarikh-i-Firoz Shahi*, Op.cit, p.103, *Futuh-us-Salatin*, Op.cit, p.156

In 1949 another *Tabaqat-i-Nasiri* was published from Qandahar by Abdul Haiy Habibi. Though incomplete, it is from the beginning to twenty first *tabaqat*. It's English translation with informatory notes and comments by Major H.G. Raverty was published in 1881 but it begins from the seventh *Tabaqah*.

Trained under the guardianship of Sultan Iltutmish, Balban also developed sympathy, kindness and love for the *Ulama*, scholars and *mashaikh*. Praising his high moral conduct, Ibn Batuta has written that Balban himself was an '*alim*' and scholar and had high regard for *Ulama* and Sufis.[79] According to Barani he had a strong desire to make his capital a great seat of learning. He once exhorted his son Bughra Khan in these words:

دارالملک خود را از علماء و مشائخ و سادات و مفسران و محدثان و حافظان و مذکران و فاضلان و ماہران

ہر ہنری پر کن تا مصر جامع گردد۔

"(Fill your capital with *Ulama*, *Mashaikh* (Sufis) *Saiyids*, commentators of the *Quran*, scholars of *hadith*, *hafizan*—those who have committed the *Quran* to memory, orators, scholars and expert of every art and science so that it may become an Egypt)".[80]

Barani further says that during Balban's age there flourished different types of scholars and artists *Ulama* and *mashaikh* and patronized all of them.[81] Ferishta has written that Balban's court was better than that of Mahmud and Sanjar and he gathered even around his son Khan Shahid several *ulama*, saints and scholars.[82] The Scholars with whom Balban was closely associated and had laid a deep impression upon him were Maulana Burhanuddin Mahmud, Allama Najmuddin Abdul Aziz, Shaikh Sirajuddin Abu Bakr, Maulana Sharafuddin, Burhanuddin Buzzaz, Qazi Ruknuddin Samanivi, Maulana Kamaluddin Zahid, Shamsuddin Khwarazmi and Fakhruddin Naqilah deserve special mention.

79 Ibn Batuta, Op.cit, pp.35-36.
80 *Tarikh-i-Firoz Shahi*, Op.cit, p.103.
81 Ibid, pp.111-12.
82 *Tarikh-i-Ferishta*, Vol.I, Op.cit, p.75.

Maulana Burhanuddin Mahmud bin Abdul Khair Balkhi was a renowned scholar of his time. He had no parallel in the fields of syntax, lexicography, jurisprudence, *Hadith* and rational science.[83]

He was well versed in spiritual sciences also.[84] He had learnt *Mashariq-ul-Anwar* from its author, Maulana Razi-ud-din Hasan Saghani, and received instruction in *Hidaya* from Maulana Burhan-u'd'din Marghinani.[85] Balban held great respect for him Barani says:

بعد از نماز جمعه با چندان کوکبه و دبدبه که سوار شدی در خانه مولانا برهان الدین بلخی فرود آمد و تعظیم ان عالم ربانی بواجبی محافظت نمودی

"(After Friday prayer, he (Balban) with full royal etiquette and pomp went to the house of Maulana Burhanuddin Balkhi, met and benefited from him respectfully)"[86]

Allama Najmuddin Abdul Aziz Damishqi was a great scholar of philosophy. He had completed his advanced studies under one of the renowned scholars of the Islamic world, Imam Fakruddin Razi. Balban held high regard for him[87] and visited him also on Friday to benefit from his company.[88] Shaikh Sirajuddin Abu Bakr, who had migrated to Delhi from Sanjar, was a renowned scholar of Arabic language and literature.[89] He always remained engaged in teaching and a large group of *Ulama* and seekers of knowledge benefited from his scholarship.[90] Balban paid visit to him also every Friday.[91]

Maulana Sharafuddin Walwaji was a great jurist (*faqih*) and known for his teaching of jurisprudence. Balban met him also very

83 *Nuzhat-u'l-Khawatir*, Vol.I, p.186.

84 *Akhbar-u'l-Akhyar*, Op.cit, p.46.

85 *Fawa'id-u'l-Fu'ad*, Op.cit, p.238-39, *Akhbar-u'l-Akhyar*, Op.cit, pp.45-46.

86 *Tarikh-i-Firoz Shahi*, Op.cit, p.46.

87 Ibid, p.46.

88 *Tarikh-i-Ferishta*, Vol.I, Op.cit, p.76.

89 Ibid.

90 *Nuzhat-u'l-Khawatir*, Vol.I, Op.cit, p.92.

91 *Tarikh-i-Ferishta*, Vol.I, Op.cit, p.76.

respectfully.[92] Similarly Burhanuddin Buzzaz and Qazi Ruknuddin Samani also were famous scholars of *Fiqh* (jurisprudence) in Delhi. Both of them were respected by Balban.[93]

Maulana Kamaluddin Zahid, also known for his piety and spirituality, had been the teacher of Shaikh Nizamuddin Auliya of Delhi. The latter had studied the famous work *Mashariq-ul-Anwar* under him. Balban held great reverence for him and wanted to appoint him the *Imam* (leader of the congregational prayers), but the Maulana declined with the remark, "Our prayer is all that is left to us. Does the Sultan want to take that also.[94] Likewise, Maulana Shamsuddin Khwarizmi also had earned great respect in Delhi for his learning and scholarship. Most of the teachers in Delhi were his pupil. The author of *Siyar-ul-Auliya* has highly praised his moral virtues and his deep affection for Shaikh Nizamuddin Auliya who studied the *Maqamat-i- Hariri* from him.[95] According to Jamali, the author of *Siyar-ul-Arifin*, Shaikh Shamsuddin Khwarazmi was the source of inspiration to the *Ulama* of Delhi and had deep insight in rational and traditional sciences.[96]

Maulana Fakhruddin Naqilah also was a distinguished scholar of Delhi in those days. He was particularly known for his deep knowledge of *Fiqh* (jurisprudence) *Usul* (science of principles of different subject) and Arabic Literature. A number of his pupils flourished in Delhi and other places. Balban had appointed him *Qazi* and *Sadr Jahan* of his empire.[97] Moreover, there were several other *Ulama* and scholars who were widely known for his deep insight in different sciences and learnings. Mention may be made of Qazi Rafi'uddin Gazruni, Qazi Shamsuddin Miraji, Qazi Jalaluddin Kashani, Qazi Sadiduddin, Qazi Zahiruddin etc.[98] Besides, Barani informs of some other *Ulama* and men of Islamic learning who had come from the Syed families of different places around Delhi.[99]

---

92 *Tarikh-i-Firoz Shahi*, Op.cit, p.46, *Nuzhat-ul-Khawatir*, Vol.I, p.125.
93 *Nuzhat-u'l Khawatir*, Vol.I, Op.cit, pp.98,119.
94 *Siyar-u'l-Auliya*, Op.cit, p.116, *Akhbar-ul-Akhyar*, Op.cit, p.72.
95 Ibid, p.573.
96 *Siyar-u'l-Arifin* (Urdu translation Ghulam Ahmad), Op.cit, p.115.
97 *Tarikh-i-Firoz Shahi*, Op.cit, p.24, *Nuzhat-u'l-Khawatir*, Vol.2, p.103.
98 *Siyar-u'l-Auliya*, Op.cit, p.582.
99 *Tarikh-i-Firoz Shahi*, Op.cit, p.111.

Balban had contact with the saints of all mystic orders.[100] He had great regard for the *Mashaikh*. It is perhaps for this reason that Nizamuddin Auliya is reported to have made high praises of this Sultan of Delhi.[101] Though the events of his deep love and respect for Shaikh Fariduddin Ganj-i-Shakar are found mentioned in different sources,[102] he is said to have close association with other saints also.

Though according to a modern scholar, Abdul Rahman Sabahuddin Balban might have obtained blessings from almost all significant contemporary Sufis like Shaikh Bahauddin Zakariya of Multan and his son Shaikh Sadruddin, Shaikh Badruddin Ghaznawi, Shaikh Abul Muwaiyid Nizamuddin, Shaikh Jamaluddin Hanswi, Shaikh Alauddin Sabir of Kaliyar, Sidi Maula, Shaikh Husamuddin Multani, Shaikh Najibuddin Firdausi, Shaikh Abu Bakr Haidar Tusi etc.[103]

Among the other famous poets of Balban's age Maulana Shamsuddin Dabir is also noteworthy. A native of qasba (town) Sunam,[104] Shamsudidn Dabir was a relative of Amir Hasan Sijzi, the compiler of the *Fawaid-u'l-Fu'ad.*[105] The author of the *Nuzhat-ul-Khawatir* has included him among the ulama of the time.[106] Maulana Dabir had studied Qazi Hamiduddin Nagauri's book *Lawaih* under Shaikh Fariduddin Ganj-i-Shakar[107] and perhaps joined the latter's mystic discipline.[108] As per information contained in the *Fawaid ul- Fu'ad*, he frequently paid visits to Baba Farid at Ajodhan.[109] For his closeness to Sultan Balban, Ziauddin Barani has provided sufficient information.[110] The famous sixteenth century historian Mulla Abdul Qadir Badayuni

100 Ibid, p.46, p.111.

101 See: *Fawa'id-u'l-Fu'ad*, Op.cit, p.99.

102 *Fawa'id-u'l-Fu'ad*, Op.cit, p.99, *Siyar-ul-Auliya*, Op.cit, pp.79-80, see Nizami, K.A, *Salatin-i-Delhi Kay Mazhabi Rujhanat*, Op.cit, pp.164-65. Nizami, K.A., *The Life and Times of Farid-u'd-din Ganj-i-Shakar*, Op.cit, pp.102-03.

103 Abdur Rahman, Syed Sabahuddin, Op.cit, pp.228-29.

104 *Tarikh-i-Ferishta*, Vol.2, p.389.

105 *Fawa'id-ul-Fu'ad*, p.128, 162.

106 *Nuzhat-u'l-Khawatir*, Vol.2, p.52.

107 *Fawa'id-u'l-Fu'ad*, Op.cit, p.128, *Tarikh-i-Ferishta*, Vol.2, Op.cit, p.389.

108 *Nuzhat-u'l-Khawatir*, Vol.2, Op.cit, p.52.

109 *Fawa'id-u'l-Fu'ad*, Op.cit, p.128.

110 *Tarikh-i-Firoz Shahi*, Op.cit, p.95.

says that Shamsuddin Dabir's deep scholarship, wide knowledge and literary as well as scientific approach is beyond description[111] shedding light on this great scholar and poet's close relations with Balban, Badauni further says:

سلطان غیاث الدین بلبن در آخر حال او را

منشی مملکت بنگاله و کامرود ساخته ....

"(Sultan Ghiyathuddin Balban made him the *Munshi-i-Mamlukat* of Bengal and Kamrud)"[112]

To show his literary and poetic greatness, he quotes Shamsuddin Dabir's several verses in his *Muntakhab-ut-Tawarikh.*[113]

Among other *Ulama* and scholars of Balban's age, Alauddin Kashli Khan also earned much fame. He was the nephew of the Sultan and worked as *barbak* in his government. Barani says that in generosity he is known as the '*Hatim Tai*' of his age.[114] Ferishta writes that scholars, *Ulama* and poets from Egypt, Syria, Baghdad, Khurasan, Turkistan and Transoxiana etc. visited him and received precious gifts and awards. He was popular for his kind and generous nature.[115] Another famous patronizer of learning at that time was Amir Ali who was the *sarjandar*, incharge of the security guards of the Sultans. According to Ziauddin Barani, he was the son of a slave of Balban.[116] He too was very kind and generous to men of arts and letters.[117] Amir Khusrau, who, after the death of Prince Muhammad had joined the service of Amir Ali Sarjandar also has highly praised the latter's generosity.[118] Barani

111 *Muntakhab-u't-Tawarikh*, Vol.I, Op.cit, p.94.

112 Ibid, p.94.

113 Ibid, pp.94-96

114 *Tarikh-i-Firoz Shahi*, Op.cit, p.113.

115 *Tarikh-i-Ferishta*, Vol.I, Op.cit, p.78.

116 *Tarikh-i-Firoz Shahi*, Op.cit, p.118.

117 Ibid, pp.118-19.

118 See: Amir Khusrau, *Qiran-u's-Sa'dain*, ed. By Maulvi Muhammad Ismail Meruti and Syed Hasan Barani, Aligarh Institute, Aligarh College Press, 1918, p.222.

informs of another patron of learning and education of the period. He was a noble known as *Malik-ul- Umara* Fakhruddin, the *kotwal* of Delhi. Twelve thousand people received stipends from him for reciting, studying and committing to memory the Holy *Quran.*[119] Moreover, the great son of Indian soil, renowned intellectual of that age and one of the most distinguished Persian poets of the Orient, Amir Khusrau, though a youth of hardly twenty years, also was a precious gem of Balban's time.

Amongst the sons of Sultan Balban, Prince Muhammad was popular for the patronization of learning. Amir Khusrau, Amir Hasan attended his *majlis*, and he held great respect for scholars.[120] No doubt Sultan Balban and his son were lovers of learning and held high regard for nobles and scholars but there is no evidence to show that they build any *madarsa* during their respective rule.

Balban paid special attention to the education of his son which has been already discussed in detail in the previous chapter. His eldest son, Sultan Muhammad had developed some special type of good characteristics.[121] It is reported that *Ulama*, scholars and poets freely attended his gatherings and the Prince discussed different literary and academic points with them.[122] Amir Khusrau and Amir Sijzi also highly admired his scholarly taste.[123] Ferishta says that his court (*majlis*) was always full of the men of learning and knowledge.[124] At Multan he visited Shaikh 'Uthman the most learned man of that age, but no presents or treaties could prevail on him to remain out of his native country Turan.[125] He twice sent messages to Shiraz to invite Shaikh Sadi, the famous Persian poet and forwarded with them some presents and also money to defray the expenses of the journey. His intention was to build a *Khanqah* (monastery) for him in Multan and endow it with villages for it's maintenance. The poet due to the feebleness of old age was unable to accept the invitations, but on both occasions sent some verses in his

119 *Tarikh-i-Firoz Shahi*, Op.cit, p.117.

120 *Tarikh-i-Firoz Shahi*, Op.cit, pp.67-69, *Tarikh-i-Ferishta* Vol. I, Op.cit, p.81, Saeed, Ahmad Rafiq, Op.cit, pp.76-78

121 Ibid, pp.67-68.

122 Ibid.

123 Ibid, p.67.

124 *Tarikh-i-Ferishta*, Vol.I, Op.cit, p.78.

125 Tarikh-i-Firoz Shahi, Op.cit, p.67.

own hand and made his apologies in writing.[126] As he died in his youth he could not fulfil his desire of creating an intellectual atmosphere in Delhi and in other parts of the Sultanate. Had he survived the literary, cultural and intellectual history of the country would be different all together. Paying his tribute to the deceased Prince, Ziauddin Barani says: "I have often heard Amir Khusrau and Amir Hasan saying with sorrow that if ours and other scholar's and artists fate had favoured, Khan Shahid would survive and grace the throne of Balban, and all of us would have been sunk in rupees. But men of learning and scholarship are ill fated, the time never looked at them with the eyes of mercy and even could not see them as rich and prosperous. The cruel sky is not so powerful as to provide a king to sit on the royal throne"[127] so that artists and scholars could flourish.

Balban's second son Bughra Khan had also been provided with best type of education and training but he could not become as learned, cultured and disciplined as was his eldest son Sultan Muhammad (Khan Shahid). Though according to Ferishta only story tellers, musicians singers and musketeers lived in his court.[128] But we come to know through the introduction (*dibachah*) of Amir Khusrau's *Ghurrat-ul-Kamal* that he too had men of learning and knowledge around him. Khusrau himself was close to this Prince and along with Amir Hasan Sijzi had accompanied him and his father Balban in 678 A.H./1279-80A.D. in an expedition to Lakhnauti[129] similarly when Bughra Khan was appointed the governor of Samana, Shams Dabir also went with him[130] and patronized artists, poets.

In 686 A.H./1287 A.D. Balban died and was succeeded by his grandson, who was only seventeen, Muizuddin Kaiqubad, the son of Bughra Khan, who continued to be an independent ruler of Bengal (Lakhnauti). The young Sultan ruled over the Delhi Sultanate for about two years. Barani says:

"سلطان معزالدین بادشاہزادہ صاحب مکارم اخلاق بود و طبع نظم و خلقے پاکیزہ و جمالے وافر داشت"

126 Ibid, p.68.
127 Ibid, pp.68-69.
128 *Tarikh-i-Ferishta*, Vol.I, Op.cit, p.75.
129 *Fawa'id-u'l-Fu'ad*, Op.cit, p.128.
130 Ibid, p.269.

(Sultan Muizuddin the Prince bore good morals, mild nature and pious habits; and he was very beautiful and sophisticated).[131]

The contemporary sources are silent about his interest in promoting education, learning and knowledge. However, he was associated to Amir Khusrau.

The founder of the Khalji dynasty Jalal-u'd-din Khalji (1290-95 A.D.) was not as popular as the other Sultans, Barani gave him the title of *Sultan-ul-Halim*[132] in view of his mild and clement nature, in sharp contrast with both Balban and 'Ala-u'd-din Khalji'. However in the Sultan's *majlis* Amir Khusrau presented a fresh ghazal every day.[133] The Sultan's interest in poetry and his poetic flair led him to compose stray verses, even full ghazals.[134] During Jalal-u'd-din Khalji's reign the royal *Darbar* had become a centre of learning for the nobles and scholars in which jurists, historians, philosophers, logicians and all sundry participated. But inspite of this intellectual scenario we do not hear of the establishment of any *madarsa*.

The first Sultan of Khalji dynasty, Jalaluddin was a poet, and was deeply interested in poetry. Several verses of this first poet king of India are found mentioned in the works of history. Once while besieging the fort of Gwalior, he built a monument there and composed a *rubai'* (quatrain) about it:

ما را کہ قدم بر سر گردوں ساید
از تودۂ سنگ و گل چہ قدر افزاید
ایں سنگ شکستہ زاں نہادیم درست
باشد کہ دل شکستہ آساید

131 *Tarikh-i-Firoz Shahi*, Op.cit, p.127.

132 Ibid., p.174.

133 Ibid, p.200.

134 Ibid, p.197.

"To me, whose feet have kissed the heaven.
Stone and clay will not be beneficial.
This broken stone that we have fixed here.
Will provide shelter to heart breakers."[135]

Barani has provided the details of the poetic meetings and free gathering at the court of Jalaluddin Khalji. However, some of the *nadims* of the Sultan, like Taj-u'd-din Iraqi, Amir Khusrau, Muwayyid Jajarmi, Amir Arsalan Kulahi, Taj Khatib and others were conspicuous for their interest in history and literature.[136]

During the reign of Alauddin Khalji (1295-1315 A.D.) as already mentioned above, Delhi had become such a rendezvous of scholars that in Baranis opinion Baghdad, Samarqand, Kaashaan, Isfahan and Shiraz. Tabriz also looked with envy towards it. This proves that the Sultan must have definitely taken keen interest in establishing mosques, *madarsas, khanqahs* and patronized scholars. In the *madarsas* such teachers were appointed that they were experts in their subjects.[137] That is precisely why not only people from different parts of the *Sultanate* but also from other countries flocked to Delhi to acquire learning and knowledge from these teachers. The evidence of the deep interest that the Sultan took in building mosques and *Madarsas* is to be found in the titles used to describe him.

For instance on the southern side of the *Alai Darwaza* the engravings on the epigraphic plate contain the following words along with the name of the Sultan:-

[138] "مؤکد منابر معالم ومساجد وموطوقواعد مدارس ومعابد"

(The Provider of strength to the foundation of mosques and *madarsas*).

Jalaluddin Khalji was succeeded by Alauddin Khalji and no doubt his period was the precedence of Emperor Akbar's period. The great

---

135 Shaikh, M, Ikram, Op.cit, p.171.
136 *Tarikh-i-Firoz Shahi*, Op.cit, p.199.
137 *Tarikh-i-Ferishta*, Vol. I, Op.cit, pp.121-22.
138 Khan, Sir Syed Ahmad, *Asar-u's-Sanadid*, Vol.3, Delhi, ed. Khaliq Anjum, Delhi, Urdu Academy Delhi, 1990, p.165.

poets like Amir Khusrau and Amir Hasan, and scholars like Ziauddin Barani flourished at that time. According to Barani, Sadruddin Aali, Fakhruddin Qawas, Hamiduddin Raja, Maulana Arif, Ubaid Hakim and Shihab Ansari were the poets of the Alai period, and were rewarded by the court for their poetry. Every one of them has his own style of poetry and a *diwan* of his own.[139] Unfortunately the *kalam* (poetry) of these *sahib-i-diwan* (having the collection of their poetry) poets is not available. If available, the *diwan* of Ubaid Hakim would be interesting. Barani writes that the company of Sa'd Mantiqi and Ubaid Hakim had made Muhammad Tughlaq a free thinker and doubtful about religion.[140] He accepted only those traditional points which he found reasonable.

Likewise there were several historians whose works are not available now, as for example Kabiruddin, son of Tajuddin Iraqi. Barani says:

درتالیف نثر عربی و پارسی ید بیضامی نمود و در فتح نامہ مجلدات پرداختہ است و داد نثر نویسی دادہ۔

"(He seemed an illumined light in Arabic and Persian prose, and produced several volumes in *Fath-namah*, and received appreciation in prose writing)".[141]

It appears from the statement of Barani that there were large number of scholars in Delhi during and before the Alai period. He writes:

و جملہ دارالملک دہلی چہ در عصر علائی و چہ پیش از عصر علائی و بعد از و مصنفان و مولفان و شاعران و فاضلانِ بسیار بودہ اند و ہستند۔

"(And in the whole capital Delhi whether during and before or after the 'Alai period,' there have been and even still are many writers, compilers, poets and scholars)".[142]

But we are now not aware of their works and biographies. It is an unfortunate event of our early literary life that the disturbance of times have totally damaged the contribution of that age. Only *tazkiras* of the Sufis, some historical works and Amir Khusrau's books have survived.

139 Ibid, pp.360-61.
140 Ibid.
141 Ibid, p.361.
142 Ibid.

Apart from the poet and writers, Barani states that there were large number of scholars as well:

'درتمامی عصر علائی در دارالملک دہلی علمای بودند کہ آن چنان استادان کہ ہر یکی علامۂ وقت ودر بخارا وسمرقند وبغداد ومصر وخوارزم ودمشق وتبریز وصفاہان ورے وروم ودر ربع مسکون نباشد ودر ہر علمی کہ فرض کنند از منقولات وتفسیر وفقہ واصول دین ونحو ولغت ومعانی وبدیع وبیان وکلام ومنطق موی می شگافتند وہر سالی چندین طالبان علم از استادان سر آمدہ بدرجۂ افادات می رسیدند ومستحق جواب دادن فتوی می شدند وبعضی ازان استادان در فنون علم وکمالات علوم بدرجہ غزالی ورازی رسیدہ بودند چنانکہ....'

(Throughout the Alai period, there were in Delhi, the *Ulama*, who were teachers of such high calibre that every one of them, was a great scholar of his time. And like them were not available in Bukhara, Samarqand, Baghdad, Egypt, Khwarizm, Damascus, Tabrez, Isfahan, Ray, Rum and other cities of the world. They showed their scholarship in every science of *Manqulat*, *Tafsir*, *Fiqh*, *Usul-i-Din*, *Nahw*, *Lughat*, *Sarf*, *Kalam* and *Mantiq* and every year many students benefited from these eminent teachers and became authority in issuing *fatwa* some of these teachers have reached to the status of Ghazali and Razi in different arts, sciences and excellence).[143] Barani afterwards gives the names of about *forty six Ulama.*[144]

Names of Forty Six Ulamas:

1. Qazi Fakhruddin Naqilah
2. Qazi Sharafuddin Sarbahi
3. Maulana Nasiruddin Ghani
4. Maulana Zahiruddin Lang
5. Qazi Mughithuddin Bayana
6. Maulana Tajuddin Muqaddam

143 Ibid, ppp.352-53.

144 Ibid, pp.353-54, In the Urdu translation of *Tarikh-i-Ferishta* there is a mention of more two ulama other than these 46 i.e. Qazi Jalaluddin who was made Qazi-ul-Mulk and Malik Hamiduddin Multani, who was given the authority of Qazi Abdul Hayy, Khwaja *Tarikh-i-Ferishta* (Urdu translation) Deoband, Maktaba Millat, 1983, p.393.

7. Maulana Ruknuddin Sunami
8. Maulana Tajuddin Kulahi
9. Maulana Zahiruddin Bhakkari
10. Qazi Muhiyuddin Kashani
11. Maulana Kamaluddin Kohli
12. Maulana Wajihuddin Paili.
13. Maulana Minhajuddin Qaini
14. Maulana Nizamuddin Kulahi
15. Maulana Nasiruddin Karah
16. Maulana Nasiruddin Sabuni
17. Maulana Alauddin Tajir
18. Maulana Karimuddin Jauhri
19. Maulana Hujjat Multani
20. Maulana Hamiduddin Mukhlis
21. Maulana Burhanuddin Bhakkhari
22. Maulana Iftikharuddin Barani
23. Maulana Husamuddin Surkh
24. Maulana Wahiduddin Malhu
25. Maulana Alauddin Karak
26. Maulana Husamuddin Ibn Shadi
27. Maulana Hamiduddin Banyani
28. Maulana Shihabuddin Multani
29. Maulana Fakhruddin Hansavi
30. Maulana Fakhruddin Saqaqil
31. Maulana Salahuddin Satriki
32. Qazi Zainuddin Naqilah
33. Maulana Wajihuddin Razi

34. Maulana Alauddin Sadr-ush-Shariah
35. Maulana Miran Marikalah
36. Maulana Najibuddin Sari
37. Maulana Shamsuddin Tam
38. Maulana Sadruddin Gandhak
39. Maulana Alauddin Lohari
40. Maulana Shamsuddin Yahya
41. Qazi Shamsuddin Garzuni
42. Maulana Sadruddin Tawi
43. Maulana Muinuddin Loni
44. Maulana Iftikharuddin Razi
45. Maulana Muizuddin Andehvi
46. Maulana Najimuddin Intishar

Perhaps no academic contribution of any of them is now available. As a matter of fact all of them belonged to the class of scholars and teachers. It may be presumed from the presence of *Shaikh-ul-mashaikh* (the great Shaikh, i.e. Nizamuddin Auliya) Amir Khusrau, Amir Hasan and Barani himself that the academic and literary style of the Alai period might have been very high. But we must not presume that there had been forty six Ghazali and Razi or perhaps one or two Shah Waliullah. It appears from their circumstances that inspite of the general literary and academic interest and the presence of large number of *Ulama* and scholars, the books were not in abundance, as the art of printing had not been introduced, and therefore it was difficult to take literary authenticity and research to its zenith. Moreover, faith and love dominated everywhere. Critical point of view had not developed. The method of *Muhaddithin* (scholars of *hadith*) through which they critically examined the traditions, had not become common in religious circles.

In connection of *Ulama* and *mashaikh*, it is necessary to mention here Khwaja Ziauddin Sunami who was the author of the *Nisab-ul-*

Ihtisab[145] and very strictly followed the *Shariah*. Although he was reprehensive to Shaikh Nizamuddin Auliya on account of his practice of hearing '*sama*'(mystical songs) the latter however held great regard for him.

Another renowned scholarly figure of that age was Amir Hasan Sijzi who was a poet like Amir Khusrau. They both were intimate friends and served under Khan Shahid. His most famous work is the *Fawaid-u'l-Fu'ad* which contains the *malfuzat* (table talks or conversations) of his *pir*, Shaikh Nizamuddin Auliya of Delhi. No other collection of *Malfuzat* received such wide recognition like this work. It is said that Amir Khusrau was so much impressed by the *Fawaid-u'l-Fuad* that he expressed the desire of exchanging all his scholarly and poetic contribution with this work. Even Amir Khusrau flourished during the Alai period.

Tibb (medicine) also developed in India during Alauddin Khalji's reign. Barani writes: "In the days of Alau-u'd-din there were physicians who in their knowledge of the subject . . . . surpassed Hippocrates and Galen, such top physicians have not been seen at any other time. The master of physicians (*Ustad-ul-Atibba*) Maulana Badr-u'd-din' Damishqi lived throughout Alauddin's reign and students of medicine in the city studied their books with him. If the urine of a man mixed with the urine of some animal was brought before him in a glass test-vessel . . . . he could declare immediately which animals urine was in the test vessel . . . . He explained the *Qanun* and the *Qanuncha* of Bu'Ali Sina and other medical works in his . . . . excellent and meaningful discourse."[146]

The successor of Sultan Alauddin Khalji i.e. Qutbuddin Mubarak Shah's reign (1315-1320 A.D.) was full of lawlessness and chaos but historians are of the view that in the field of education and learning the tradition of patronization of scholars continued in his reign also. The

145 *Nisab-ul-Ihtisab*, written by Ziauddin Umar Ibn Muhammad al-Sunami commonly known as Ziauddin Barani is an Arabic treatise related to *misbah* (censure of public morality), the well known institution of Islamic state, For biographical notices of the author see: *Akhbar-ul-Akhyar*, Op.cit, p.109, *Tazkirat-i-Ulama-i-Hind*, Op.cit, pp.97-98, *Fuqah-i-Hind*, Op.cit, pp.254-56.

146 *Tarikh-i-Firoz Shahi*, Op.cit, p.362.

Sultan was very generous in providing *jagirs* and *wazaifs* and the jagirs of those *Ulama* and *mashaikh* which were taken away during the preceding period were returned back.[147] This enabled the promotion of learning and the process of teaching and learning progressed extensively. Near Alauddin khalji's *maqbara* (which was built by Qutbuddin Mubarak Shah in 1317 A.D.) there is an evidence of a *madarsa* near *Quwwat-ul-Islam Mosque* but there is no precise information on who built it? Either Qutb-u'd-din Aibek, Iltutmish or Qutb-u'd-din Mubarak Khalji, one of these have built it during their respective reign. Some historians are of the opinion that it was built by Qutbuddin Mubarak Shah but some are of the view that, it was Iltutmish who while building the *Quwwat-ul-Islam* mosque built this *Madarsa* close to it.[148]

Alauddin Khalji was succeeded by Qutbuddin Mubarak Khalji in 1316 A.D. He changed the entire scene of Alauddin's court. Except prohibition which he continued, he terminated all regulations of his father so far as state patronage to *'Ulama* was concerned, the situation slightly improved under Mubarak Khalji. But apart from increasing their stipends[149] he did not take any interest in academic matters and spent most of his time in pleasure pursuits.

The Tughlaq Sultans were great patrons of learning and literature. The Tughlaq period put an end to the moral degradation that had crept in amongst the aristocracy towards the end of the Khalji period. They brought in massive growth and development by improving the moral culture of society, encouraging philosophy and jurisprudence and promoting projects of public welfare.

The first ruler of the Tughlaq dynasty was Sultan Ghiyasuddin Tughlaq. He hardly ruled for five years. Most of the scholars of his period were of the Alai period. He was on the best of terms with the *'Ulama* and the *Masha'ikh* of his day. He used to send gifts to them when a child was born in his *harem* or when he received news about the victory of his armies.[150]

147 *Tarikh-i-Firoz Shahi*, Op.cit, p.382.

148 Nadvi, Abul Hasnat, Op.cit, p.21, Syed,Sir Ahmad Khan, *Asar-us-Sanadid*, vol.I p. 320.

149 *Tarikh-i-Firoz Shahi*, Op.cit, pp.382-83.

150 For details see: Nizami, K.A;, *Salatin-i-Delhi Kay Mazhabi Rujhanat*, Op.cit, pp.314-21.

Sultan Ghiyasuddin Tughlaq (1320-1325 A.D.) was famous for his love for learning, religious leanings and patronization. He held great respect for nobles and scholars. He invited them to his court at every good occasion and presented gifts and rewards to them.[151] No. historian has mentioned of the establishment of any *madarsa* during his reign. Some of them think that a little away from Tughlaqabad, the Barbar's fort (*Nai-Ka-Qila*) was infact a *Madarsa* built by Ghiyasuddin Tughlaq.[152]

Shaikh Abdul Haq Muhaddith states the scarcity of *Ulama* and scholars during the reign of Muhammad bin Tughlaq. However, there had been several eminent personalities to be mentioned here. For example, Ziauddin Barani, Ibn Batuta, the traveller, Zahiruddin who was an architect, Shihabuddin Abul Abbas Ahmad who was unique in the art of eloquence. The most popular poet and *Malik-us-Shuara* (poet laureate) was Badr Chach who belonged to Chach, i.e. Tashqand. The Sultan respected him a lot and bestowed on him the title of *Fakr-uz-Zama*' (pride of the time). Almost all the *qasaid* (long poems) of Badr Chach are in praise of Muhammad Tughlaq. As some of them point out historical events and there is lack of material regarding this time (Tughlaq period), historians use these *qasidas* as source material of history. Elliot has translated some of them in his work. But on account of its unpopular style of writing, abundance of complicated matter, difficult words, twisted and subtle similies and metaphors, everyone cannot understand them. Besides *qasidas*, Badr Chach wrote (composed) a *mathnawi* entitled '*Shah Namah*'.

Ghiyasuddin Tughlaq's successor Muhammad bin Tughlaq (1325-1351 A.D.) who took keen interest in the rational sciences but yet we find the evidence of the study of *Fiqh* and other religious sciences in the contemporary historical literature of his period. In order to invite the *Ulama* of foreign countries to Hindustan the Sultan sent his special envoys and for the expenditure of their travel allotted a large sum of money.[153] According to Prof. Gibb, Ibn Batuta, the famous traveller of

151 *Tarikh-i-Firoz Shahi*, Op.cit, p.435.

152 Law, N.N., Op.cit, p.42, Fanshawe, H.C., *Delhi, Past and present*, London, John Murray, Albermarle Street, 1902, p.291, Zaki Muhammad, *The Arab accounts of India During the fourteenth century*, Delhi, Idarah-i-Adabyat-i-Delli, 1981, p.85.

153 Al 'Umari, Shahabuddin, *Masalik-ul-Absar-fi-Mumalik-ul-Amsar*,pp.42-43.

Islam, 'had already made up his mind to seek his fortune in India to which the boundless munificence of the reigning sovereign of Delhi was attracting numbers of scholars and theologians from other countries.[154] When the Sultan laid the foundation of the city of Khurramabad near Delhi he also established a *Madarsa* there. The famous poet Badrchach has specially mentioned about this *Madarsa* in one of his *qasidas* and has presented a *Q'ita* on its builder, one of it's is (verses) is this.

رئیس مدرسہ او معلم ادریس امام مسجد او طوطی شکر گفتار [155]

"The head of the *madarsa*, *Muallim* (Professor) Idris, also a *Imam* of his mosque, was a sweet speaking person like nightingale".

We know that there were not less than one thousand *madarsas* in Delhi during his reign which proves that *madarsas* flourished to a large extent inspite of this upheaval (transfer of capital). The same authority i.e. Ibn Batuta, the most energetic globe trotter of Tangier who visited India in 1341 A.D. and was cordially received by the Sultan also testifies to the loss caused by the transfer of capital from Delhi to Daulatabad: Delhi says he, one of the greatest and most magnificent cities in the world, was at the time like a desert and had the fewest inhabitants.[156] The above words reflect the utter ruin caused to Delhi which was the most popular centre of higher learning during the Sultanate period.

Sultan Muhammad bin Tughlaq had a great liking for men of learning and loved to associate with the *'Ulama*, the *Mashaikh* (Saints), the Sufis and the philosophers. He had great respect for saints like Shaikh Rukn-ud-din Multani and Shaikh Nizamuddin Auliya. It was from them that he drew his inspiration, and to them he was indebted for his initiation into Sufism.[157] Sultan Muhammad Tughlaq himself was a poet. He composed the following verses at the time (of the agony) of his death:

---

154 Gibb, H.A.R., *Travels of Ibn Batuta* 1325-1354 A.D., (Introduction pp.5&6), Vol. I, New Delhi, Munshiram Manoharlal Pub. Pvt. Ltd, 1993 (Introduction pp.5&6)

155 Badr-u'd-din Chach, *Qasa'id Badr Chach*, Kanpur, Nawal Kishore, 1877, p.10.

156 Law, N.N., Op.cit, p.47.

157 Mahdi Husain, *Rise and Fall of Muhammad bin Tughlaq*, Delhi, Idarah-i- Adabiyat-i-Delhi, 1972, p.23.

بسیار دریں جہاں طپیدیم بسیار نعیم و ناز دیدیم

اسپان بلند برنشستیم ترکان گراں بہا خریدیم

کردیم بسے نشاط و آخر چوں قامتِ ماہ نو خمیدیم [158]

"I deeply observed this world by passing through great difficulties; and I experienced all sorts of luxurious life.

I rode many high class horses; and purchased costly Turkish slaves.

I availed great comfort and at last when entered into old age, found myself totally helpless".

The famous Moroccan traveller Ibn Batuta came to India during the reign of Sultan Muhammad bin Tughlaq. The Sultan had great reverence for him and appointed him the *Qazi* of Delhi. Later he sent him as his ambassador to the king of China. He (Ibn Batuta), therefore (on account of his journey from India to China) got an opportunity to see, not only the North and Central India, but Malabar, Maldives, Ceylon, Mabar, Bengal, Arakan, Sumatra and famous coastal areas of China. He has mentioned the interesting events of all the places in his travelling account. Janab Maulvi Abdul Rahman Sahib has published the Urdu translation of this *Safar- Namah* with detailed and scholarly notes and explanation.[159] A renowned scholar of that time was Maulana Muinuddin Umrani, who wrote marginal notes— (*hawashi*) on *Kanz, Manar, Husami, Talkis* and *Miftah*.[160] Muhammad bin Tughlaq, it appears also knew about the literary activities of other Islamic cultural centres, like Shiraz, Samarqand, etc. he sent Maulana Muinuddin Umrani to Qazi Azd with a request to visit India and dedicate his work *Matan Muwafiq* to him. Sultan Abu Ishaq of Shiraz who had great respect for Qazi 'Azd did not allow him to leave his realm.[161] The Sultan is reported to have sent

158 Shaikh, M.Ikram, Op.cit, p.424.

159 For details see: Ibn Batuta, *Safar Namah*, Urdu ed. and translation by Janab Maulvi Abdul Rehman Saheb, Delhi, Maktaba Burhan, 1964, also Ibn Batuta, *Safar Namah*, ed. and translated by Rais Ahmad Jafri, Karachi, Nafis Academy, 1961.

160 Shaikh, M., Ikram, Op.cit, p.424.

161 *Akhbar-u'l-Akhyar*, Op.cit, p.142, *Ma'athir-u'l-Kiram*, Op.cit, pp.184-85.

Shaikh Abu Bakr b. Khallal, along with some other scholars to Samarqand to persuade Shaikh Burhan-u'd-din Sagharji to come to India. He gave to this team of scholars forty thousand *tankas* as travel expenses.[162]

Zia Bakshi of Badayun was a more popular figure than Maulana Muinuddin Umrani. Though he passed his life in seclusion, he left several works as his memorial, some of them are still intact. One of his works *Gulrez* has been published by the Royal Asiatic society. Another famous work is the *Silk-us-Suluk*. Its Urdu translation has been published from Lahore with the title *Allah Walon ki Qawmi Dukan* and original Persian too has been printed. With regard to *Silk-us-Suluk*, Shaikh Abdul Haq Muhaddith Dehlavi writes:

سلک السلوک او بغایت کتاب شیریں و رنگین است۔ بزبانِ لطیف و موثر مشتملبر حکایات مشائخ و کلمات ایشان و اکثر تصنیفات وی مملوست بہ قطعہ ہا کہ ہمہ بہ یک طریق و یک نہج واقعہ اند۔ چنانکہ قطعہ

بخشی! خیز وبا زمانہ بہ ساز
ورنہ خود را نشانہ ساختن است
عاقلان زمانہ می گویند
عاقلی با زمانہ ساختن است

(His *Silk-us-Suluk* is very sweet and colourful in subtle, delicate and effective language. It consists of the stories of *Mashaikh* (Sufis) and their sayings. Most of his works are full of stanzas which are all equal in pattern and style. Accordingly the *qitah* (stanza):

> "Rise, O' Bakhshi and do in accordance with the time;
> Other wise you yourself will be your target;
> Wisemen of the time do say;
> Wisdom is to mix with the time".[163]

162 Otto Spies, Op.cit, pp.42-53.
163 *Akhbar-u'l-Akhyar*, Op.cit, p.105.

More popular than his *Silk-us-Suluk* is his *Tuti Namah*[164] which contains the fifty stories told by a parrot which have been translated into German, English and Deccani. The Urdu prose book *Tota-Kahani*, which was compiled by Syed Haider Bakhsh Haidari on the request of Dr. Gil Graist, the principal of the Fort William College is the translation of the *Tuti Namah*. Maulana Ziauddin Bakhshi was a poet also. He was a pupil of the famous poet Shihabuddin Mehmara of Badayun in the art of poetry. He died in 1350 A.D.

Another contemporary of Sultan Muhammad Tughlaq was Ziauddin Barani renowned historian of the time whose *Tarikh-i-Firoz Shah*[165] is a precious treasure of the events of that age. He was born in 684 A.H./ 1282 A.D. in Baran, now known as Buland Shahar. His father and other relatives were associated with the royal court. He was intelligent with a sharp intellect and was imparted with good education. Having joined the mystic discipline of *Sultan-ul-Mashaikh*, Shaikh Nizamuddin Auliya, he too took his residence in Ghiyaspur. On his *pir's* death and when Sultan Muhammad bin Tughlaq ascended the throne, Barani, on account of his quick wittiness (*Hazir jawabi*) and the art of companionship (*fan-i-nadimi*), made good place in the eyes and heart of the Sultan. It appears from his work—the *Tarikh-i- Firoz Shahi* that the Sultan, on several critical occasions sought his advice or at least told him his problems. It is written in the *Siyar-ul-Auliya* that "On account of his pleasantness of nature, he was matchless in the art of companionship (*fan-i-nadimi*). And ultimately, due to having mastery in this art, he was appointed the *nadim-i-khas* (chief companion) of Sultan Muhammad Tughlaq and earned a lot out of this .... world". On reaching the age of seventy he relinquished the royal service, took to a life of seclusion and started the writing and compilation of significant and matchless works.[166]

When Firoz Shah became the Sultan, Barani named his book after his (Sultan's) name as '*Tarikh-i-Firoz Shahi*' but the Sultan was for some reason angry with him and he (Barani) was not given any (special)

164 Ibid.

165 *Tarikh-i-Firoz Shahi* is a history of the Sultans of Delhi from Balban A.H. 662/1263 A.D. to Firoz Shah's sixth year, A.H.758/1357 A.D. forming a continuation of the *Tabaqat-i-Nasiri*, see: Storey, C.A., Vol.I, part.I, p.507.

166 *Siyar-u'l-Auliya*, Op.cit, p.323.

position. But later he issued a stipend which was not sufficient for Barani. And he died in 758 A.H./1357A.D. due to restlessness. But according to *Siyar-ul-Auliya* "He had no money with him at the end of his life. He had distributed all his garments (among needy and poor people) in the way of God. Accordingly, there were just a mat (boriya), and a small sheet of old cloth on his dead-body."[167]

The *Tarikh-i-Firozi Shahi* is infact the completion or appendix (takmilah) of the *Tabaqat-i-Nasiri* and contains the events from the accession of Sultan Ghiyathuddin Balban, i.e. 664 A.H./1246 A.D. till the events of the sixth regnal year of Sultan Firoz Shah i.e. 758 A.H./ 1357A.D. In comparison to Minhaj, Barani describes more interesting events and his style of writing also is very beautiful. Therefore, the *Tarikh-i-Firoz Shahi* is more popular than the *Tabaqat-i-Nasiri.*

Barani has a special point of view regarding the art of historiography. Though he attaches importance to the description of the events, yet he pays more attention in deriving conclusion from those events and through that in highlighting the art and principles of administration and government. He himself writes:

"اگراین تالیف را تاریخ خوانند اخبار سلاطین وملوک دریابند۔ واگر درین تالیف احکام انتظام والتیام جویند، ازانہم خالی نیابند۔
واگر دریں تالیف مواعظ ونصائح جہانبانان وجہانداران طلبند، بیشتر وبہتر از تالیفات دیگر مطالعہ فرمایند۔"

["If they (people) hold this work as a history, they will get the news of Sultans and kings in it. And if they trace the principles of administration they will not find (this work) without them. And if they seek or require the good sayings and beautiful advices of sovereigns and rulers in this compilation (*talif*), they will study these things more and better than in other works."][168]

In political affairs and in the affairs of state also, Barani has a special point of view. And it was difficult for him to make an assessment of those rulers, (for instance Alauddin Khalji), whose events of life were not in accordance with his point of view. However in the line of our

167 Ibid.

168 *Tarikh-i-Firoz Shahi*, Op.cit, p.21.

historians Barani holds an unique place.[169] Although his concept of history was limited and advisable (*mahdud and nasihatanah*), yet he was fully aware of the responsibilities. In his work, the historiography is not just the description of events but has reached the level of a creative art, and that too without giving up or sacrificing the accuracy of statement. Moreover, the active and living pictures of some extraordinary figures, like Balban, Alauddin Khalji, Muhammad bin Tughlaq, in the *Tarikh-i-Firoz Shahi*, may not be seen in other old works of history.

Another historian of this age is Isami who wrote a *Mathnawi* entitled as the *Futuh-us-Salatin*[170] consisting of twelve thousand verses during the last year of Muhammad bin Tughlaq's reign (1350 A.D.). It contains the events of the lives and conquests of Ghaznavides, Ghurids, Slaves, Khaljis and first two Sultans of the Tughlaq dynasty have been described in versified form.

Isami was born in Delhi in 1310 A.D. His real name is known but he says that his ancestor who first came to India was Fakhr-ul Mulk Isami. He had been the *Wazir* of the Caliphs of Baghdad but having been grieved on some remark of Caliph of time (*Khalifa-i- Waqt*), he left his place and came to Delhi via Multan along with his family. At that time, the ruler of Delhi was Sultan Shamsuddin Iltutmish who venerated the *Ulama*, scholars and eminent persons who migrated from the Islamic countries to Delhi as a result of the Mongol irruption. He warmly received *Fakr-ul-Mulk* and entrusted on him the post of minister. The grandson of Fakhrul Mulk, Izuddin Isami, a military officer in Balban's time, was the grand-father of the author of the *Futuh-us-Salatin*. This grandfather

---

169 Many modern historians attempted to study Ziauddin Barani and his *Tarikh-i- Firoz Shahi*. Peter Hardy, for instance, is of the opinion that Barani conceived history to have a didactic religious purpose and treats history as a branch of theology, Hardy Peter, *Historians in Medieval India*, London, Luzac & Company Ltd., 1960, pp.23, 39. Mohibbul Hasan is of the opinion that the *Tarikh-i-Firoz Shahi* is a much more complicated study which requires as much an examination of the basic categories of Barani's thought as analysis of his fluctuating emotions, Mohibbul Hasan, *Historians of Medieval India*, Delhi, Meenakshi Prakashan, 1968, p.39.

170 *Futuh-us-Salatin* is an epic poem on the rulers of India from Ghaznavides to the date of composition i.e. 1349-50 A.D. composed by Isami and dedicated to Muzaffar Bahman Shah, the first ruler of Bahmani dynasty, Storey, C.A., Vol.I part.I, Op.cit, p.433.

brought him up. Isami writes that at the ripe age of ninety he and his grandfather had to decide to leave for Daulatabad on the instructions of Sultan Muhammad bin Tughlaq but it was in the beginning of this journey, that the old man died.

During the completion of the *Futuh-us-Salatin*, Isami fully benefited from the library of the founder of the Bahmani dynasty, Bahman Shah. And he composed events with care and gave vivid explanations. As he is a semi contemporary for the Khalji and Tughlaq dynasties, and had direct access to people who migrated in large numbers to Daulatabad, who had been eye witness of the events in northern India. Therefore his *mathnavi* is of great historical significance. His personal life is behind curtains. It reveals from the *Futuh-us-Salatin* that he was very displeased with the contemporary conditions and wanted to shift to the Illumined city (*Madina Munawwara*) i.e. Madina. As there is no trace of him after the compilation of the *Futuh-us-Salatin*, it is thought he might have settled in Hejaz.

According to Qalqashandi two hundred jurists were always there with Sultan Muhammad at his dinner.[171] When the Sultan went on campaigns *imams* and *Ulama* encircled him. The Sultan was also interested in the religious education of the people. He appointed thousands of jurists in *maktabs* to teach *qirat* etc.[172] He arranged philosophical and religious discussions to satisfy his own intellectual curiosity and to break the rigid thinking.[173] Muhammad bin Tughlaq came under the influence of Ibn Taimmiya's movement of religious reform and regeneration. His policy towards contemporary mystics was largely due to his commitment of Ibn Taimmiya's ideology.[174]

---

171 Otto spies, Op.cit, p.33, Ishwari Prasad is of the opinion that Mohammad like other oriental monarchs maintained splendid court which was an inevitable necessity in middle ages, Prasad Ishwari, *A History of Qaraunah Turks in India*, Allahabad, Central Book Depot, 1974, p.297.

172 Ibid, p.39.

173 *Tarikh-i-Firoz Shahi*, Op.cit, p.465, Nizami K.A., *State and Culture in Medieval India*, Op.cit, p.117.

174 For details see: Nizami, K.A., "*The impact of Ibn Taimmiya on South Asia*", in Journal of Islamic Studies, Vol.I, Oxford, 1990, pp.125-35.

It was after the death of Muhammad Tughlaq that the nobles and the *Ulama* selected Firoz, the nephew of Ghiyathuddin Tughlaq, for the throne of Delhi. The reign of this Sultan is remembered in the history of India for peace and public welfare. The first thing he did was that he released those prisoners whom Muhammad Tughlaq had thrown into prison. He gave compensations to the survivors of those who had been murdered on the instruction of Muhammad bin Tughlaq.

Sultan Firoz Shah Tuglaq (1351-88 A.D.) was a highly accomplished and versatile man of literary and artistic tastes. In his devotion to learning, literature, and architecture he surpassed all other Sultans of Delhi. Himself a fairly educated monarch, he devoted his energies to the spread of Islamic learning and literature. The establishment of many *madarsas* and the lavish grant of subsistence allowances and stipends to the learned greatly enhanced his reputation as a patron of learning. Not only did he built new *madarsas* but also renovated and repaired the old buildings, mosques and *madarsas* of his predecessors which he has mentioned in his *Futuhat-i-Firoz Shahi* where he writes, "One of the favours of God, bestowed on the humble servant (was that) he was enabled to construct works of public utility, I erected numerous mosques, *madarsas* (colleges) and *Khanqahs* so that the *alims* and *mashaikh*, devotees and pious men might devote themselves to the worship of the true God and help with prayer the founder of charitable institutions.[175]

It is interesting to hear from the Sultan himself some particulars about the provisions made for building operations:-

"Provisions for the future repairs and rebuilding of these *madarsas* and tombs was made from their old endowments, which were to remain attached to their respective institutions. And where no income had been settled before, I assigned villages whose revenues are always to be used in meeting the needs of visitors and for providing, carpets, light and other requirements of the places concerned."

175 *Futuhat Firoz Shahi*, Op.cit, p.11.

"Again, thus I contributed the grants of villages, lands and old endowments attached to *madarsas*, tombs and graves of the victorious Sultans of the past and the great *mashaikh* for meeting the needs of visitors and providing necessary materials required for the holy places. In addition if there was no endowment or other provision at any place, an assignment was made for it so that the noble work might continue for ever and travellers learned and holy men might rest there and remembered them and me in their prayers.[176]

He further informs us, "Portions of the *madarsa* of Sultan Iltutmish with whom God may be pleased had fallen down. These were likewise, rebuilt and furnished with sandalwood doors." "In the mausoleum of Sultan Ruknuddin a son of Sultan Shamsuddin which is situated in Malikpur, the enclosure was repaired, a dome was built and a *Khanqah* constructed."[177] Also Sultan Alauddin Khalji's mausoleum was repaired and furnished with doors of sandalwood. Walls of the water reservoir and the western walls of the mosque which is within the *madarsa* and ground floor were repaired.[178]

According to the testimony of Nizamuddin Bakhshi and Ferishta,[179] the Sultan established no less than thirty *madarsas*, appointed qualified professors there and provided them a handsome pay. However Abdul Baqi Nahawandi has recorded in his *Maathir-i-Rahimi*, that he opened as many as fifty *madarsas*.[180] Although the number of *madarsas* differs in different accounts there were definitely several of them existing in a flourishing state, but the exact number is not known.

The *madarsas* of Firoz Tughlaq's period became popular because of the high standard of education and excellent coaching arrangements.

---

176 Ibid, p.15.

177 Ibid, p.13.

178 Ibid, p. 14.

179 According to Nizamuddin Ahmad and *Ferishta*, Firoz Shah built 30 Madarsas, *Tabaqat-i-Akbari*, p.121, *Tarikh-i-Ferishta*, Vol. I, Op.cit, p.151.

180 According to the *Ma'athir-i-Rahimi* he erected 50 Madarsahs, Abdul Baqi Nahawandi *Ma'athir-i-Rahimi*, Vol. I, ed. M. Hidayat Husain, Calcutta, A.S.B., 1924, p.30. There is no denying the fact that. Firoz Shah erected a large number of *Madarsahs*, but it is very difficult to give the exact number on the basis of the accounts of later authorities.

The *Firozi Madarsa* and the *Madarsa-i-Shahzada Buzurg*[181] were known throughout the country.

Perhaps the only detailed account of a Madarsa founded by a Sultan of Delhi is that of *Firozi Madarsa* of Delhi. On the southern bank of the *Hauz-i-Khas*,[182] Firoz Shah built this *madarsa*[184] in 1352 A.D.[184] It was the most magnificent *madarsa* of its time, "Its magnificence," writes Barani, "architectural proportions and pleasant air make it so unique among the great buildings of the world that it would be justifiable if it claimed superiority over the Khwarnaq built by Simar or the palace of Kisra."[185]

The Firozi Madarsa was a double storied building with arched dalans projecting windows overlooking the tank.[186] As soon as one entered the doorway he found himself in a blooming garden adorned with pathways and passages.[187] This two storied structure was in itself a fine example in the art of building. It stood on strong pillars and there were many domes made over it. The location of this *madarsa* was excellent and it

181 Anonymous, *Sirat-i-Firoz Shahi*, (Facsimile edition), Patna, Khuda Baksh Oriental Public Library', 1999, p.208

182 An extensive tank covering an area over 70 acres of land, constructed by 'Alauddin Khalji in 1296. It was later repaired and cleansed by Firoz Shah. See Carr Stephen, *The Archeological and Monumental Remains* of Delhi, Allahabad, Kitab Mahal, 1967, p.83.

183 Sirhindi, Yahya bin Ahmad Bin Abdullah, *Tarikh-i-Mubarakshahi*, tr.by Basu K.K., Karachi, Karimsons, 1977, p.127. The remains of the *Madarsas* possess a historical or Quranic epigraph and the only inscriptional decorations one comes across in it are the plastered discs inscribed with one or the other of the following phrases: *Hasbi Allah, Sultan Allah, ul Mulk Allah*, see Memoirs of the Archaeological Survey of India, No: 47, p.77. A record of all the Quranic and non historical epigraphs on the protected monuments in the Delhi Province, by Maulvi Muhammad Ashraf Husain, Calcutta, Govt. of India, 1936, p.77.

184 *Tarikh-i-Firoz Shahi*, however is silent about the date of establishment of this madarsa K.A. Nizami mentions 1352 A.D. in his *Studies in Medieval Indian History and Culture*, Allahabad, Kitab Mahal, 1966, pp.73, but Sir Syed's *Asar-us-Sanadid*, has given the date as 1354 A.D. Khan Sir Syed, *Asar-us-Sanadid*, Vol. I, ed. Khaliq Anjum, Delhi, Urdu Academy, Delhi, 1990, p.329.

185 Nizami, K.A., *Studies in Medieval Indian History and Culture*, Allahabad, Kitab Mahal, 1966, pp.73, Jauhri, R.C., Op.cit, p.171.

186 Zafar, Hasan, *Monuments of Delhi, Lasting splendour of the great Mughals and others*, Vol. III, (Mehrauli Zail), New Delhi, Aryan Books International, 1920 rept 1997, pp.179-80, Alavi, Azra, Op.cit, p.14.

187 *Diwan-i-Mutahhar*, Oriental College Magazine, May, 1935, p.136

was built on a large, extensive campus. There were spacious courtyards in between the different buildings of the *madarsa*, it had wide galleries and corridors. The scenic beauty, gardens laiden with beautiful colourful flowers added explicit charm to this *madarsa*.

Barani describes the beauty of this *madarsa* in the following words:-

"از بناهای مبارک خداوند عالم مدرسه فیروز شاهیست که بس بوالعجب عمارتی برسر حوض علائی بنا شده است وعمارت
مدرسه مذکور از رفعت گنبدها وشیرینی عمارتها وموازین صحنها ولطافت نشست جاشهاے ومحلهای مروج وصفهای
دلآویز گوی لطافت از عمارتهای که در عالم معروف است ربوده است.... از شیرینی عمارت وموازین عمارت
وهوای دل کشای ازان بناهانادره است"
188

"What greatly God gifted is the *Madarsa-i-Firoz Shahi* that wonderful buildings are situated near the Alai Tank. The buildings of the *madarsa*, because of the glory of their domes, sweetness of their construction, open courtyards, comfortable seats, beautiful palaces and attractive lines of students, have left behind the buildings of other places in the world. In attraction and comparison, and also from the point of view of air, these monuments are rare."

Another beautiful description of this *madarsa* in poetic form has been done by the famous poet Mutahhar of Kara[189] who praises the Firozi Madarsa in these words:-

صحن او روح فزا ساحت او جاں
خاک او مشک فشان نکہت او عنبر بار
سبزه وسنبل وریحان وگل ولاله درو
رسته وآراسته چندانک کند با تو کار

"Its courtyard, because of its construction is very comfortable, Its dust is scented with musk, its air is ambergrised, There are greenery, spikenard, sweet basil, rose and popy flower inside it, All its ways are beautifully decorated"

188 *Tarikh-i-Firoz Shahi*, Op.cit, pp.562-63.

189 *Diwan-i-Mutahhar*, Op.cit, p.136.

The *Firozi Madarsa* covered a capacious area besides several lecture halls, it had within its campus, commodious hostels for both teachers and the taught, guest houses for casual visitors, a huge mosque, rooms for *imams* and *mu'azzins* and *hujrahs* (small rooms) for those who wished to spend their time in meditations.[190] Comfy and pleasant looking carpets of Shiraz, Yemen and Damascus were spread in every corner of the *madarsa*.[191] In the words of Mutahhar:

وز بساط یمن مفرش شیراز ودمشق

همه آراسته بیرون ودرونش چو نگار

"Its carpets have been brought from Yeman, Shiraz and Damascus, Both its outside and inside are beautifully decorated"

Other than its beauty, magnificence and excellence in building the *madarsa* was famous for its cultured and experienced teachers who were experts in their subjects. Amongst the most famous was Maulana Jalal-u'd-din Rumi (not the famous philosopher and author of the *Mathnawi*, Jalal-u'd din Rumi of (1273 A.D.). Barani has used the title (استاد متفنن) i.e. teacher of different arts and crafts for him.[192] But in Mutahhar's *Diwan* it is clearly evident that Jalal-u'd-din Rumi was the principal of this *madarsa* from the following words:

صدر آن محفل وسر دفتر آن استادی

که زسر تا بقدم صورت عقل ست و وقار

گفتم این عالمِ آفاق جلال الدین است

که رومی آن کزنسبتش رے کند و روم فخار[193]

"The head of the gathering and the incharge of its office is a teacher; Who, from top to bottom, is the face of intellect and honour.

---

190 *Tarikh-i-Firoz Shahi*, Op.cit, pp.563-65.

191 Diwan-i-Mutahhar, Op.cit, p.137.

192 *Tarikh-i-Firoz Shahi*, Op.cit, p.564.

193 Diwan Mutahhar, p.137.

I said this world-fame teacher is Jalaluddin Rumi,
Of whose genealogy the cities of Ray and Rum, take pride."

Mutahhar has called him a past master in *Quran*, *Hadith*, *Fiqh* and has acknowledged of himself benefiting from the teachings of Jalaluddin Rumi.

راوی ہفت قراء ت سند چاردہ علم
شارح پنج سنن مفتی مذہب چار
پس شنیدم زگفتارش انواع علوم
اخذ کردیم ز تفسیر واصول واخبار[194]

"He knows seven dialects of *qirat* and he is authority in fourteen sciences,

He is interpreter of the five collection of *hadith* and the *mufti* of all four schools of jurisprudence.

In short, I heard from him about different sciences, I derived lot from his *tafsir*, *usul* and *hadith*".

Sir Syed Ahmad Khan and other modern writers[195] have named Syed Yusuf Bin Jamal Haseeni as the most famous and renowned teacher of the *Firozi Madarsa* and have even said that he was buried in the courtyard of this *madarsa*. Others have mentioned, him as the principal teacher of the *madarsa* which was built close to Hauz Alai but was some other *madarsa* and not the *Firozi Madarsa*.[196] The syllabus of the *Madarsa-i-Firoz Shahi* included both traditional (*manqulat*) and rational (*ma'qulat*) sciences. Barani particularly refers to the teaching of *tafsir* (Quranic exegesis), *hadith* (Traditions of the Prophet) and *Fiqh* (Muslim jurisprudence).[197] As Firoz Shah was keenly interested in

194 Ibid, p.137.

195 Syed, Abdul Hayy, Op.cit, p.159.

196 *Akbar-ul-Akhyar*, Op.cit., p.150, Rafiq, Sai'd Ahmad, Op.cit, p.93.

197 *Tarikh-i-Firoz Shahi*, Op.cit, p.564.

astronomy, history, medicine, there is a possibility that these subjects were taught in this *madarsa*.

No information on the uniform of the students is available but the teachers of this institution wore the Syrian *jubbah* and the Egyptian *dastar*.[198]

Contemporary sources bring out the fact that other than teaching and learning the process of holding debates and seminars was present in the *Firozi Madarsa* and the students were given opportunity to debate on a particular topic of significance. Khaliq Nizami[199] has narrated that the Muslim method of middle ages laid great emphasis on seminars and mutual discussions amongst the students. The purpose was to make use of their intelligence and improve their standard as intellectuals. The Firozi Madarsa did not neglect this very important method of imparting knowledge. To prove this Nizami has used this particular verse of Mutahhar:-

ہم چنان یک دگراز طالب علمان ہر سوی بر فلک بر دہ صدا غلغل بحث و تکرار [200]

Liberal grants were provided by the state to finance this *madarsa* and meet all the expenses of the teachers and the students. Royal arrangements were made for the boarding and lodging of students. According to Mutahhar the following dishes were served at the meals: "Pheasants, partridges, herons, fish, roasted fowl and bulky kids, fried loaves, sweets of different kinds, and other things, were heaped everywhere in large quantities." Pomegranate syrup, prepared with the mixture of sorrel, was served as a drink. Betel-nuts were brought in gold and silver dishes after the meal.[201]

Barani writes about the religious atmosphere prevailing at the *madarsa*:

198 Diwan-i-Mutahhar, p.137.

199 Nizami, K.A., *Studies in Medieval Indian History and Culture*, Op.cit, p.77

200 *Diwan-i-Mutahhar*, p.137

201 Ibid, p.138.

”واز انکه مدرسه فیروز شاهی معدن خیرات وحسنات است ودر او عبادت لازمه وهم عبادت متعدیه مومی شود
وفرایض خمسه بجماعت مسنون می گذارند وصوفیان نماز چاشت واشراق وفی زوال واوابین وتهجد ادا می کنند
ولیلا ونهارا ذکر میگویند وبدعا وثنای بادشاه مشغول می باشند ...وهر روز حافظان در ختمهای قرآن مشغول می باشند
ومسافران آواز تکبیر بآسمان می رسانند“

“Because this *madarsa* is a monument of good works and public benefaction, prayers obligatory and supererogatory are constantly being offered within its precincts. The five compulsory prayers are offered in congregation according to *Sunnah*. The Sufis offer the *Chasht* Prayer (offered between sunrise and meridian), *Ishraq* (prayer offered soon after sunrise), *Fayaz-Zawal* (prayer offered immediately after sunset) and *Tahajjud* (prayer offered in the latter part of the night), praise God, night and day and send benediction on and sing and praise the Sultan constantly. People who know the *Quran* by heart recite the full text every day; the travellers raise their voices to the heavens when they cry Allah-o-Akbar”.[202]

Barani writes that the beauty of the *Firozi Madarsa* was par excellence and the satisfaction and peace that one experiences after entering this *madarsa* could not be availed or felt in any other place which he expresses in the following words:-

”واگرچه دارالملک دهلی بادشاهان گذشته طاب ثراهم عمارتها بسیار کرده اند مالهائے بے اندازه دران خرچ شده
ومواطن دیوان وپریان گشته ام شیرینی، روحی وراحتی که مدرسه فیروز شاهی دارد هیچ بنائے نیست وبدین زیبائی
عمارتی مشاهده نشده است“ [203]

“Although the former rulers have built a number of attractive monuments in Delhi and spent heavy amount in their beautification and decoration, yet the prettiness, pleasure and comfort which are in the *Madarsa-i-Firoz Shahi* are not seen elsewhere.”

202 *Tarikh-i-Firoz Shahi*, Op.cit, pp.563-564.

203 Ibid, p.565.

The *Firozi Madarsa* was a great centre of Muslim learning in the East, and people gathered there from different parts of the country, simply to have a look at it:-

از پے نظارہ دیدار او شرق و غرب

کاروان در کاروان و قافلہ در قافلہ

[With a view to have a look at it (people from) the east and the west (come) in caravan after caravan].[204]

The second *madarsa* of the Firozian period was built at Siri which also has been praised by Barani who records that Maulana Syed Najm-ul-Millat Waddin Samarqandi, a great scholar of the time was the principal of this *madarsa*.[205]

Another very famous seat of learning in Delhi was the *Madarsa-i-Shahzada Buzurg*.[206] It was named after the eldest son of Firoz Shah, Fath Khan, who died in 1374 A.D. A footprint of the Prophet was placed at the grave.[207] The area therefore came to be known as *Qadam Sharif*.[208] Within the enclosure the Sultan built a charity house (*Langar Khana*), a *madarsa* and a mosque consisting of three chambers, covered with domes with a courtyard attached to it surrounded by walls.[209]

The doorway of this *madarsa* was engraved with the following lines:-

"The guide of those who have lost (their way) Muhammad

"The Preachers of Preacher Muhammad

---

204 Ibid, p.564, Nizami, K.A., *Studies in Medieval Indian History and Culture*, Op.cit, p.56.

205 Ibid, p.565.

206 Sirat, p.208.

207 Zafar Hasan, *Monuments of Delhi lasting splendour of the great Mughals and others*, New Delhi, Aryan Books International, 1919, rept 1997, p.241. It is related that Firoz Shah secured it as a gift from the Prophet by sending his spiritual guide *Makhdum Jahanian Jahan Gasht*, to him. The Sultan received this relic with great reverence and expressed his desire that after his death it should be placed over his grave. But when his favourite son Fath Khan died before him in 1374 A.D. it was placed on his grave.

208 Thomas, E, *The Chronicles of Pathan kings of Delhi*, New Delhi, Munshiram Manoharlal (Oriental Publishers), 1967, pp.297-98.

209 Zafar Hasan, Vol. II, Op.cit, pp.242-44, Corr Stephen, pp.147-78.

"Glorious is the *madarsa*, the pulpit and the house
"In the midst of which is read the praise of Muhammad
"For the broken hearts he is (Healing) balm
"For the afflicted in the heart Muhammad is a comfort etc.[210]

Apart from the *madarsa* established by the Sultans themselves, there were large number of other institutions whose teachers and students received grants from the Sultan. Nobles also emulated the Sultans in helping educational institutions and encouraging educational activities.

The above discussion on the educational centres of Islamic higher learning shows that these centres were found all over the Sultanate and imparted education in different branches of learning at higher level.

Amongst the scholars of this period was the compiler of the famous Arabic dictionary *Qamus*, Maulana Majduddin Firozabadi who came to India in this period. Three other people worth mentioning of the Firoz Shahi period were Maulana Ahmad Thaneshwari, Maulana Khwajaji, who was the teacher of Qazi Shihabuddin Daulatabadi, and Qazi Abdul Muqtadir Dehlawi. The most famous amongst Sufi (*mashaikh*) was Makhdum Nasiruddin Chiragh of Delhi.[211] Sultan Muhammad bin Tughlaq had disrespected him but Firoz Shah paid him great honour. It was the *Shaikh* who, after the death of Muhammad bin Tughlaq persuaded Firoz Shah, who was intending to leave for Hajj and other pilgrimages, to become the Sultan of Delhi. Firoz, on becoming the Sultan, sought his advice on several occasions. Shaikh Sadruddin Multani was another famous *Shaikh* (Sufi) of that time whom the Sultan had granted the title of *Shaikh-ul- Islam.*

It appears that poetry and the compositions of verses was not popular in Firoz's reign as compared to others. However, some famous poets of the time are found mentioned in the sources, one of them was Masud Bak, who is said to be a relative of Firoz Shah. His *diwan*, the collection of his verses and poems has been published from Hyderabad, Deccan. His real name was Sher Khan. Perhaps Masud Bak was his title. For a

210 Carr Stephen, Op.cit, p.147.

211 Shaikh, M., Ikram, Op.cit, p.430, Jauhri, R.C., Firoz Tughlaq (1351-88 A.D.), Agra, Shivalal Agrawal & Company, 1968, p.158.

long time he lived the life of aristocracy. Later he felt attracted to the *darveshi* (the mystical life) and joined the discipline, (became a *murid*-disciple) of Shaikh Ruknuddin bin Shaikh Shihabuddin. He wrote several works on Sufism (*Tasawwuf*), as for example the *Tamhidat* and the *Mirat-ul-Arifin*. Shaikh Abdul Haqq Muhaddith Dehlavi writes about him:

"در سلسلۂ چشتیہ ہیچ کس این چنین اسرار حقیقت را افاش نگفتہ، و مستی نہ کردہ کہ او کردہ"

(In the Chishti order nobody disclosed the secrets of reality and drank with the love of God as he did).[212]

The other poet was Hamid Qalandar who compiled the *Khair-ul-Majalis*,[213] the *Malfuzat* of *Hazrat Chiragh-i-Delhi*. Amir Khusrau's son Amir Ahmad was also a poet of pleasing nature but we do not come across any *Diwan* of his.[214] In the same period, Shihabi, who was a physician, composed a *mathnawi* entitled as the *Tibb-i- Shihabi*. But the best poet of that time was Mutahhar who belonged to Kara (near Allahabad). He praised Firoz immensely and was an eulogist of Firoz Shah and his time. A nobel known as *Malik-ul- Sharq*, Malik Ain-ul-Mulk, whose *Insha-i-Mahru*[215] is famous, was also one of the celebrated personalities whom he praised. Badayuni writes that the *diwan* of Mutahhar consisted of fifteen to sixteenth thousand verses.[216] But it was not easily available even in the time of Shaikh Abdul Haq Muhaddith. Fortunately, a copy of this diwan has been discovered by Dr. Wahid Mirza. The latter and Maulvi Muhammad Shafi, principle, Oriental College, Lahore wrote invaluable articles in the Oriental College Magazine and revived the name of the poet.[217]

---

212 *Akhbar-ul-Akhyar*, Op.cit, p.169

213 The *Khair-u'l-Majalis* is a record of one hundred mystic gatherings of Shaikh Nasir-u'd-din *Chiragh-i-Delhi*, For details see: Hamid Qalandar, *Khair-u'l-Majalis*, ed. Nizami, K.A., Aligarh, Dept. of History, 1959. Not only is it a source of information of the lives of several Indo-Muslim saints but also supplies information on the political and economic conditions of the time'.

214 *Muntakhab-u't-Tawarikh*, Vol.I, Op.cit, pp.255-56.

215 The *Insha-i-Mahru* is collection of 134 documents drafted by Ain-u'l-Mulk, some for himself, some on behalf of the government and some for others. For details see: Ain-ul-Mulk Mahru *Insha-i-Mahru*, ed by S.A. Rashid, Aligarh, AMU, 1954.

216 *Muntakhab-ut-Tawarikh*, Vol.I, Op.cit, p.257.

217 Muhammad Shafi, Diwan-i-Mutahhar, *Oriental College Magazine*, Lahore, May, 1935.

Besides composition of verses and poetry, *fiqh* (jurisprudence) also was highly developed in those days. Alauddin Khalji was not very interested in religious learnings and sciences and the supporters of the *Shariah* (Ulama), were not paid much respect. But when Sultan Ghiyasuddin Tughlaq ascended the throne he paid due respect to *Shariah* and its admirers. Barani writes:

"وازبرای جریان احکام شریعت قاضیان ودا ہک ومحتسبانِ عہد اورا آبروی بس بسیار واشنائی تمام پیدا آمدہ بود"

(For the circulation of the Injunctions of the Shariah, *qazis*, *muftis* and censors of his time received very much respect and association with him).[218]

Afterwards, there was much emphasis on the sciences of *fiqh* and preaching of the Shariah. We are informed of several famous works of *fiqh* (jurisprudence) of the Firozi period. Among the old works of Indian *Fiqh* the *Fiqh-i-Firoz Shahi* (also known as *Fatawa i-Firoz Shahi*[219] is very famous. Moreover, *Khan-i-Azam* Tatar Khan, who was a noble of Firoz and died few years after 1357 A.D., got edited monumental works of religious science. One of them is the exegesis—(*tafsir*), of the *Quran* and the other is concerned with the *fiqh* (jurisprudence) which contains thousands of problems of *fiqh*, differences amongst the jurists and their *fatawas* about every problem. A copy of this work, consisting of nine volumes and translated during the ninth century, is preserved in the *Kutub-Khana-i-Asafiyah*, the Asafiya Library-Hyderabad. This work is entitled as the "*Al Fatawa-i- Tatarkhaniyah.* Its compiler's name is Maulana Alam bin Alauddin Hanafi. People of that age were so much interested in *fiqh* that a *murid*-(disciple); of Shaikh Nasiruddin Chiragh wrote a long *mathnawi* concerning the subject of *fiqh* with the title *Tarfat-ul-Fuqaha.* There are more than thirty thousand verses in it.[220]

218 *Tarikh-i-Firoz Shahi,* Op.cit, p.441.

219 The work is a revision and enlargement of the original draft of Sayyed Yaqub Muzaffar Kuhrami. This is a comprehensive work on Islamic law compiled to give guidance to the *qazis* and *muftis* in particular and to the Muslims in general, Zafarul Islam, *Fatawa-Literature of the Sultanate period,* New Delhi, Kanishka Publishers, 2005, pp.21, 22.

220 Shaikh, M., Ikram, Op.cit, p.433.

According to the author of *Sirat-i-Firoz Shahi*, he had listened from beginning to end most books on jurisprudence. The *Fatawa-i- Firoz Shahi* was prepared at his instance. The *Fawa'id-i-Firoz Shahi*[221] of Maulana Sharaf Ibn Muhammad al-'Atai was another book on *fiqh* dedicated to Firoz Shah, considered in the broad perspective of trends in Muslim religious scholarship, the age of Firoz Shah was pre-eminent in the production of *Fiqh* literature. Firoz Shah was responsible for encouraging these trends.[222]

Another worth mentioning event of Firoz Shah's riegn was the translation of Sanskrit works into Persian. Badayuni has mentioned several such works of different subjects. One of them is the *Dalail-i-Firoz Shahi* (apparently an astrologically oriented work)[223] which he (Badayuni) studied in Lahore in 1000 A.H./1591 A.D.

Firoz Shah was also interested in providing education to his slaves. Thousands of his slaves were instructed in different subjects and became artisans of different types. Afif informs us: "Some of the slaves spent their time in reading and committing to memory the holy book, others in religious studies, some others in copying books. Some were placed under tradesmen and were taught mechanical arts, so that about 12,000 slaves became artisans (hasib of various kinds)"[224] Firoz Shah's slave establishment is sometimes subjected to unmerited criticism. He raised the social, intellectual and economic status of his slaves and made then useful members of society.

During Firoz Shah's reign there was considerable development in the field of medicine also. The *Sirat-i-Firoz Shahi*[225] gives a list of diseases and medicines indicating the Sultan's interest in the subject. The science

221 The manuscript of the work, are preserved in the Maulana Azad Literary, A.M.U., (Subhanallah collection No.293.2/27, Jawahar Collection, No. 687). Asiatic society of Bengal, Calcutta, (catalogue, pp.517-18 No.1069) and Khuda Baksh O.P. Library (Catalogue Vol.XIV/1225).

222 Nizami, K.A., *Salatin-i-Dehli Kay Mazhabi Rujhanat*, Op.cit, pp.396-98.

223 *Sirat-i-Firoz Shahi*, Op.cit, p.301.

224 *Tarikh-i-Firoz Shahi* (Afif), Op.cit, p.270, Havell, E.B., *The History of Aryan rule in India (From the earliest time to the death of Akbar*, London, George G. Harrap & Company Limited, 1974, p.321.

225 For details see: *Sirat-i-Firoz Shahi*, Op.cit, pp.93-97, pp.236-41, pp.320-55.

of surgery was also developed. New instruments of operation were also devised. There was an instrument which was used to find out the position of a child in the womb of the mother.[226] He also established a hospital (*Dar-ul-Shifa*) where the general public were treated, infact Firoz adopted a modern approach by gathering mentally ill patients and having them detained in the hospital for treatment.[227] There was progress in the fields of astronomy, and mechanical sciences also.

During the reign of Sultan Firoz Shah, men of learning and talent who had specialized in different sciences, including medical were patronized, and looks were written at the instance of the Sultan. However, only two of the books have been discovered the *Rahat-ul-Insan* written by Ilyas bin Shahab in A.D. 1385 and the *Tib-i-Firozshahi.* The Tib-i-Firozshahi deals with diseases that birds suffer from and contains prescriptions for their treatments unlike this, the Rahat-ul Insan deals exclusively with the treatment of human beings. Along with prescriptions for different ailments, it also contains charms with Quranic verses and talismans, casting light on the superstitions that people believed in.[228]

The development in the mechanical science can be gauged from the list of mechanical devices listed by Afif:[229]

1. *Tas ghariyal*, a gong, meant to regulate the time of prayers. It was prepared by Firoz Shah in cooperation with astronomers and was placed on the *darbar* hall of Firozabad.
2. Large size revolving *cauldrons*, for cooking ten fat sheep.
3. *Claundron stands*, with ten legs to carry the 'revolving cauldrons.
4. *White dome*, with a special portico (*fariza*), a part of royal camp.
5. *Azhdar Peel*, fixed on the backs of elephants.

226 Ibid, pp.320-21.

227 Ibid, pp.336, 338, that Physicians were employed in the Hospital (*Shifakhana*) and medicines were distributed is clearly stated in the detailed accounts of the hospital, Ibid, pp.235-42 and *Tarikh-i-Firoz Shahi* (Afif), Op.cit, pp.357-59.

228 Siddiqui, Iqtedar Husain, Composite Culture under the Sultanate of Delhi, Primus Books, New Delhi, 2012, pp.50-51.

229 *Tarikh-i-Firoz Shahi* (Afif),Op.cit, pp.255, 369-70, Jauhri, R.C., Op.cit, p.179.

6. Huge drums tied to the backs of elephants during hunting expeditions.
7. Two *astrolabes* (usturlabs) indicating direction.

Education of Women:

The education of woman is an important aspect of society which can not be ignored.

Islam stands for equality of humankind and gives an exalted place to women in society. A perusal of the Holy *Quran* enables one to understand the Prophet's (PBUH) views on women. The *Quran* speaks highly of women and holds them responsible for forming the character of children. The Prophet of Islam laid the foundation of education in the following terms, *Talab-ul-Ilmul-Farzaton ala Kulle Muslim was Muslimah.*[230]

طلب العلم فريضة علىٰ كل مسلم و مسلمة

Acquisition of knowledge (in the right sense) is incumbent upon all the faithful men (Muslim) as well as women (Muslimah).

According to Islamic laws,[231] no discrimination is to be made between man and woman in the field of education and learning. Education, which was, prior to Islam, the monopoly of men was now open to women also. Women excelled themselves in various faculties.[232] It was the duty of parents to educate their daughters in order to enable them to develop their abilities. During childhood, they received education along with boys[233] in institutions generally associated with mosques.[234] Perhaps the seclusion of women was not in vogue in the early stages of life but

230 Meena Bhargava and Kalyaani Dutta, *Women, Education and Politics*, (New Delhi: Oxford University Press, 2005), p.1.

231 AmeerAli, *Spirit of Islam,* Delhi, Idarah-i-Adabiyat-i-Delhi, 1922, reprinted 1978, pp.254-55.

232 A.M.A. Shustery, *Outlines of Islamic Culture* (Bangalore: Bangalore Printing and Publishing Co. Ltd., 1954), pp.120-21.

233 Ibid., p.525.

234 Ibid., p.125.

it was, on attaining womanhood, that they had to restrict themselves within the four walls of the house. This in no way dampened their spirits to pursue their education. The presence of lady teachers asserts that women did carry on their education after attaining puberty.[235] There were special institutions for female education located at various places such as Cairo, Baghdad and Damascus.[236]

Women were also instructed in various arts as sewing, spinning, embroidery, music, poetry, theology[237] and in other spheres of learning. Fazl, an eminent poetess, flourished under Mutawwakil. Zainab, grand daughter of the Prophet, was a famous lady jurist of her time. Ummul Muhmmayyid, who lived in the 12th century of the Christian era (6th century AH) received diplomas of competence from learned persons. She used to teach law. Takieh, during the time of Saladin, delivered lectures on traditions.[238]

Arab ladies were extremely fond of poetry and recitation and some of them have left their compositions.[239] Many ladies participated in poetic contests and discussions in the reign of Harun and Mamun.[240] Zubieda, the wife of Harun, was herself a famous poetess and was also an accomplished speaker. She rivalled her husband in building hospitals, colleges and other public institutions.[241] Oilayya excelled in music and poetry.[242] Sukaina, the daughter of Husain and the grand daughter of Ali, served as a solace of poets, jurists and learned scholars.[243]

The princesses of the royal families during the Sultanate period were educated by learned teachers. But the details regarding the mode of education is insufficient. Contemporary historians refrain from making public mention of them. No doubt, their political, religious and

235 *Ibid.*
236 *Ibid.*, p.513.
237 *Ibid.*, p.525.
238 Ameer Ali, *A Short History of Saracens*, New Delhi: Kitab Bhawan, 1977, p.456.
239 Ameer, Ali, *Spirit of Islam*, p.202.
240 Ameer, Ali, *A Short of History of Saracens*, p.455.
241 A.M.A. Shustery, Op.cit., p.588.
242 Ameer Ali, *A Short History of Saracens*, p.457.
243 A.M.A. Shustery, Op.cit., p.587.

literary contributions have been narrated by the Persian chronicles but the social and cultural aspects of Muslim women have been avoided.

The Persian chronicles unknowingly or under compulsion did not deal with women's affairs but concentrated their compositions on the political affairs of the empire, the military exploits and the magnificence of the royal courts.

In India, the Turks, who had fully assimilated the political traditions of the Persians, and had accepted the right of females to sovereignty had already raised a lady, Razia, to the throne and thereby had taken a very progressive step. The example of Razia encouraged the ladies of royalty to take an active part in politics. Razia's nomination to the throne was objected by the *Ulama* as it was contrary to Islamic practice. As late as the 16th century Shaikh Abdul Haq Muhaddith Dehlavi in his *Tarikh-i-Haqqi* expressed surprise at the attitude of the *Ulama*. The contemporary historian Minhaj Siraj who was a distinguished theologian and jurist of the period is silent about this aspect of the problem.[244] This practice continued throughout the Turkish rule in India and even the Afghans seems to have allowed their ladies to have some say in political matters.

The patronage, which the institution of harem enjoyed under the Sultanate of Delhi, gave women of royalty enough impetus to further their ambition in carrying out administration, leading troops to the battle field, dispatching and receiving envoys, signing treaties and dealing sternly and tactfully with disruptive forces in the Sultanate. The earliest reference to a lady who participated in political activities in the Sultanate period is that of Khudavanda-i-Jahan, Shah Turkan, Chief Queen of Sultan Iltutmish, Raziya, eldest daughter of Sultan Iltutmish, being a woman of intellectual aptitude, she worked for the encouragement of education and patronized men of letters.[245] Minhaj was entrusted the supervision of *Madarsa-i-Nasiriyah*[246] which became

244 Habib Mohammad and Nizami, K.A. (ed.) *The Comprehensive History of India, the Delhi Sultanate*, Vol.5, Op.cit, p.237.

245 Siraj Minhajudin, *Tabaqat-i-Nasiri*, Vol.1, trans. by H.G. Raverty, New Delhi: Oriental reprints Corporation, reprint 1970, p.637.

246 *Ibid.*, p.644.

a centre of learning in her reign. During the Khalji period, Malika-i-Jahan, wife of Sultan Jalaludidn Khalji, dominated the political scenario.[247] The Tughlaq period witnessed the political influence of Makhdama-i-Jahan and Khudavandzada, the mother and sister of Sultan Muhammad binTughlaq respectively.[248] The influence of women in the political sphere varied according to their personality, family connections, political situation and the character of the Sultan. As the Sultan's wife, mother or sister, they often played an important role in matters of succession, war and peace. By virtue of their tact, intelligence and diplomacy they often strengthened the Sultanate.[249]

Learning and literature was highly developed in Sultan Firoz Shah's reign. But unfortunately the Sultanate of Delhi declined after his death. It was on account of chaotic condition that many scholars dispersed from Delhi and nothing could be written about the development of *ilm wa adab* (learning and literature). But whatever information is available in the contemporary *tazkiras* and in the *Akhbar-ul-Akhyar* and in Badayuni's work tells us that this reign was not less worthy than the Alai period in knowledge and scholarship.

We see that the numerous institutions established by the Sultans and their nobles such as the *Firozi Madarsa* provided boarding and lodging to the teachers and students. Handsome stipends were paid to students. These centres of higher learning along with other educational institutions discussed in the preceding pages have explained the large network of education that was put up by the Sultans.

Thus the patronization of scholars and intellectuals played a pivotal role in creating a congenial atmosphere for the stimulation of learning and literature. Due to the keen interest taken by the Sultans not only the religious sciences but also the rational sciences like astronomy, medicine, mechanical, arts etc. were developed and promoted. Besides making occasional grants, some of the Delhi Sultans and the nobles of

---

247 Muhammad Habib, *The Campaigns of Ala'uddin Khilji (Khazai'-inul-Futuh of Amir Khusrau)* Madras: D.B. Taraporewala, 1931, p.38.

248 Ibn Batuta, *The Rehla of Ibn Batuta*, Eng. Trans. by Mahdi Husain, Vadodara: Oriental Institute of Baroda, 1976, p.118.

249 For details see, *Composite Culture Under the Sultanate of Delhi*, Op.cit., p.151-162.

the state were enlightened enough to realize the importance of learning, and as such they started educational institutions with rich endowments. The education of women, a gender specific issue, was also not neglected, especially women of the royal household took active part in the promotion and patronization of education and learning. As a result of such impetus given by the Sultan, the people were sure to imbibe a great love for education and knowledge, and hence we find that distinguished scholars from all over the Muslim world were invited and encouraged to live in India by the inducement of pensions and conferment of distinctions. The state granted pensions and jagirs to a selected few, while others were patronized by the nobles of the state, for such patronage was considered a virtuos deed.

Chapter-VI

Scholars and Their Contribution in the Field of Muslim Education

The *ulama* i.e. the scholars played a crucial role in the promotion of education and learning. Due to their personal effort, hard work, sincerity and dedication, they were successful in creating an atmosphere congenial for learning. The teachers of the period under review were very intelligent and dedicated their complete lives for the promotion and progress in learning. They had indepth knowledge of the sciences both external (*Ulum-i-Zahiri*) and internal (*Ulum-i-Batini).* Moreover there were also scholars who studied the rational sciences. For the sake of acquisition of knowledge the scholars travelled to different places. They were so deeply involved in this process of teaching and learning that the method of indepth study and research came in vogue. Seminars and discussions were conducted which further enhanced the study of thought provoking topics. The standard of intelligence had reached such a height that most of these scholars penned down their thoughts and brought about voluminous compilations and compositions which provided further incentive to study. The purpose and aim of these scholars was to either attain spiritual gain or acquire maximum knowledge and not to achieve commercial benefits. These scholars belonged to different strata and category, they could be nobles, Sufis, common men etc. as education was open to all and anybody who desired to study could attain education and learning. The *Malfuzat* are a rich source to know about the scholars and their accomplishments and in the following pages the scholars have been discussed in detail so as to derive at their contribution in the field of education.

Qazi Hamiduddin Nagauri (ob.641 A.H) was entitled Muhammad bin A'ta and became famous as one of the great *Mashaikh* of Hindustan. He knew the external sciences (*Ulum-i- Zahiri*) and the internal sciences (*Ulum-i-Batini*) very well. He was the *khalifa* of Shaikh Shahabuddin Suhrawardi was extremely fond of *sama* and was an active participant of the *Sama* gatherings. Due to his liking for *Sama* the *ulama* of the period presented a *Mahzar* against him to the Sultan in reign. His famous compilation is *Tawali-Shumusi*. He had complete knowledge of the *Shariya* (Law of Islam) and *Tariqat* (spiritual path)[1]. He authored the *Lawaih*[2] and many other treatises. Nizamuddin Auliya once said to his students after going through the works of Qazi Hamiduddin Nagauri, 'Every thing of what you have yet to study is also herein. And further I confess that what I have studied and what I have not studied I find all of that in these pages[3]. Viewing this statement of Shaikh Nizamuddin

Auliya it can be surmised that Shaikh Hamiduddin Nagauri was a scholar of high stature and his knowledge was par excellence.

Shaikh Jalaluddin Tabrizi belonged to the Suhrawardi *silsilah* and was a disciple of Shaikh Shihabuddin Suhrawardi. When young Shaikh Fariduddin Ganj Shakar met Shaikh Jalaluddin Tabrizi, his trouser (*sarawil*) was in shreds and he had continually to hide one hole or the other. Shaikh Jalaluddin realized his anxiety and said "There was a *darwesh* in Bukhara who was busy in education. For seven years he had no trousers (*izar*) and was only on a lion cloth (*futah*). Don't be worried see what happens"[4]. According to Shaikh Nizamuddin this *darwesh* was Shaikh Jalaluddin Tabrizi himself.

Shaikh Jalaluddin Tabrizi once explained the status and functions of the '*ulama*'. He said, their utmost desire is confined to be engaged in

1 *Akhbar-ul-Akhyar*, Op.cit, 37.

2 *Fawa'id-u'l-Fu'ad*, Op.cit, p. 128.

3 Ibid, p. 241.

4 *Siyaru'l-Auliya*, Op.cit, pp. 62, 63.

teaching and imparting knowledge to others or to be appointed as *qazi* or *Sadr-i-Jahan*. Their aspiration is limited to only that. But the darweshes aspire for more than that and their status is manifold and much higher.[5] It may be presumed that the darwesh's motive was a selfless and pure desire to serve the people in anyway possible, but the *ulama* desired to attain big official positions through which material and commercial gains could be achieved.

Shaikh Burhanuddin Mahmud was a contemporary of Balban and belonged to the second half of the 13th century. He was a senior *alim* who studied the *Mashariq-ul-Anwar* from it's author. Shaikh Burhanuddin Mahmud used to say that when he was six or seven years old he was going somewhere along with his father, he came across Burhanuddin Marghinani author of '*Hidaya*' and greeted him respectfully, the *Shaikh* stared at him and blessed him saying that Allah is making him say that one day this boy will become a great scholar that seekers of knowledge will come at his door to acquire learning.[6] It is surprising that the scholar and *Shaikh* of the medieval period had reached such spiritual heights that they could forecast the future of others which astonishingly turned out to be true.

Shaikh Fariduddin Ganj-i-Shakar (1175-1265 AD) belonged to the Chishti *silsilah*. Very rightly does Isami call him "the ruler of the realm of spiritual discipline (*Shah-i-Mulk-i-Suluk*).[7] After finishing his early education in Kathwal, Baba Farid proceeded to Multan.[8] He was then only 18 years of age. He joined the *madarsa* in the mosque of Maulana Minhaj-u'd-din Tirmidhi. Here he committed to memory that entire text of *Quran* and began to recite it once in twenty four hours.[9] He completed his spiritual training in Delhi under Shaikh Qutb-u'd-din Bakhtiar Kaki. The *Jamaat Khana* at Ajodhan of Shaikh Farid where his disciples slept, prayed and studied was one of the greatest centres of spiritual culture in Medieval India.[10]

5 *Fawa'id-u'l-Fu'ad*, Op. cit, p. 237.
6 *Akhbar-ul-Akhyar*, Op.cit, p. 47.
7 *Futuh-u's-Salatin*, Op.cit, p.8.
8 *Siyar-u'l-Auliya*, Op.cit, p.60.
9 *Khair-u'l-Majalis*, Op.cit, p.220.
10 For details see: Nizami, K.A., *The Life and Times of Farid-u'd-din Ganj-i-Shakar*, Delhi, Idarah-i- Adabyat-i-Delli, 1973, pp.46-55.

Baba Farid's main subject of study was the *Quran*. He had devoted much of his time to it. He taught six parts of the *Quran* to Shaikh Nizamuddin Auliya who could never, during his life forget the Shaikhs enchanting manner of reciting it.[11] Besides he had wide and extensive knowledge of the mystic literature. He laid special emphasis on the *Awarif-u'l-Ma'arif* of Shaikh Shihabuddin Suhrawardi and considered it to be an indispensable study for a mystic selected by his master for the grant of *khilafat*. The credit of making this book a part of the mystic syllabus goes to him. He was also interested in the works of Qazi Hamiduddin Nagauri, a close friend of his master Qutbuddin Bakhtiar Kaki. He taught *'Lawaih'* to Shams Dabir.[12] Baba Farid was keenly interested in books and it seems that he had a library[13] of standard works on religion and mysticism. His anecdotes in the *Siyar-u'l-Auliya* prove that he had a very thorough knowledge of Arabic Grammar.[14] He said to his disciples that religious knowledge and learning is a prerequisite to spiritual discipline. All those mystics whom Shaikh Farid gave his *khilafat Namas* were required to get the document endorsed by his senior disciples, particularly, Shaikh Jamal-u'd-din Hansawi.[15]

Shaikh Jamal-u'd-din Hanswi was the oldest disciple of Baba Farid and belonged to the 13th century. He was a *khatib* when he joined the discipline of Baba Farid. He was a man of great learning. His two works are a Persian *Diwan*[16] and an Arabic treatise-*Mulhamat*[17] which have survived.

11 *Siyar-u'l-Auliya*, Op.cit, p.448, *Fawa'id-u'l-Fu'ad*, Op.cit, p.65.

12 *Fawa'id-u'l-Fu'ad*, Op.cit, p.128.

13 *Siyar-u'l-Auliya*, Op.cit, p.197.

14 Ibid, p.107.

15 Ibid, pp.117-118.

16 This *Diwan* is in two volumes. One volume contains ghazals , the other contains ruba's and qit'ahs (printed by Pirji Rafi-u'd-din, Tahsildar, Delhi, 1889, in the Chashmah-i-Faid Press Delhi) A Ms of the *Diwan* is preserved in the library of the University of Uppsala (Bibliotheca No.360). See Islamic Research Association Miscellany, Vol. I, 1948, pp.167-174.

17 *Mulhamat* was published in 1306 A.H. from Alwar (Yusufi Press) It is full of Sufistic aphorism.

Shaikh Najimuddin Mutawakkil was the youngest brother of Shaikh Farid and belonged to the 13th century. He had come to acquire education in Delhi but decided to settle there permanently. He was granted *khilafat* by Shaikh Farid. He lived in abject poverty thus when he desired to have a copy of *Jawami-al-Hikayat* transcribed for himself he experienced difficulties due to the shortage of resource. But due to the help of a scribe named Hamid he got the *Jawami-al-Hikayat* transcribed for himself.[18] We can infer from this that he was a man of scholarly temperament.

Maulana Badr-u'd-din Ishaq, a resident of Delhi of the 13th century was the *khalifa* of Shaikh Farid. He acquired his education and scholarship here itself. He desired to gain complete knowledge of all sciences and arts but while studying sciences he came across some doubts and difficulties which even the great *ulama* of Delhi could not solve. Thus he decided to travel to Bukhara to solve his problems from the *ulama* there. On his way when he reached Ajodhan (Pakpattan) he saw that Shaikh Farid's fame had reached far and wide and people from all over used to come to visit him to solve their queries. One of his close friends suggested him to meet Baba Farid. When Badruddin Ishaq saw Baba Farid he was surprised to see his enlightened preaching and magical sermons and spiritual power by which he won the hearts of people. All the doubts of Badruddin Ishaq were cleared after listening to the discussions and preachings of Baba Farid and he gave up the idea of going to Bukhara and became a murid of Shaikh Farid.[19] Later he married Baba Farid's daughter Bibi Fatima. The brochure '*Asrar-ul-Auliya*'[20] (Mysteries of the Saints) is his compilation in which he collected the *malfuzat* of Baba Farid and also wrote a scholarly work on Arabic Grammar '*Tasrif-i-Badari*'[21]

18 *Fawa'id-u'l-Fu'ad*, Op.cit, p.28.19

19 *Siyar-u'l-Auliya,* Op.cit, pp.179-80.

20 *Akhbar-ul-Akhyar,* Op.cit, pp.67-8.

21 However Muhammad Habib and K.A. Nizami do not consider '*Asrar-ul-Auliya*' amongst the genuine malfuzat on the ground that it bears wrong dates, mistakes about the names of persons places and their period, M.Habib 'Chishti records of the Sultanate period', Medieval India Quarterly, Vol.I, No:2, October, 1950, pp.25-8, Nizami, K.A., *The Life and Times of Fariduddin Ganj Shakar,* Op.cit, pp.119-20.

This example of Badruddin Ishaq's desire to go abroad for study bespeaks of the keen desire and desperation of the scholars to travel far and wide to quench their intellectual thirst and also shows how the scholars of India were on par with scholars of Bukhara and sometimes even better than them.

Maulana Alauddin Inderpati was a great scholar, famous for his scholarship and learning and lived in the second half of the 13th century. He was a *Hafiz-i-Quran* and many close associates of Shaikh Nizam-u'd-din Auliya memorized the Quran from him. Mir Khurd and his two uncles were his students. He spent his life in *Tilawat* (worship) and Sufi living.[22]

Maulana Kamaluddin Zahid was the erudite scholar of the second half of the 13th century who was not attached to any *silsilah* as such and K.A. Nizami has listed him in the category of 'starving teachers' (i.e. an *alim* who devoted his whole life to teaching), was a distinguished Traditionalist of Delhi, pious, scholarly and simple originally a native of Marigala, he settled in Delhi. He was a pupil of Maulana Mahmud Ali al Hasan As'ad Balkhi,[23] a pupil of Maulana Razi-ud-din Saghani. When Balban came to know about his piety and scholarship, he called him to his court and requested him to accept the duty of leading his prayers. "Our prayer is all that is left to us", replied the Maulana, "Does he want to take that also from us". Balban was dumbfounded and did not pursue his request further.[24]

Nizamuddin received instruction in *Mashariq-ul-Anwar* from him and committed the whole book to memory.[25] The refusal of Maulana Kamaluddin Zahid of Balban's proposal of government post to him shows the pure intention of the scholars of medieval age to work for the welfare and serve mankind with out any greed of material gains.

Maulana Badruddin Nasafi was a famous *danishmand* of 13th century and was not associated to any *silsilah*. If anybody came to acquire education from him he put three conditions:

22 *Siyar-u'l-Auliya*, Op.cit, p.316.

23. Ibid, p.115.

24. Ibid, p.116.

25 *Siyar-u'l-Auliya*, Op.cit, p.111, *Akhbar-ul-Akhyar*, Op.cit, p.72.

a) Firstly you will eat only once a day so that there is place for the desire of knowledge.

b) You will not miss classes, if you miss any day, I will not teach the next day.

c) If you meet me on the street, you will only greet Salaam and involve in no formalities and waste time.[26]

It can be gathered from these rules laid down by Shaikh Badruddin Nasafi for his students, that immense amount of discipline was maintained while conducting the process of teaching during the medieval period.

Maulana Aalauddin Usuli was a pious, erudite and dedicated scholar of the 13th century. He did not belong to any specific *silsilah* and K.A. Nizami has listed him also in category of 'starving teachers'. Shaikh Nizamuddin learnt from him the value of dedicating one's life to higher ideals, regardless, of the pangs of poverty. He used to refer to him in his conversation, very affectionately as "my teacher."[27] It appears that Maulana Usuli was basically a teacher of *Fiqh* (Islamic law) and though blessed by Jalal-u'd-din Tabrizi, had not formally been initiated in any mystic discipline.[28] Maulana Usuli instructed Shaikh Nizamuddin in *Hidaya.*[29] Maulana Usuli's own life had an element of dramatic thrill in it. When he was young he was roaming on the streets of Badaon. He happened to pass by a house where Shaikh Jalal-u'd-din Tabrizi, a distinguished saint was staying. Shaikh Tabrizi who was sitting in the *dehliz* (entrance) of the house looked at the wandering youth and saw in him signs of future greatness. He called him in, gifted him the robe that he was himself wearing and this episode completely changed his life. 'Ala-u'd-din took to studies with all the zest of a reformed youth. In course of time he so distinguished himself that he came to be looked upon as the most erudite scholar of Badaon.[30] He looked upon teaching

26 *Siyar-u'l-Auliya*, Op.cit, p.536, *Akhbar-ul-Akhyar*, Op.cit, p.77.

27 *Fawa'id-u'l-Fu'ad*, Op.cit, p.165.

28 Ibid, p.165.

29 Ibid, p.166.

30 *Fawa'id-u'l-Fu'ad*,Op.cit, p.165, *Akhbar-ul-Akhyar*, Op.cit, pp.77-78.

as a co-operative work in which the teacher and the taught both participated.[31] Once when Malik Yar was appointed *Imam* of the Jama Masjid of Badaon, some people objected to it as he lacked requisite learning. On hearing about this objection Maulana Ala-u'd-din Usuli said that even if the *Imamate* of the Jama Masjid of Baghdad was assigned to him, it would be nothing compared to his capabilities.[32]

The Shaikh felt that it was not only formal education but a developed and delicate sensitivity which mattered.

Shaikh Nizamuddin Auliya (1244-1325 AD) was the *khalifa* of Shaikh Farid and his name was Muhammad bin Ahmad bin Bukhari and he was entitled *Sultan-ul-Mashaikh.*[33] When Shaikh Nizamuddin Auliya became 12 years old, his mother put him in a *madarsa* where he studied *Quran* and other subjects. At the same time he studied *Lughat* and *Adab.*[34] He had studied one verse of *Quran* from Shadi Muqri and due to that *Barqat* he remembered the whole *Quran.* Shadi Muqri was a '*qari*' an experienced and able teacher, a *hafiz*, who could recite the *Quran* according to its seven methods of recitation.[35]

Maulana Alauddin Usuli instructed Shaikh Nizamuddin in '*Hidaya*'[36] and '*Quduri*'.[37] When Nizamuddin finished *Quduri*, the Maulana declared him to be qualified for putting the 'turban of scholarship' (*dastar-i-fazilat*) on his head. In those days this declaration was usually made in a function which resembled present day convocation and was called '*Dastar bandi.*[38] He went to Delhi from Badaun and studied *Maqamat-i-Hariri* and *Hadith* from Shamsul Mulk[39], since he was an expert of *Mantiq*, he came to be called '*Nizamuddin Mantaqi*' by other students. Then he

31. Ibid, p.165.

32. Ibid, p.166.

33. *Akhbar-ul-Akhyar*, Op.cit, p.54.

34. Ibid, p.55.

35. *Siyar-u'l-Auliya*, Op.cit, pp.110-11.

36 *Fawa'id-u'l-Fu'ad*, Op.cit, p.166.

37 Ibid, p.166, Abul Hasan b. Muhammad al-Quduri (972-1037) was a distinguished author on Muslim jurisprudence. His two well known books are: *al Muktasar* and *Kitab al Tajrid.*

38 For details see: *Siyar-u'l-Auliya*, Op.cit, pp.105-06.

39. *Akhbar-ul-Akhyar*, Op.cit, p.78.

went to Pakpattan and met Shaikh Farid, then he was only twenty, he studied 6 parts of the *Quran*, 6 chapters of *Awarif* and *'Tamhid'* of Abu Shakoor Salimi.[40] He received a *khilafat Nama* or *Ijazat Nama*, from Maulana Kamaluddin Zahid.[41] He also received another *Khilafat Nama* from his spiritual mentor, Shaikh Fariduddin Masud Ganj-i-Shakar which accorded him permission to teach *'Tamhidat'* of Abu Shakoor Salimi.[42] The *khanqah* of Nizam-u'd-din Auliya stood by the side of the river Jamna. Enormous futuh (unasked for presents) flowed into his hospice, in Ghiyaspur, as uninterrupted as the Jumna flowed near his door.[43] It was at the instance of Baba Farid that Shaikh Nizamuddin committed the *Quran* to memory later and displayed keen personal interest in developing Quranic studies in his own *khanqah*.[44] This khanqah was open to all kinds of people and proved to be a great centre of learning.[45]

Shaikh Nizamuddin Auliya himself did not write or compile any *Malfuz* of his spiritual Master, Shaikh Farid, but some of the random jottings he made on the sayings or on any matter preached by Shaikh Farid were available to Amir Khurd when he wrote his *Siyar- u'l-Auliya*.[46]

Maulana Qasim Bin 'Umar' was the son of a nephew of Shaikh Nizam and wrote a *Tafsir* entitled *Lata'if-ul-Tafsir*. In the introduction of his *Tafsir* he gives details of his education. He was initiated into education in a *Maktab* by Shaikh Nizamuddin who blessed him with a long life and acquisition of knowledge. He was twelve when he committed the *Quran* to memory and then he was sent to Maulana Jalaluddin where he spent nearly fifty years and studied all sciences from start to end and obtained the permission to teach *Bazdawi*, *Kashshaf*, *Hidaya*,

40 *Akhbar-ul-Akhyar*, Op.cit, p.55, *Siyar-u'l-Auliya*, Op.cit, pp.115-16, *Fawa'id-u'l- Fu'ad*, Op.cit, p.75. Teaching a few chapters of the book carefully and then leaving the rest for the independent study of the student was a practice of medieval Muslim scholarship.

41. *Siyar-u'l-Auliya*, Op.cit, pp.114-15.

42 Ibid, pp.129-31., For the English translation of both these *khilafat namas* refer: Nizami, K.A., *The Life and Times of Shaikh Nizamuddin Auliya*, Delhi, Idarah-i-Adabiyat, Delli,1991, pp.187-90.

43 *Khair-u'l-Majalis*, Op.cit, p.257.

44 Nizami, K.A., *Tarikh-i-Mashaikh-i-Chisht*, Vol.I, Delhi, Idarah-i-Adabiyat Delli, 1980, pp.406-07.

45 For details see, Nizami, K.A., *The Life and Times of Nizamuddin Auliya*, Op.cit, pp.57-79.

46 *Siyar-u'l-Auliya*, Op.cit, pp.332, 392, 393, 496 etc.

Mashariq and *Masabih* and after studying the Arabic and Persian *Tafsirs* and understanding the meaning and all details of it, he thought that he should write a *Tafsir* based on other *Tafsirs* so that people benefit out of it's study and thus the *Lataif-ul-Tafsir* came into being.[47]

Khwaja Azizuddin belonged to the 13th century, and the son of Khwaja Abu Bakr was known for his piety and scholarship. He collected Shaikh Nizamuddin's conversations in his *Majmu-u'l- Fawa'id.* He recited the whole *Quran* during Friday nights.[48]

Khwaja Aziz-u'd-din, grandson of Shaikh Farid, was a pupil of Muhi-u'd-din Kashan,[49] eminent disciple and *Khalifa* of Nizam-u'd- din Auliya. He was an excellent calligraphist[50] and recorded the conversation of Nizam-u'd-din Auliya under the title: *'Tuhfat-u'l- Abrar-fi-Karmat-u'l-Akhyar'*.[51]

Khwaja Muhammad flourished in the 13th century, was the son of Shaikh Badruddin Ishaq, grandson of Shaikh Farid, his upbringing took place under the supervision of Shaikh Nizamuddin, was trained by him and became his *khalifa,* was very close to him and actively participated in Shaikh Nizam's *Majlis.* He wrote a book based on Shaikh Nizamuddin's *malfuzat* entitled *'Anwar-ul-Majalis'*. He spent most of his time in prayers and listening to *sama* in which he had deep interest. All kinds of *Qawwal,* Persian as well as Hindi would be present for him. He was such an expert in music that during that period nobody was as good as him. He was a *Hafiz* of Quran. He had knowledge of *Ma'ani, Bayan,* and *music.* He would become so emotional during *sama* that his eyes would always be overflowing with tears.[52]

Khwaja Musa also lived during the 13th century, was the younger son of Badruddin Ishaq and grandson of Shaikh Fariduddin Ganj-i-Shakar. From childhood he was trained under Shaikh Nizamuddin's

47. Ibid, pp.215-17.
48 Ibid, p.217.
49 *Khair-u'l-Majalis,* Op.cit, pp.150-51, 202-03.
50 *Siyar-u'l-Auliya,* Op.cit, p.202, *Akhbar-ul-Akhyar,* Op.cit, p.95.
51 This malfuz is extinct now.
52 *Siyar-u'l-Auliya,* Op.cit, p.210

guidance and knew most of the sciences very well and in some subjects he was an expert. In *Usul-i-Fiqh* he studied *Bazdawi* from Maulana Wajihuddin Paili. He was *Hafiz* of Quran. He was efficient in Arabic and Persian poetry, used to read ghazals and was an expert in the field of music. He had mastered *ilm-i-Hikmat* and developed it even more by his experience. In the absence of his elder brother he did the *Imamate* also and used to read the *Quran* with clear intonations.[53]

Syed Khamosh a Sufi of the 13th century, was the son of Syed Muhammad Kirmani (Mir Khurd's uncle). He was brought up under the supervision of Shaikh Nizam-u'd-din Auliya. He used to study the *Khamsa-i-Nizami* in the *majlis* of Shaikh Nizam-u'd-din and held a respectable position in his *khanqah*. All those visitors who came to visit Shaikh Nizamuddin would during nights halt at his residence.

All kinds of foods and comforts were provided to these visitors and servants were present all the time for them. The doors of his house were always open for the *Umara*, *Fuzala*, *Badshah* and people from all strata of society and category came to his house. He used to feed about 200 *darweshes* in his house.[54]

Maulana Shamsuddin Yahya was an eminent scholar of the13th century.[55] He was an elder *khalifa* of Shaikh Nizamuddin. It appears he wrote a commentary of *Mashariq*. He came from Awadh to Delhi for acquiring education.[56] He and his cousin Sadruddin Nawli used to study the '*Bazdawi*' from Maulana Zahiruddin Bhakkari.[57] But after coming to Delhi he was so impressed by Shaikh Nizamuddin Auliya's discussion

53. Ibid, pp.211-12.
54. Ibid, p.229.
55. *Tarikh-i-Firoz Shahi*, Op.cit, p.353.
56. *Akhbar-ul-Akhyar*, Op.cit, p.97.
57 *Siyar-u'l-Auliya*, Op.cit, pp.234-35. Maulana Zahiruddin Bhakri was a resident of Bhakr in Sindh. Barani Ziauddin in his *Tarikh-i-Firoz Shahi* has written about the *ulama* of the Alai period that some of them had acquired such knowledge of all sciences and arts that they were on par with Ghazzali and Razi. In the list which *Tarikh-i-Firoz Shahi* presents, Maulana Zahiruddin Bhakri's name is also mentioned. In *Nuzhat-ul-Khawatir* it is stated that nobody was equal to him in *Nahv*, *Lughat*, *Fiqh* and *Usul-i-Fiqh*, and many benefited from him such as Shamsuddin bin Muhammad Yahya who studied *Fiqh* and *Usuli Fiqh* from him, *Nuzhat-u'l-Khawatir*, Vol.2, p.66.

in his *majlis* that he became a murid. He started teaching the '*Majma-ul-Bahrain*' and '*Tasrif-i-Maliki*' which did not have commentaries and due to this, both these books became very popular in the academic circles.[58] He was the eminent teacher of Shaikh Nasiruddin Chiragh of Delhi.[59]

Maulana Shamsuddin Yahya and Sadruddin Nawli from their early stage of education were very popular for their intellectual discussions, presence of mind and active role in the *majlis*. Maulana Shamsuddin writes that they would conduct deep study and research for all the topics related to such subjects as *Fiqh*, *Usul-i-Fiqh*, *Ma'ani* and *Bayaan*.[60] He was such a popular teacher that it was thought that any student who enrolled under him would acquire great knowledge of religion and other subjects of study and people would feel privileged to attend his *majlis*.

Shaikh Nasiruddin Chiragh Dehlavi (circa 1276-77-1356 A.D.) succeeded his master, Shaikh Nizamuddin Auliya as the head of the Chishti *silsilah* in 1325 A.D. His first teacher was Maulana 'Abdul Karim Sherwani'.[61] He taught '*Hidaya*'[62] and '*Bazdawi*'[63] to him, but the Shaikh himself one day informed his audience that he had studied '*Bazdawi*' with Qazi Muhi-u'd-din Kashani.[64] He gained massive knowledge of *Fiqh* and after his teacher's death joined the discourses of Maulana Iftikhar-u'd-din Muhammad Gilani[65] at whose feet he completed his education of external sciences (*Ulum-i-Zahiri*).

---

58 *Siyar-u'l-Auliya*, Op.cit, p.278.

59 *Siyar-u'l-Auliya*, Op.cit, p.235, *Ma'asir-u'l-Kiram*, Op.cit, p.182.

60 *Siyar-u'l-Auliya*, Op.cit, p.236.

61 *Khair-u'l-Majalis*, Op.cit, supplement, p.282.

62 An Encyclopedia of Muslim Theology and Law by Maulana Burhanuddin Marghinani (ob.1197 A.D.) published from Cairo in 1326 A.D.

63 A well known work on the principles of Islamic law by Ali b. Muhammad Bazdawi, an eminent jurist of Hanafi law (ob.1089 A.D.)

64 *Khair-u'l-Majalis*, Op.cit,. p.150. Qazi Muhi-ud-din Kashani was an eminent disciple of Shaikh Nizam-u'd-din Auliya. He was one of the most distinguished scholars of the Alai period, *Tarikh-i- Firoz Shahi*, Op.cit, p.353.

65 *Khair-u'l-Majalis*, Op.cit, p.282.

He committed the *Quran* to memory at the age of twelve. During this period he also completed the study of *Panj Ganj*[66] and *Hariri*[67] Maulana Fakhr-u'd-din Zarradi and his brother Kamaluddin were his classmates.[68]

So far as his exegetical studies are concerned he was particularly inclined towards *Kashshaf*[69] frequently referred to the *Mashariq-ul-Anwar*, a popular work of *Hadith* in those days.[70] Imam Ghazzali's works particularly *Ihya-ul-ulum*[71] and *Minhaj-u'l-Abidin*[72] were deeply appreciated by him. Shaikh Shihabuddin Suhrawardi's *'Awarif-ul-Ma'arif* was also his favourable book.[73] He has referred to *Sharh-i-Ta'arruf* in his discourses,[74] on questions of *Fiqh* he is found referring to *Hidaya, Sharh Aqida*[75] and *Muqaddamat-u's- Salat.*[76] He was interested in the poetry of Sanai, Nizami, Ahmad Jam and Sa'di. The *Mathnawi* of Maulana Jala-u'd-din Rumi has been referred to for the first time in India in his discourses.[77]

All sorts of people came to meet Shaikh Nasiruddin Mahmud, scholars, students, teachers, religious orators etc.[78] The Shaikh received them cordially and attended to their problems with deep sympathy.

Maulana Husam-u'd-din Multani was another distinguished *khalifa* of Shaikh Nizam-u'd-din Auliya, was well known for his insight in literature of *Fiqh* (Muslims Jurisprudence). He remembered by heart large parts of *Hidayah.* Besides he was well versed in *Qut-u'l- Qulub* and *Ihya-ul-'ulum'.*[79]

---

66 A book of Grammar, etymology. It continued to be prescribed in the syllabus through out the medieval period. It was included in *Dars-Nizami*, Sufi, G.M.D., Op.cit, p.73.
67 The *Maqamat-i-Hariri* is esteemed as a great literary treasure in the Arabic language.
68 *Khair-u'l-Majalis*, Op.cit, p.63.
69 Ibid, pp.65, 83, 120.
70 Ibid, pp.94, 114, 136, 207.
71 Ibid, p.68.
72 Ibid, pp.56. 212.
73 Ibid, p.58, 123, 155, 178, 249.
74 Ibid, p.207.
75 Ibid, p.239.
76 Ibid, p.29.
77 Ibid, p.163.
78 For details see: Nizami, K.A., *The Life and Times of Shaikh Nasiruddin Chiragh*, Delhi, Idarah-i-Adabyat-i-Delli, 1991, pp.44-51.
79 *Siyar-u'l-Auliya*, Op.cit, p.266, *Akhbar-ul-Akhyar*, Op.cit, pp.89-90.

Qazi Sharfuddin was a friend of Maulana Husamuddin Multani. He had completely memorized the *Quran*. He knew many sciences and was an embodiment of scholarship. Amir Khurd learnt '*Diwan-Ahsan-Hasan*' from him.[80]

Maulana Wajihuddin Paili was the *khalifa* of Shaikh Nizam- u'd-din Auliya and an accomplished scholar, who had excellent knowledge of '*Kashshaf*' and '*Daqaiq*'. It is said that once he went to Ajodhan to meet Shaikh Farid and he was addressed as '*Abu Hanifa Paili*' by the Shaikh because his insight in *Fiqh* was unrivalled.[81]

Maulana Fakhruddin Zarradi was the *khalifa* of Shaikh Nizamuddin Auliya and acquired education from Maulana Fakhruddin Hanswi in Delhi. He became very famous because of his intelligence and eloquence of speech.[82] Mir Khurd's father once rented a house close to Shaikh Nizamuddin's house and opened a *madarsa* there in which learned people and students would gather. He himself would teach in this *madarsa*. Maulana Fakhruddin Zarradi would also after his *Chasht* prayers attend the *majlis* here and would teach the *Hidaya* to Maulana Ruknuddin Inderpati.[83] Maulana Kamaluddin Samani, a famous *ulama* of Delhi writes that Maulana Fakhruddin Zarradi challenged the *ulama* on the question of *sama*. He was such an excellent debater that nobody could win over him and his arguments were very meaningful and reflected his intelligence.[84]

Shaikh Nasiruddin Mahmud writes whatever he and his associates took one or two months to study, he grasped within an hour. During Muhammad Tughlaq's reign when people emigrated to Deogir, Maulana Zarradi also went there, from there he went to Baghdad and studied books on *Hadith* in great detail. Then he decided to return to Delhi for which he boarded a ship which sank and he died in this accident.[85]

Maulana Alauddin Nili was among the great *alims* of Awadh, belonging to the 13th century, pious and sincere. He studied the *Tafsir*

80 *Siyar-u'l-Auliya*, Op.cit, pp.308-09.
81 Ibid, p.296.
82 *Akhbar-ul-Akhyar*, Op.cit, p.91.
83 *Siyar-u'l-Auliya*, Op.cit, p.278.
84 Ibid, p.280.
85 *Akhbar-ul-Akhyar*, Op.cit, p.91.

Kashshaf from Delhi's Shaikh-u'l-Islam, Maulana Fariduddin. He had transcribed the *Fawaid-u'l-Fu'ad* with his own hands and busied himself most of the time in reciting it. People asked him that inspite of so many books with himself why he always read the *Fawaid-ul-Fu'ad*, he answered that the peace and solace he experiences after reading it, he will not find anywhere.[86]

Shaikh Alauddin Nili was a *Hafiz* and was known for his mastery over the religious sciences. He was a very powerful orator and his lectures on *Kashshaf* were appreciated for their clear analysis of exegetical problems. Shaikh Nizamuddin Auliya was particularly impressed by his recitation of the *Quran* while leading the prayers. Once he was so pleased with his recitation that he granted his prayer carpet to him.[87] Ibn Batuta who attended his Friday sermons says: "Many listeners of his sermons repent at his hand, shave their heads and become men of ecstasy."[88]

Qazi Muhi-u'd-din Kashani was the grandson of Qazi Qutbuddin Kashani, and was a renowned scholar of the 13th century. He was the *khalifa* of Shaikh Nizamuddin Auliya who respected him so much that he stood up when he saw Qazi Muhi-u'd-din Kashani. The moment he would come Shaikh Nizamuddin would conclude his *majlis* and solve the difficulties and doubts of Qazi Saheb. The *wazifa* he received from the administration he gave it up in front of Shaikh Nizamuddin and spent his life in practice and worship.[89] He studied from Shaikh Shamsuddin Qaushji and other teachers of Delhi.[90]

Maulana Fasihuddin Dehlavi was a great scholar and during his studentship days would often attend Shaikh Nizamuddin Auliya's *majlis* and ask him many doubts and solve them. Qazi Muhi-u'd-din Kashani was his classmate. He was a famous *Fuqaha* and had studied *Usul-i-Fiqh* from Maulana Shamsuddin Qaushji and other sciences from other famous *ulama*[91] Sultan Balban appointed him teacher for his sons and

86. Ibid, pp.93-94.
87 *Siyar-ul-Auliya*, op. cit, pp. 285-86.
88. Ibn Batuta, Op.cit, p.30.
89. *Siyar-u'l-Auliya*, Op.cit, p.294, *Akhbar-ul-Akhyar*, Op.cit, p.97.
90. *Nuzhat-u'l-Khawatir*, Vol.2, p.111.
91. *Siyar-u'l-Auliya*, Op.cit, p.299.

for a long time he served Balban but later got attracted towards Kamaluddin Zahid and became a murid of Shaikh Nizamuddin Auliya and died during the lifetime of his mentor.[92]

Maulana Mu'in-u'd-din 'Imrani was a profound scholar of the 13th century and was deeply respected in the academic circles. Shaikh Abdul Haqq calls him an outstanding scholar and teacher of the city. He wrote commentaries on *Kanz, Husami, Miftah-ul-'ulum, al-manar* etc. His insight in *Fiqh* literature was unrivalled. Maulana Khwaja ji learnt at his feet, Muhammad bin Tughlaq sent him to Shiraz to invite Qazi Azd to India and request him to dedicate his *Matan Muwafiq* to him but when Qazi 'Azd met Maulana Mu'in-u'd-din Imarani, he refused to come saying, what is the need for me when there are already such great intellectuals in India.[93]

Syed Jalaluddin (ob. 1291 A.D.) was the *khalifa* of Shaikh Bahauddin Zakariya. Having received his early education at Uchch under the guidance of Shaikh Jamal Khandan Ru and Shaikh Bahauddin, the *Qazi* of Uchch. He then went to Multan to join the seminary in the shrine of Bahauddin Zakariya where he stayed for a year and studied *Hidaya* and *Bazdawi* under the guidance of Shaikh Musa and Maulana Majiduddin, both of them, the renowned scholars and famous teachers of this seminary. From there he went to Mecca and Medina and benefited from the scholarly and spiritual excellence of Shaikh Abdullah Yafai and Shaikh Abdulla Mutri.[94]

Shaikh Abdul Haq Muhaddith Dehlawi says, "He travelled widely and received blessings and benedictions from saints" (*Siyahat Bisyar kard wa bisyari az Auliya ne'mat wa barkat yaft*).[95] On account of his visits and journeys he came to be known as *Jahan Gasht-* (world Traveller). The Makhdum studied the *Awarif-u'l- Ma'arif* under Shaikh Sharafuddin Mahmud Tastari and received the *Khilafat Nama.*[96] He was

92 Mir Khurd, *Siyar-ul-Auliya*, Urdu translation and published by Khwaja Islamuddin Nizam, Delhi, 1985, pp.521-522.
93 *Akhbar-ul-Akhyar*, Op.cit, p.144.
94. For details see: Qadiri, Muhammad Ayyub, *Makhdum-i-Jahanian Jahan gasht*, Karachi, H.M. Said Company, 1975, pp.65-70.
95 *Akhbar-ul-Akhyar*, Op.cit, p.142.
96 For details see: Qadiri, Muhammad Ayyub, Op.cit, pp.89-91.

a prolific writer, the collection of letters known as *Muqarrir Nama*, his Persian translations of the Holy Quran and Qutbuddin Damishqi's *Risala-i-Makkiya* are his famous literary and scholarly achievement[97] so far as his conversations, malfuzat are concerned, about eight collections are found referred to by scholars in medieval and modern works. The most renowned amongst these collections is the '*Jami'-ul-ulum*'[98] related to his stay at Delhi.

Another famous collection is the *Siraj-ul-Hidaya.*[99] It contains considerable information of historical significance both political and cultural.[100] *Khazain-i-Jalali* (compiler: Baha bin Hasan bin Mahmud bin Sulaiman) is also one of the collections of *Makhdum-i-Jahanian*, its original full name is the *Khaznat-ul-Fawaid-ul-Jalaliya.*[101]

Another voluminous collection of his is the *Jawahar-i-Jalali* which was compiled by one of his khalifas, Fazlullah bin Ziya al Abbasi, in 1379A.D.[102] *Mazhar-i-Jalali* is another famous collection of the *Malfuzat* of Makhdum Syed Jalaluddin Bukhari. Its compiler's name is not known. Another collection is the '*Manaqib-i-Makhdum-i- Jahaniyan*' which supplies valuable information of some political events of Firoz Shah's time.[103] Another collection is the *Fawaid-ul-Mukhlisin* compiled by Muhammad Jafar Tumasi.[104] According to Charles A. Storey there is one more collection of his entitled *Mahbubia.* Its compiler's name was Yusufi.[105] Likewise some brochures and treatises are also mentioned, the *Arabain Sufia* (Forty Sufis). It is said *Makhdum-i-Jahanian* compiled this work during his stay at Makka. The other work is the *Asrar-ul Arifin* in which inner and spiritual knowledge of Sufis has been

97 Ibid, p.187.

98 Ibid,

99. Ibid, pp.188-89.

100. Nizami, K.A., *On History and Historians of Medieval India*, New Delhi, Munshiram Manoharlal, 1983, p.189.

101. Ibid, pp.197-98.

102. Ibid, pp.199-201.

103. Ibid, p.203.

104. Ibid, p.206.

105. Storey C.A., Vol.I, Op.cit, pp.953-54.

discussed. Similarly, *A'mal wa Ashghal* too is a work of *Makhdum-i-Jahanian*, compiled by Ja'far Badr 'Alam bin Jalaluddin Maqsud Alam.[106]

Makhdum-i-Jahanian established a permanent educational centre known as *Madarsa-i-Jalali* in his *khanqah* in Uchch. The *Quran* and *Hadith* were taught here. Instead of *Tafsir-i-Kashshaf* the *Tafsir Madarik* was preferred. *Qirat* was taught here. The famous collections of a *hadith Sahih-al-Bukhari, Sahih Muslim, Tirmizi, Sunan-i-Abu Daud* and *Mishkat-ul-Masabih* were frequently taught. The *Jami-i-Saghir* was taught regularly. The famous work of *fiqh, Hidaya* was specially taught. The *Makhdum* also paid attention to *Sarf wa Nahv* (conjugation and syntax i.e. grammar), and *lughat* (lexicography), so that it could be easy for students to learn Arabic language.[107] *Makhdum-i-Jahanian* had his personal collection of books and possessed a personal library.

Maulana Khwaja Gi was the *khalifa* of Shaikh Nasiruddin Mahmud Dehlavi. He was the pupil of Maulana Muin-u'd-din Imrani and teacher of Qazi Shihabuddin Daulatabadi, he was an eminent scholar of his day and carried on instructional work in Delhi with great enthusiasm and attracted large number of pupils to his seminary.[108]

Qazi Abdul Muqtadir was the *khalifa* of Shaikh Nasiruddin Mahmud, and teacher of Qazi Shahabuddin. His compilations were popular for elegance of style and eloquence. He taught '*Shamsiya*' and had attained knowledge of both internal (*ulum-i-batini*) and external (*ulum-i-zahiri*) sciences. His student wrote a book '*Manaqib- ul-Siddiqin*' in which he described the circumstances of sufis. He was a distinguished scholar and poet of Arabic. He wrote the '*Qasidat-al- Lamiyyah*' composed in imitation of *Lamiyyat-ul-'Ajam* which was admired in the literary circles.[109]

Syed Yusuf Ibn-Syed Jamal-ul-Hanswi belonged to the 13th century. His ancestors came from Mashad and settled in Multan. He came to Delhi during the reign of Sultan Firoz Shah Tughlaq and joined his army as a soldier. But after seeing his piety and scholarly traits

106. Qadiri, Op.cit, p.206

107. Ibid, pp.152-53.

108. Ibid, pp.143-44.

109 Ibid, pp.150-51.

Sultan Firoz appointed him teacher in his *madarsa* built on the *Hauz Khas Alai* (*Firozi madarsa*). For many years he taught in this *madarsa* and imparted knowledge to all. He wrote the commentary of the famous book of Qazi Nasiruddin Baizawi '*Lab-ul-Lubab fi Ilm ul Au'rab* which became famous with the name '*Yusuf*'. He also wrote the commentary of '*Minar*' entitled '*Taiyih-al-Afkar*'. His teacher was Maulana Jalaluddin Rumi who was amongst the pupils of Maulana Qutbuddin Razi who wrote the keys to '*Shamsiya*' and '*Mutala*'. Syed Yusuf's *tomb* is at Hauz Alai.[110]

Thus we can infer from the above discussion more than the institutions of learning the personal efforts of scholars played a pivotal role in promoting education and learning. The basic feature of Muslim educational system was that it was traditional in its disposition and theological in context. The curriculum was broadly divided into two categories, the *manqulat* and *maqulat*, the former dealing with traditional sciences and the latter with rational sciences was emphasized, but gradually the rational science began to receive greater attention. But this emphasis on *maqulat* did not lead to much scientific and technological advancement like nowadays.

110 Ibid, p.150.

Conclusion

The traditions of Muslim education in India were in general the same as the Abbasids of Baghdad. They were transplanted in India by the scholars and literati of Muslim lands who migrated to India as a result of the Mongol invasion. The Sultanate of Delhi within just a century of its foundation had reached an unrivalled position in the field of Muslim education.

Qutbuddin Aibek founded the Sultanate in 1206 A.D. and was the first ruler of the Slave dynasty. He built many mosques which were not only centres of religious worship but also of education. In the memory of his son Nasiruddin Mahmud, Iltutmish founded the *Nasiriyah Madarsa*. Qazi Minhaj Siraj, the historian was appointed as its principal. Sultan Iltutmish during his absence appointed his daughter Razia Sultan his regent and also during his lifetime declared her his successor to the throne. Driven by the hordes of Changiz Khan, learned men from places such as Turkey, Mawara-ul-Nahr, Khurasan, Iraq, Azarbaijan etc. found an honourable place in the court at Delhi. Balban's son Sultan Muhammad was deeply interested in education and learning. The most learned and accomplished men of the time visited his court quite frequently.

Sultan Alauddin Khalji was also a great appreciator and patron of talent. By the time of Alauddin Khalji's reign (1296-1316 A.D.) Delhi became an important metropolitan city for the migrants coming from the Muslim East. The migrant scholars from far-off lands such as Bukhara, Samarqand, Iraq and Iran were not able to carry their invaluable collection of books and manuscripts to India with the result that stress was laid on such subjects as poetry, contemporary local history, law, grammar etc. which did not require the use of libraries. However, there were a large number of schools and colleges in all important cities. Delhi alone had one thousand *Madarsas* in the fourteenth century A.D.

The Sultanate of Delhi attained a very high level in the field of Muslim education just within a century of its foundation. According to Ziauddin Barani, the scholars of the reign were on par with Ghazali and Razi. After the close of Alauddin's rule, the high standard of wisdom and learning sank to an inferior level. Although Sultan Muhammad Tughlaq appreciated all sorts of learning yet the number of learned men during the period were comparatively less.

Amongst the Tughlaqs, the first three rulers of this dynasty were themselves distinguished scholars. Although Ghiyasuddin Tughlaq's learning was generally religious but that of his son Muhammad Tughlaq was almost encyclopaedic and his appetite for knowledge was insatiable. He was so well versed in the rational as well as theological sciences that even his worst critics recognized his high intellectual calibre. The *Futuhat-i-Firoz Shahi* by Sultan Firoz mentions that Firoz Shah Tughlaq repaired and rebuilt structures of former rulers which were ruined due to the lapse of time. He built the magnificent '*Firozi Madarsa*', Ziauddin Barani, the contemporary historian, has praised this building and says that Maulana Jalaluddin Rumi a scholar of great repute, was appointed to teach commentaries on the *Quran*, *Hadith* (tradition) and *fiqh* (Muslim law and jurisprudence) in the *Madarsa*. During Firoz Shah's reign a syllabus was introduced of fourteen subjects which included traditional as well as rational sciences. He was deeply interested in astronomy and medicine. The *Sirat-i-Firoz Shahi* enumerates in detail the development in the field of astronomy and medicine. The study of medicine developed to a great extent during the reign of Sultan Alauddin Khalji, Muhammad bin Tughlaq and Firoz Shah Tughlaq.

The Delhi Sultans took a keen interest in the promotion of learning, many books were written under their patronage, scholars were recognized, many Sanskrit books were translated into Persian, *Madarsas* were established, endowment and grants were made so as to make provision for the maintenance of these educational institutions. But this does not mean that Muslim settlements in India began after the Ghurid invasions. Long before Shihabuddin appeared on the scene many Musalmans had been living for generations in India under the Hindu Rais. There were Muslim colonies in Badaon, Bahraich, Ajmer, Nagaur, Qanauj and other places. For example, Maulana Raziuddin Hasan Saghani, the famous author of *Mashariq-ul-Anwar* was born in Badaun in 1181 A.D., learnt the *ahadith* there and when he went to Baghdad he was soon acknowledged as a leading scholar of the Traditions of the Prophet which means even before the coming of the Sultanate there was some kind of indigenous education and institutions of the same. Secondly the development and progress of education did not depend on the Sultan's patronage alone and the *Madarsas* established by him. Whether there was patronization of education or not, Muslim education was always there.

With the establishment of Muslim rule in India, a need was felt for the erection of mosques, which also fulfilled the function of the centres of learning. It is a striking feature to note that since the rise of Islam, mosques played an important part in the promotion of education and learning. It was the meeting place of the learned men, the place of devotion and worship, study and discussion not strictly organized but open to every Muslim.

In India too, as in other Muslim countries, mosques continued to function as centres of learning even after the establishment of regular *Madarsas*. During the Sultanate period also a large number of mosques were constructed throughout the length and breath of the land. Learned men who came to India either of their own volition or were invited by the ruling monarchs, usually had close links with these mosques. In teaching, they did not adopt any new method but followed the traditional system which was prevalent in other Islamic countries. The religious basis remained in force as it was in other countries.

A study of Muslim education during the Sultanate period helps us to understand that Islamic education did contain a co-ordination between secular and religious elements. Though education was influenced by religion, at times the *ulama* and scholars established the importance and indispensability of education for practical life. Provision of education in arts, crafts, architecture, agriculture, medicine and commerce and such other subjects of practical utility defined the essential aim of education to be a harmonization between secular and religious education.

It is very difficult to estimate the extent of Muslim education in India in early times. We have no accurate estimate as to the average number of students attending a college. Probably this varied considerably from just a few students with one teacher, to a large number with many teachers in the more important centres of learning. Probably most mosques had attached to them, if not a *madarsa* then a *maktab* or primary school. All Muslim children were supposed to attend a *maktab* in order to learn the portions of the *Quran* required for the Muslims daily devotion but we cannot be sure that they always did so.

Under the Islamic system, education was considered to be indispensable for life. The religious background enhanced the indispensability and universality of education. Another important feature of Islamic education was that politics, literature and history made appreciably good progress during the period. Before this period the tendency to produce the historical work had not freely evolved under the ancient Indian education system whatever little history we get, it is in the form of legendary and mythological tales and epics.

We are able to obtain less of true and authentic accounts of historical events in chronological order before the advent of the Muslims. Rajatarangini written by Kalhana can be placed in the category of history. But during the Muslim period history was written in the form of *memoirs* and the Sultans extended patronage to famous historians in their courts. *Belles letters* of the period owed its existence especially to the high aesthetic sense of the Sultans. Therefore, different aspects of literature such as prose, verse, fiction and poetry were included in the curricula of contemporary education.

Like the ancient Indian system of education, it is a special feature of the Islamic educational system that it effected a close personal contact between the teacher and pupil. Most teachers either the one's of the *maktabs* and *Madarsas* or private teachers paid individual attention to the students. Rote learning in *maktabs* was given importance, and the principal aim of the teacher was to pass on the pupil the learned traditions which he himself had received. Every student proceeded with his lesson independently according to his level of intelligence and personal capability.

Despite its merits, Islamic education was not immune from certain glaring defects. Though religious education formed an integral part of the primary curriculum and the study of the *Quran* was compulsory yet a very high level of spiritualism was difficult to attain. Prompted by religious and social prestige, the rulers had established *maktabs* and *Madarsas* but after the death of the founders, usually the institutions deteriorated but this does not mean that Muslim education deteriorated, because the individual centres run by scholars kept functioning as institutes to impart education.

Right from childhood, in the elementary or primary stage itself, children were taught the Persian alphabet in *maktabs*. The medium of instruction in *Madarsas* was Persian. Persian was the court language and was compulsorily studied, although Arabic grammar and language was also taught. Although according to the tenets of Islam, the acquisition of knowledge is considered an important duty, Islamic education in India could not be 'universal'. Infact, the state did not establish any regular well organized body like the Department of Education aiming to educate the masses and to spread knowledge among them.

Due to the strict Pardah system, women usually remained confined to their homes and were deprived of education. No doubt, the princesses and other girls belonging to aristocratic households received education inside their own palaces and some of them acquired a considerable amount of learning but there was no proper arrangement for the girls of the general masses. Only few girls learnt reading and writing in the local mosques with boys. According to some writers, this neglect of female education was due to adversity of circumstances and not due to any inherent defect in the system.

The patronage, which the institution of *harem* enjoyed under the *Sultanate* of Delhi, gave women of royalty enough inducement to further their ambition in carrying out administration, leading troops to the battle field, despatching and receiving of envoys, signing treaties and dealing sternly and tactfully with disruptive forces in the Sultanate. Women belonging to the royal household such as Khudawanda-i-Jahan, Shah Turkan, Chief queen of Sultan Iltutmish, Razia Sultan, eldest daughter of Sultan Iltutmish, Malika-i Jahan, wife of Sultan Jalaluddin Khalji, Makhduma-i-Jahan and Khudavandzada, mother and sister of Sultan Muhamamad bin Tughlaq patronized education and learning.

The effective role of these women in politics and administration displays that they must have been fairly educated. But contemporary historians abstain from making public mention of them. No doubt their political, religious and literary contributions have been narrated by the Persian chronicles but the social and cultural aspects of Muslim women have been evaded. The Persian chronicles knowingly or unknowingly or under compulsion did not deal with women's affairs but concentrated their compositions on the political affairs of the empire, the military exploits and the magnificence of the royal courts. The system of mass education for girls was however not present in the Sultanate period, though education among the ladies of the royal families was quite intensive and progressive, especially in case of ladies who displayed high intellectual potential. But during the medieval period there was hardly any mass education, worth the name. despite the fact that Muslim ladies remained behind Pardah with not many facilities for a liberal education, yet the progress made by some women is indeed admirable.

Dr. Nasim Akhtar in his article 'Islam, Women Education and Indian *Madarsas'* infers 'The role of women's *Madarsas* in transformation of the Muslim society in general and women folk in particular from the grip of superstition, un-islamic rituals and innovations, is highly appreciable but they need many changes in their education system. In north Indian *Madarsas* modern education does not have its due share in religious curriculum, while in south Indian *Madarsas*, both the education: traditional and modern go simultaneously. In the religious *Madarsas* of Andhra Pradesh, Tamil Nadu and Kerala, the women *Madarsas* have the system to manage both the educations. Some of them have included English and Sciences in their curricula, while others do manage to teach modern subjects in evening in the same building. After completing the course of Arabic and Islamic Studies, a girl does cover the syllabus of government School upto matriculation level and appears in the state government examination. In the first shift they do study English, Urdu, and any local language. These subjects also help them in the government school's examination. He points out that in this system one problem remains unsolved i.e., the problem of extra load of modern education. He suggests that this problem can be solved to some extent, if the difficult book of Arabic and Islamic Studies are replaced by simple ones, and this is not practically impossible. It needs reformulating the curricula.[1]

Although the aim of receiving education was mainly religious and moral training, it may be stated that the Muslim religious scholarship during the medieval period was not hostile to the study of rational, metaphysical or practical subjects. Its main concern was to ensure that the religious dimension of the personality did not weaken as a result of the emphasis on philosophic studies. The tradition of rational and philosophic studies was respected to the extent, that it did not erode the foundations of religion. The Mu'tazilite *Kashshaf*, the rationalist *Tafsir-i-Kabir* of Razi and the works of Abu 'Ali'ibn Sina continued to enjoy a place in Islamic studies of Medieval India.

Other than the *maktabs, Madarsas* and *khanqahs* there were also other agencies through which education was imparted. The individual centres of education, academic assemblies and Sufi *majlis* were also channels through which knowledge was imparted. The individual centres were the most popular medium for imparting knowledge. The observatories and astrolabes functioned as a medium to provide knowledge in astronomy and hospitals functioned as institutes for the provision of medical knowledge and *karkhanas* functioned as a medium to provide technical knowledge and develop industrial skill and craftsmanship. Some of the *Sufi Jama'at Khanas* (hospices) also created an atmosphere conducive to the progress of learning. The thirteenth and fourteenth century Sufis of *Suhrawardi* and the *Chishti* and *Firdausi Silsilahs* attracted intellectuals, delivered discourses and held discussion on matters related to religion, metaphysical philosophy and poetry.[2]

The *Madarsas* in Medieval India had hardly any fixed syllabus. The inclusion of books in the curricula depended on several considerations, personal predilections of a teacher, availability of books, adherence to traditional approach and utility in some specific context. It is also worth recalling that the *Madarsas* and its teacher performed an important role in enhancing upward social mobility. The doors of the *Madarsa* were thrown open to all classes, even though there was opposition from a section of the ruling elite to the education of low born Muslim children. The brief information extracted from Ibn Batuta's *Rehla* and Barani's *Tarikh-i-Firozshahi* about the carreer of Ratan the Babar, tends to suggest that low caste Hindus could also have their children educated in Persian language and popular sciences. During Sultan Muhammad Tughlaq's reign Ratan made rapid progress and ultimately attained the rank of a high noble.[3] There were teachers who were known for their special insight in certain classical works and students came to them to receive instruction in that particular book and obtained certificates (*ijazah*) which entitled them to teach the book to others.

As stated earlier there was no uniform syllabus for all institutions, Shaikh Farid Ganj Shakar (ob.1265) taught to his disciples the *Qur'an* the *Tamhidat* of Abu Shakoor Salimi and the *Awarif-al-Ma'arif* of Shaikh Shihab-al-Din Suhrawardi. His objective was pragmatic, the *Quran* was to act as the source of all religious inspiration, the *Tamhidat* was to serve as a guide book for *Fiqh*, and the *Awarif* a manual for *Khanqah* organization. Maulana Kamal-al-din Zahid taught *Mashariq-al-Anwar* to his students and Maulana Farid-al-Din Shafi, Shaikh-ul-Islam of Awadh taught *al-Kashshaf* to his pupils. Eminent scholars of the period who had special insight in some branch of learning usually taught a few selected books and granted certificates (*ijazah*) to their pupils.

Moreover in the Sufi *majlis* the most commonly used Tafsir were the *Tafsir Madarik*, *Tafsir Kashshaf*, *Tafsir Razi*, *Tafsir Zahiri*, *Tafsir Nasiri*, *Tafsir Basara*, and *Arais-ul-Bayan*. It appears that in the Chishti circle the most popularly used *Tafsir* was the *Tafsir Madarik*. During our period of study the *Awarif-ul-Ma'arif*, *Fusus-ul-Hikam*, *Kashf-ul-Mahjub* and *Qut-ul-Qulub* were the famous *Tasawwuf* books taught in the Sufi *Majlis*.

The institutions run by state had a more comprehensive syllabus and included subjects like, *Ilm-i-Tabi'i*, *Ilm-i-Riyadi*, *Ilm-i-Nazar* etc. some books were compiled on specific themes by persons who were specialists in that area. Maulana Diya-al-Din al-Din Sunnami, who held charge of the Department of Censor of Public morals during the reign of Alauddin Khalji wrote in Arabic *Nisab-al- Ihtisab* for the guidance and instruction of those who had to perform the duties of a *muhtasib* (sensor of morals). Maulana Abd-al-Hamid Muharrir Ghaznawi wrote during the time of Firoz Shah Tughlaq, a manual *'Ilm-al-Hisab* for the instruction of those who had to keep records and maintain accounts. The selection of certain books like *Tahdib-al-Mantiq, Hikmat al-Ishraqiyyah, Khulasat-ul Hisab* etc. for preparation of commentaries and annotations was dictated by the needs of students studying those books.

The use of paper is likely to have facilitated the copying of books and book trade. It also enabled larger collections of books to be accumulated by individuals. The foundation of the Sultanate and the educated Muslim's love for books gave a boost to the book trade and also promoted a library culture.[4] It also led to the progress to the craft of paper making in the country on the one hand and provided job opportunities to the people in the Urban Centres. The scribes, bookbinders, and those who dealt in the trade of the books also benefited from it.[5] Thus the libraries not only enhanced the diffusion of knowledge but also promoted intellectual culture. The habit of the nobles and scholars of collecting books and maintaining libraries in the pre Mughal India encouraged and influenced the later generations to promote intellectual fervour during the Mughal period and even afterwards.

The fourteenth century saw the largest production of *Fiqh* literature in India. *Fatawa-i-Firoz Shahi, Fawa'id-i-Firoz Shahi, Fatawa-i-Tatar Khaniyah* were the popular works of Fiqh compiled during this period.

As a result of the Mongol invasion, after the Ghurian conquest in India (c. 1200) access to the massive richness to Arabic Sciences was now achieved but under increasing intellectual and religious restraints. Sultan Muhammad-bin-Tughlaq was a follower of the rationalist thinkers and Barani as his courtier was also regarded a rationalist and underwent imprisonment for being the late Sultan's close associate. On his release, Barani compiled the *Tarikh-i-Firoz shahi* in order to please Firoz Shah but in vain. But the defence of Muhammad-bin-Tughlaq's state policies and the praise of the rationalist scholars antagonized the reactionaries, who had gained ascendancy at court. Being a predicament Barani then revised the *Tarikh* in his own defence condemning the rationlist thinkers.[6] Ziauddin Barni (1351 A.D.) vehemently criticized Muhammad bin Tughlaq for upholding Reason and Rational approach to be superior to the dictates of the sacred texts and for keeping company with scientists and philosophers.

In India two areas in which interest was mainly shown were astronomy and medicine especially during the reign of Alauddin Khalji, Muhammad Tughlaq and Firoz Shah Tughlaq which has been discussed in detail in chapter V of this book.

With regard to modern survivals of Quranic schools in India, the Quinquennial review of education quotes De la Fosse as saying that these "are usually attached to a mosque.......the scholars commence by studying the Arabic alphabet, and as soon as they can read are made to recite suras, or chapters of the *Quran*. Neither writing nor arithmetic is taught. So far as my experience, instruction is usually confined to reading and memorizing but some times an attempt is also made to explain the meaning of what is read. This however is rare.[7]

William Adam, in his report on education in Bengal (1835-1838 A.D.) says with regard to the *Madarsas*, "In the Arabic schools, the course of study takes a much wider range. The grammatical works are numerous, systematized and profound. Complete courses of reading on rhetoric, logic and law are embraced. The external observances and fundamental doctrines of Islam and Ptolemy on astronomy in translation, are not unknown. Other branches of natural philosophy are also taught, and the whole course is crowned by the presence of treatises on metaphysics, deemed the highest attainment of the instructed scholar.[8]

In the contemporary world the significance of curriculum and its survey has increased to the extent that the relation of education with religion and culture has become very strong and firm and it has also developed a deep relationship with the economic life of the people. No doubt this relationship was also found in the past but it was not so deep rooted and commercialized as it is in the present day and age. This is the reason why the consideration and interest of people has increased in the curriculum of the *Madarsas* and other religious institutions of Muslims. A lot of discussions and debates take place on the need for amendment and reform and in different ways the expression of thoughts still persists. One such attempt was made by Prof. S.M. Azizudin Husain by organizing a seminar on '*Madarsa* Education in India from 11 to 21st century' in 2002 which he later edited and published as a book.[9]

From the detailed discussion on the curriculum in this work, entitled "Muslim Education and Learning During the Delhi Sultanate (13th and 14th Centuries)" it can be deduced that whatever was the course of studies it was perhaps dominated by various books of study. The selection of books in the process of teaching was such that after their completion a student would develop the quality of grasping the meaning of the subject and the ability of comprehending the different sciences and arts would enhance.

It is however not correct to compare the method of teaching adopted in the *Madarsas* of that period to the modern *Madarsas* of nowadays. Especially considering the difference in thinking and administration of both the periods, it is not right to form a hasty opinion. No doubt just like during the *Sultanate* period different sciences and arts were taught similarly in the curriculum of the modern *Madarsas* along with religious sciences other sciences can be taught.

While comparing the administration of education of both the periods usually this aspect is neglected that during the medieval period there was no fixed time or period for the acquisition of knowledge, instead the love of learning and deep interest was such that the process of derivation of knowledge continued throughout their lives, thus it was not very difficult to attain specialization in a particular subject. Usually after obtaining excellence and mastery in one field of studies, the scholars would change to another field of studies. But nowadays the circumstances are such that the student after reaching a particular stage or level of education or after completing a definite course, in order to fulfill the economic needs or other necessaries of life or to fulfill other demands of life gives up education. In other words education during the medieval period was not job-oriented like these days and it was not so deeply related to earning a livelihood or gaining employment as it is nowadays. Also the differences in the courses of teaching of subjects were not so inherent as it is today. That is why under one administration the study of different subjects at the same time was possible or it was comparatively convenient to study the rational as well as traditional sciences simultaneously. Moreover nowadays with the massive technological and technical advancement and advanced research, the sciences have developed to such high levels beyond measure, that it would be foolhardy to expect an individual to acquire knowledge of several subjects at a time.

As Muslim thought developed from the seventh century onwards there were in almost every subject a number of opposed schools. But discussion gradually reconciled the idea of these schools, or else left (as in mystical thought) two opposed schools in the field. Under the medieval circumstances of life and specially the conditions of teaching, it is not surprising to find that academic progress led to acceptance of one standard work, or if reconciliation of opposed ideas was not possible to two standard works, one representing the orthodox, and the other the critically minded. Thus Quranic commentaries found their fulfillment in two works the *Kashshaf* of Zamakhshari for the critically minded and the *Tafsir-i-Kabir* of Imam Fakhruddin Razi for the orthodox. Similarly in mysticism, the centrist school of Shaikh Junaid found its final expression in the *'Awarif-ul-Ma'arif* of Shaikh Shihabuddin Suhrawardi, while the thoughts of the leftist schools who had suffered persecution for centuries, were expressed in the *Futuhat-i-Makkiya* of his contemporary, of Shaikh Muhiuddin Ibn 'Arabi. In other subjects, where continued disagreement would have been disastrous, a single work obtained general acceptance for eg. the *Qanun-i-Shifa* of Shaikh Abu Ali Sina in medicine and the *Hidaya* of Maulana Burhanuddin Marghinani in law. These great works preserved the achievements of the past but they crushed initiative, for they were accepted as final in their own spheres.

Muslim civilization in all spheres had developed to its maximum stature before the establishment of the empire of Delhi. The Indian Musalmans during the Sultanate period did not contribute much to the ideology of Islam. Their contributions are limited to the sphere of applied arts and the reduction of theory to practice. But within this limited field, their achievements are commendable.

The *Madarsa* peformed an important role during medieval times not only in the diffusion of knowledge that took place in the urban centres, but also social mobility. Thirteenth and fourteenth century writers in Persian produced significant literary works. They also inspired scholars during the subsequent period and helped maintain a literary tradition that forms part of India's intellectual heritage.[10]

Prof. Mujeeb Ashraf after conducting a detailed survey of *Madarsa-i-Rahimiah* draws upon some interesting conclusions and gives some very practical suggestions. He states 'The first and foremost fact revealed is that the *Madarsas* cannot have a system of education completely devoid of religious courses, secondly, the Muslim education system has never been static and monolithic. It passed through the phases of changes in pattern and character; thirdly, Islam never prohibits the learning of rational and' natural sciences or the languages other than Arabic, Persian, Urdu etal. However the *Ulama*, in view of the exigency, arising out of the political upheavals advised Muslims to be extremely careful and cautious lest it effects their very basis of faith or *Iman*; fourthly, Muslims have never been averse to changes except, that they would accept it to be surely in tune with their religious beliefs, aims and objectives. As a result, we find that the phases of *Manqulat* or religious education were followed by the phases of *maqulat* or rational sciences.[11] Also elementary education imparted in *maktabs* including the learning of alphabets and 3R: reading writing and arithmetics has played a positive role in spreading literacy and atleast providing primary education among a majority section of Muslim population which otherwise would have remained deprived of even rudimentary education. In the present situation this significant role performed by *Maktabs* and *Madarsas* for provision of literacy amongst the Muslim Community deserves greater appreciation.

References

1 Azizuddin Husain, S.M. *Madarsa Education in India* (11 th to 21 st Century), Kanishka Publishers, New Delhi , 2005, p. 104.

2 Siddiqui, Iqtidar Husain, *Delhi Sultanate, Urbanization and Social Change*, Viva Books, New Delhi, 2009, p. 143.

3 Ibid, p. 143.

4 Ibid, p. 154.

[5] Ibid, p. 160.

[6] Ibid, p. 147.

[7] Keay, F.E., *Indian Education in Ancient and Later Times*, London, Oxford University Press, 1942, pp. 137-39.

[8] Ibid, p. 139.

[9] Azizuddin Husain, S.M. *Madarsa Education in India* (11 th to 21 st century) New Delhi, Kanishka Publishers, 2005.

[10] *Delhi Sultanate, Urbanization and Social Change*, Op.cit, p. 148.

[11] *Madarsa Education in* India , Op. cit, pp. 70-17.

Appendix-I

An Ijazat Namah (School Certificate)

The teacher in medieval India could not set up an educational institution and instruct people in different religious sciences unless he had obtained an *ijazat-namah* from an authority on the subjects he intended to teach. The *ijazat namah* was the medieval form of the modern certificates and diploma.

The following certificate was granted to Shaikh Nizam-u'd-din Auliya by his teacher, Maulana Kamal-u'd-din Zahid, a renowned *muhaddith* of Delhi in 679 A.H./1280 A.D.

This *Ijazat Namah* thus establishes the instructional *silsilah* of Shaikh Nizam-u'd-din Auliya with the author of *Mashariq-u'l-Anwar*.

Maulana Razi-u'd-din Hasan Saghani

↓

Maulana Burhan-u'd-din Mahmud As'ad al-Balkhi,

↓

Maulana Kamal-u'd-din Zahid

↓

Shaikh Nizam-u'd-dn Auliya

بسم الله الرحمن الرحيم

الحمد لمن له الاهتداء والاعطاء و الصباح والرواح٠ والمدح لمن له الآلاء والنعماء والصباح والمداح، والصلوة الفصاح على ذی الفضائل السماء والكلمة والكلام المفتاح والمناقب العليا والاحاديث الصحاح صلوة تدوم دوام الصباح والرواح و بعد فان الله تعالى وفق الشيخ الامام العالم الناسک السالک نظام الدين محمد بن احمد بن علی مع وفور فضله فی العلم و بلوغ قدرة ذروة الحلم مقبول المشائخ الكبار منظور العلماء الاخيار والابرار بان قرأ هذالاصل المستخرج من الصحيحين على ساطر هذه السطور فی زمن الزمن الحار و درو الامطار من اوله الى آخره قراءة بحث و اتقان و تنقيح معانيه و تنقير مبانيه و كاتب السطور يرويه قراءة و سماعاً عن الشيخين الامامين العالمين الكاملين احد الشيخين مولف شرح اثار النيرين فی اخبار الصحيحين والاخر صاحب الدرسين المنيرين الامام الاجل الكامل مالک رقاب النظم والنثر برهان الملة والدين محمود بن ابی الحسن اسعد البلخی رحمة الله عليهما رحمة و اسعة كتابة و شفاهة و هما يرويانه عن مولفه و اجزته ان يروی على كما هو المشروط فی هذا الباب، و الله اعلم بالصواب، و اوصيته ان لا ينسانی و اولادی فی دعواته فی خلوته وصح له القراءة والسماع فی المسجد المنسوب الى نجم الدين ابی بكر التواسی رحمة الله فی بلدة دهلی صانها الله عن الآفات و العاهات

از نعيم طرب و شادمانی و رحيق نشاط و كامرانی حظی كامل و نصيبی شامل بر گيرند و دعائی دولت قاهرهٔ ما كه حامی بيضه اسلام و مسلمانی و حارس حوزهٔ ايمانی است، فی آناء الليل و اطراف النهار ورد وقت و حرز حال خود سازند تا بحسن عقائدآن دعا گويان غيبت كه مخلصان بی ريب اند و بركات دعوات صالحهٔ ايشان در صباح و مساء عزائم غزوات كه در مستقبل ايام به نيت صادقهٔ اتساع اسلام و استيصال كفرهٔ هفت اقليم مصمم خواهد شد يا بشارت فتح و فيروزی اكتفا پذيرد بمشية الله وعونه۔

* *Siyar-ul-Auliya*, Op.cit, pp. 104-105

Appendix-II

A Khilafat-cum-ijazat Namah

The following *khilafat-cum-Ijazat Namah* was granted to Shaikh Nizam-u'd-din Auliya by his spiritual master Shaikh Farid- u'd-din Ganj-i-Shakar. It confers spiritual authority on Shaikh Nizam- u'd-din Auliya and accords permission to teach *Tamhidat* of Abu Shakoor Salimi, a book dealing with the fundamentals of faith.

بسم الله الرحمن الرحيم

الحمدلله الذى قدم احسانه على ملة و اخر شكره على نعمة هوالأول هوالآخر و الظاهر والباطن لا مؤخر لما قدم ولا مقدم لما اخر ولا معلن لما ابطن ولا مخفى لما اظهر ولا يكاد نطق الوائل والا - و اخرملى ديمومة اعتجاراً او تقابلاً والصلوة على رسوله المصطفى محمد و آله و اهل الودود الارتضاء و بعد فان الشروع فى الاصول يوسع دعاء الشهود و يحصر لمن يكرع ملها محارق الورد على ان الطريق مخوف والعقبة وكود - و نعم الكتاب فى هذا الفن تمهيد المهتدى ابى شكور برد الله مضجعه وقد قرأ ملدى الولد الرشيد الامام اللقى العالم الرضى نظام الملة و الدين محمد بن احمد زين الائمة والعلماء مفخر الاجلة والا تقياء اعانه الله على ابتغاء مرضاته و اناله ملتهى رحمته و اعلى در جاته سبقاً بعد سبق من اوله الى اخره قراءة تدبرو ايقان مستجمع رعاية سمع و دراية جنان و كما حصل الوقوف على حسن استعداده

كذالک وفور تهياة اجزته ان يدرس فيه المتعلمين بشرط المجانبة عن التصحيف والغلط والتحريف و بذل الجد و الاجتهاد فى التصحيح والتلقيح عن الزلل و عنته المعول والله العالم و كان ذالک يوم الاربعاء من الشهر المبارک رمضان عظمه الله بركته بالاشارة العالية ادام الله العلى اسحاق بن على بن اسحاق الدهلوى بمشافهته حامدا و مصليا فاجزت له ايضاً بان يروى على جميع ما استفاده وحوى وسمع ذالک منى ودعى والسلام على من اتبع الهدى و اجزت له ايضاً ان يلازم الخلوة فى مسجد اقيمت فيه الجماعة ولا يخل بشرائطها التى بها حصول الزيادة و برفضها تكون الاقدام عاتله ناصية و ذالک تجريد المقاصد من مفاسد ها و تفريد الهمة عما تغفلها و بيان ذالک ما قال رسول الله صلى الله عليه وسلم كن فى الدنيا كانک غريب او كعابرى سبيل وعد نفسک من اصحاب القبور " الحديث " فعلد ذالک صح قصده و اجتمع همته و صارت الهمم - المختلفه همة واحدة فليدخل الخلوة مفترا نفسه معدماً للخلق عالما بعجزهم تاركا للدنيا و شهواتها و اقفاً على مضارها و امليتها واتكن خلوته معمورة بانواع العبادات اذا سئمت نفسه عن احتمال الاعلى يلزلها الى الادنى ادان حجت فليلزلها اما بعمل يسير او بالنوم فان فيه احترازا من هواجس النفس وليحترز اطالة فانها تقسى القلوب والله تعالى على ذالک اعانه و يحفظه عما شانه و رحمه و هو ارحم الراحمين صلى الله على محمد وآله وايضاً اذا استوفر حظه من الخلوة و انفتحت بها عين الحكمة و اجتمعت خلواته بمناد ياته وصل اليه من لم يقدر الوصول الينا يستوفى اليه اياه فيده العزيزة نائبة عن يدنا و هو من جماة خلفائنا و التزام حكمه فى امرالدين والدنيا من جماة تعظيمنافرحم الله من اكرمه وعظم من اكرمناء و اتهان من لم يحفظ حق من حفظنا صح ذالک كله من الفقيرالمسعود تم .بعون الله و حسن توفيه والله اعلم - C *

---

* *Siyar-ul-Auliya*, Op.cit, pp. 117-119

Alai Darwaza

Firozi Madarsa -Front View

Firozi Madarsa-double Storey Building

Firozshah's Tomb-beside the Firozi Madarsa

Jami Mosque

Jami Mosque-Siri Fort

Qadam Sharif

Siri Fort

Bibliography

A) Persian Sources:

I. Early Medieval Period:

1) Awfi, Muhammad, *Lubab-ul-Albab*, Isfahan, Ibn Sina Kitab Khana, 1333 Shamsi.
2) Fakr-i-Mudabbir, *Tarikh-i-Fakhruddin Mubarak Shahi*, (also known as Tarikh-i-Fakhr Muddabir, ed. Denision Ross London, R.A.S. Forlong Fund, 1927.
3) Juzjani, Minhajuddin Siraj, *Tabaqat-i-Nasiri*, Vol.I, ed. Abdul Hayy Habibi, Kabul, Anjuman-i-Tarikh-i-Afghanistan, 1342 Shamsi.
4) Syed, Muhammad Masum, *Tarikh-i-Masumi*, Bombay, Matba'-i-Qayyama, 1938.

II. Later Medieval Period:

1) Afif Shams Siraj, *Tarikh-i-Firoz Shahi*, ed. M. Wilayat Husain, Calcutta, Asiatic Society of Bengal, 1891.
2) Anonymous, *Sirat-i-Firoz Shahi* (Fascimile edition of the manuscript) Patna, Khudabaksh Oriental Public Library, 1999.
3) Badayuni, Abdul Qadir, *Muntakhab-ut-Tawarikh*, Vol.I, ed. M. Kabiruddin Ahmad Ali, Calcutta, Asiatic Society of Bengal, 1868.

4) Badayuni, Abdul Qadir, *Muntakhab-ut-Tawarikh*, Vol.II, ed. M. Kabiruddin Ahmad Ali, Calcutta, Asiatic Society of Bengal, 1869./

5) Barani, Ziauddin, *Tarikh-i-Firoz Shahi*, ed., Sir Syed Ahmad Khan, Aligarh, Sir Syed Academy, AMU, 2005.

6) Bilgrami, Gulam Ali Azad, *Ma'athir-ul-Kiram*, Agra, Mufid Am Press, 1910.

7) Ferishta, Muhammad Qasim, *Tarikh-i-Ferishta*, Vol.I & II, Lucknow, Nawal Kishore, 1864-65.

8) Isami, *Futuhus-Salatin*, ed. Usha, A.S., Madras, University of Madras, 1948.

9) Khusrau, Amir, *Qiran-us-Sa'dain*, ed. Maulvi Muhammad Ismail Meruti and Syed Hasan Barani, Aligarh, Aligarh College Press, 1918.

10) Khusrau, Amir, *Hasht-Bihisht*, ed. Sulaiman Arif, Aligarh, Institute Press, 1918.

11) Khusrau, Amir, *Dewal Rani Khizr Khani*, ed.: Rashid Ahmad Ansari, Aligarh, Madarsat-ul-um, 1917.

12) Khusrau, Amir, *Ijaz-i-Khusrawi*, Vol.II, Lucknow, Nawal Kishore, 1876.

13) Nahavandi, Abdul Baqi, *Ma'athir-i-Rahimi*, Vol.I, ed. M. Hidayat Husain, Calcutta, Asiatic Society of Bengal, 1924.

14) Nizamuddin Ahmad, *Tabaqat-i-Akbari*, Lucknow, Nawal Kishore, 1875.

15) Sirhindi, Yahya bin Ahmad bin Abdullah, *Tarikh-i-Mubarak Shahi*, ed. M. Hidayat Husain Calcutta, Asiatic Society of Bengal, 1931.

16) Tughlaq, Firoz Shah, *Futuhat-i-Firoz Shahi*, ed. Shaikh Abdur Rashid, Aligarh, Department of History, 1954.

III. Tazkiras:

1) Dehlavi, Shaikh Abdul Haqq Muhaddith, *Akhbar-ul-Akhyar*, Delhi, Matba-i-Mujtabai, 1332 A.H.

2) Mir Khurd, *Siyar-u'l-Auliya*, Delhi, Matba-Muhibb-i-Hind, 1302 A.H., 1885 A.D.

3) Rahman Ali, *Tazkira-i-ulama-i-Hind*, Lucknow, Nawal Kishore, 1914.

IV) Malfuzat:

1) Makhdumdaza 'Abdullah, *Siraj-u'l-Hidaya*, ed. Sajjad Husain, Delhi, Indian Council of Historical Research, 1983.

2) Sijzi, Amir Hasan, *Fawaid-u'l-Fu'ad*, Lucknow, Nawal Kishore, 1894.

3) Qalandar Hamid, *Khair-u'l-Majalis*, ed. Nizami, K.A., Aligarh, Muslim University, Department of History, 1959.

V) Urdu Translations:

1) Ferishta, Muhammad Qasim, *Tarikh-i-Ferishta*, Urdu translation: Abdul Hayy Khwaja, Deoband, Maqtaba-i-Millat, 1983.

2) Jamali, Hamid bin Fazl Allah *Siyar-ul-Arifin*, Urdu translation by Ghulam Ahmad, Moradabad, Shams-u'd-Mataba', 1901.

3) Jamali, Hamid bin Fazl Allah, *Siyar-ul-Arifin*, Urdu translation by Mohammad Ayyub Qadri, Lahore, Urdu Science Academy, 1989.

4) Mir Khurd, *Siyar-ul-Auliya*, Urdu translation and Publication by Khwaja Islamuddin Nizami, Delhi, 1985.

VI) English Translation:

1) Elliot H.M. and Dowson J., *History of India As Told By It's Own Historians*, (Taj-u'l-Maathir), Vol.II, Delhi, Low Price Publications, Sept., 2001.

2) Habib, Muhammad and Khan, Afsar Umar Salim, *The Political Theory of the Delhi Sultanate*, Delhi, Kitab Mahal, n.d.

3) Habib Muhammad, *The Campaigns of Ala-ud-din Khilji, (Khazai-inul-Futuh of Amir Khusrau)*, Madras, D.B. taraporewala, 1931.

4) Husain, Agha Mahdi, *Futuh-us-Salatin*, Vol.II, Aligarh, Department of History, 1976.

5) Raverty H.G., *Tabaqat-i-Nasiri*, Vol.I, New Delhi, Oriental Books, 1970.

6) Basu, K.K., *Tarikh-i-Mubarkshahi*, Karachi, Karimsons, 1977.

B) Arabic Sources:

1) Abdul Barr, Ibn, *Jami' bayan-ul-Ilm-wa-Fazala*, Urdu translation: by Malihabad, Abdur Razzaq entitled as *'Al-Ilm-wa- Al-ulama*, Delhi, Nadwat-ul-Musaniffin, 1953.

2) Al Kattani,Al Shaikh Abdul Hajj, *Nizam-Al-Hukumat Al-Nabawiyah Al Taratib Al Idariyah*, Vol.I, Beirut, (Pub. Hasan Jata) n.d.

3) Allama, Abdu'l Hayy b. Fakhru'd-Din-al-Hasani, *Nuzhathu'l-Khawatir*, Vol.I, Hyderabad, Osmania Oriental Publications Bureau, 1962.

4) Allama, Abdu'l Hayy b. Fakhru'd-Din-al-Hasani, *Nuzhathu'l-Khawatir*, Vol.II, Hyderabad, Osmania Oriental Publications Bureau, 1966.

5) Zahabi, Muhammad Husain-ul-Zahabi, *Al-Tafsir wa-al-Mufsiron*, Vol.3, Alqahra, Darul Kutub-ul-Hadisa, 1962.

Modern Works In English

Modern Works On Religion:

1) Arnold, Sir Thomas and Gillaume Alfred, *The Legacy of Islam*, London, Oxford University Press, 1968.

2) Bosworth, Clifford Edmund, *The Islamic Dynasties*, Edinburg, University Press, 1967.

3) Bhargava, K.D., K.D.*A Survey of Islamic Culture and Institutions*, Allahabad, Kitab Mahal, 1960.

4) K.Ali, *A Study of Islamic History*, New Delhi, Adam Publishers and Distributors, 2003.

5) Masudul Hasan, *History of Islam*, Vol.I, Delhi, Adam Publishers, 2002.

6) Muhammad Ali, *Early Caliphate*, Lahore, Ahmadiyya-i-Isha'at-i-Islam, 1932.

7) Philby, H.S.T.J.B., *Harun-al-Rashid*, Edinburg, Peter Davies Lte., 1933.

8) Sayyid, Fayyaz Mahmud, *A Short History of Islam*, Oxford University Press, 1960.

9) Shustery, A.M.A., Outlines of Islamic Culture, Bangalore, Bangalore Printing and Publishing Co. Ltd., 1954.

10) Syed, Ameer Ali, The spirit of Islam, Delhi, Idarah-i-Adabyat-i-Delhi, 1978.

11) Syed Ameer Ali, *A Short History of Saracens*, New Delhi, Kitab Bhawan, 1977.

12) Syed, Mahmudunasir, Islam and it's concepts and History, New Delhi, Kitab Bhawan, 1983.

Modern Works in History and Literature:

1) Ahmad Aziz, *An Intellectual History of Islam in India*, Edinburg, T & A. Constable, 1969.

2) Alavi Azra, (ed) *Futuhat-i-Firoz Shahi*, Delhi, Idarah-i-Adabyat, 1996.

3) Azizuddin Husain, S.M. (ed.) *Madarsa Education in Inda* (11th to 21st century), New Delhi, Kanishka Publishers, 2005.

4. Banerjee, *J.M., History of Firoz Shah Tughlaq*, Delhi, Oriental Publishers, 1967.

5) Barthold, V.V., *Mussulman Culture*, translation from Russian by Shahid Suhrawardy, Calcutta, University of Calcutta, 1934.

6) Barthold, W, *Turkestan Down the Mongol Invasion*, London, Luzac and Co. Ltd., 1968.

7) Bhargav Meena and Dutta Kalyani, *Women Education and Politics*, New Delhi, Oxford University Press, 2005.

8) Bosworth, C.E., *The Ghaznavids, their Empire in Afghanistan and Eastern Iran*, 994-1040,Edinburg, University Press, 1963.

9) Elphinstone, Monstruat, *History of India, The Hindu and MohammedanDynasties*, Allahabad, Kitab Mahal, Pvt. Ltd., 1966.

10) Ghani Muhammad Abdu'l, *Pre-Mughal Persian in Hindustan*, Vol.I, New Delhi, Vintage Books, 1994.

11) Habib Muhammad, *Sultan Mahmud of Ghaznin*, New Delhi, S. Chand and Co.,1967.

12) Habib Muhammad and Nizami, K.A. ed., *The Comprehensive History of India*, The Delhi Sultanate, Vol.V, New Delhi, People's Publishing House, 1970.

13) Habibullah, A.B.M., *The Foundation of Muslim Rule in India*, Allahabad, Central Book Depot, 1976.

14) Hardy Peter, *Historians in Medieval India*, London, Luzac & Company Ltd., 1960.

15) Hasan, Mohibbul, *Historians of Medieval India*, Delhi, Meenakshi Prakashan, 1968.

16) Havell, E.B., *The History of Aryan rule in India*, (*From the Earliest Times To the Death of Akbar*), London, George G. Harrap & Co. Ltd., 1974.

17) Hitti, Philip, K. History of Arabs, London, Macmillan and Co. Ltd., 1970.Huart, Element, *History of Arabic Literature*, New Delhi, Deep & Deep Publication, 1990.

18) Husain Agha, Mahdi, *Tughlaq Dynasty*, New Delhi, S. Chand & Co., Pvt., Ltd., 1976.

19) Husain, Agha Mahdi, Rise and Fall of the *Muhammad bin Tughlaq*, Delhi, Idarah-i-Adabyat-i-Delhi, 1972.

20) Husain, Yusuf, *Glimpses of Medieval Indian Culture*, Bombay, Asia Publishing House, 1957.

21) Ira Lapidus, *A History of Islamic Society*, United Kingdom, Cambridge University Press, 1999.

22) Jaffar, S.M., Some Cultural Aspects of Muslim Rule in India, Peshawar, S. Mohd. Sadiq, 1939.

23) Jaffar, S.M., *Medieval India under Muslim Kings* (*The Rise and Fall of Ghaznawids*), Delhi, Idarah-i-Adabyat, 1972.

24) Jauhri, R.C., *Firoz Tughlaq* (1351-88 A.D.), Agra, Shivalal Agarwala & Co., 1968.

25) Lal Kishori Saran, *History of the Khaljis*, A.D. 1290-1320, New Delhi, Munshiram Manoharlal, 1980.

26) Lanepoole, Stanley, *History of India*, New Delhi, Asian Education Services, 1987.

27) Lanepoole, Stanley, *History of Medieval India*, Vol.3, New Delhi, Asian Educational Services, 1987.

28) Law, N.N. *Promotion of Learning in India, During the Mohammedan Rule*, Delhi, Idarah-i-Adabyat-i-Delhi, 1963.

29) Najibullah, *Islamic Literature*, New York, Washington Square Press, INC, 1963.

30) Nazim, Muhammad, *The Life and Times of Sultan Mahmud of Ghazna*, New Delhi, Munshiram Manoharlal, 1971.

31) Niazi, Ghulam Sarwar Khan, The Life and Works on Alauddin Khalji, Lahore, Institute of Islamic Culture, 1990.

32) Nicholson, R.A., A Literary History of The Arabs, Cambridge, University Press, 1969.

33) Nicholson, R.A., *Islamic Mysticism*, New Delhi, Aryan Book, 2002.

34) Nizami, K.A., *Royalty in Medieval India*, New Delhi, Munshiram Manoharlal, 1997.

35) Nizami, K.A., *State and Culture in Medieval India*, New Delhi, Adam Publishers, 1985.

36) Nizami, K.A., *Some Aspects of Religion and Politics in India during the thirteenth century*, Delhi, Idara-i-Adabyat-i-Delhi, 1974.

37) Nizami, K.A., *Studies in Medieval Indian History and Culture*, Allahabad, Kitab Mahal, 1966.

38) Nizami, K.A., *The Life of Times of Farid-ud-din Ganj-i-Shakar*, Delhi, Idarah-i-Adabyat-i-Delhi, 1973.

39) Nizami, K.A., *The Life and Times of Shaikh Nizam-u'd-din Auliya*, Delhi, Idarah-i-Adabyat-i-Delhi, 1991.

40) Nizami, K.A., *The Life and Times of Shaikh Nasir-u'd-din Chiragh-i-Delhi*, Delhi, Idarah-i-Adabyat-i-Delhi, 1991.

41) Powel Price, J.C., *A History of India*, London Thomas Nelson & sons Ltd., 1955.

42) Prasad Ishwari, *History of Medieval India*, Allahabad, The Indian Press, 1966.

43) Prasad, Ishwari, *A History of the Qaraunah Turks in India*, Allahabad, Central Book Depot, 1974.

44) Ray, Krishnalal, *Education in Medieval India*, Delhi, B.R. Publishing Corporation, 1984.

45) Sarton, George, *Introduction to the History of Science*, Vol.I, Baltimore, William and Welkins Co., 1927.

46) Sarton, George, *Introduction to the History of Science*, Vol.II, Part.II,1931.

47) Sayyed Hussin Nasr, *Islamic Science, An Illustrated Study*, Westerham, World of Islamic Festival Publishing Company, 1976.

48) Siddiqui, Iqtidar Husain, *Composite Culture Under the Sultanate of Delhi,* New Delhi, Primus Book, 2012.

49) Siddiqui, Iqtidar Husain, *Delhi Sultanate-Urbanization and Social Change,* New Delhi, Viva Book, 2009.

50) Siddiqui, Iqtidar Husain, *Medieval India: Essays in Intellectual Thought and Culture,* New Delhi, Manohar Publishers, 2003.

51) Sufi, G.M.D., *The Evolution of Curriculum*, Delhi, Idarah-i-Adabyat-i-Delhi, 1977.

52) Thomas, E, *The Chronicles of Pathan Kings of Delhi*, New Delhi, Munshiram Manoharlal Oriental Publishers, 1966.

53) Zafarul Islam, *Fatawa Literature of the Sultanate period*, New Delhi, Kanishka Publishers, 2005.

Travellers Accounts and Travelogues:

1) Ibn Batuta, *The Rehla of Ibn Batuta*, English translation and commentary: Agha Mahdi Husain, Baroda, Oriental Institute of Baroda, 1976.

2) Ibn Batuta, Travels of Ibn Batuta (1325-54 A.D.), Vol.I, English translation: Gibb, G.A.R., New Delhi, Munshiram Manoharlal Pvt. Ltd., 1993.

3) Shahabuddin Al Umari, *Masalik ul Absar-Fi Mumalik-ul-Amsar*, English translation: by Otto Spies, Aligarh, Department of History, 1943.

4) Zaki, Muhammad, *The Arab Accounts of India*, During the fourteenth century, Delhi, Idarah-i-Adabyat-i-Delhi, 1981.

Archaeology and Archaeological Reports:

1) Carr, Stephen, *The Archaeological and Monumental Remains of Delhi*, Allahabad, Kitab Mahal, 1967.
2) Fanshawe, H.C., *Delhi Past and Present*, London, John Murray, Albermarb Street,1902.
3) Husain, Maulvi Muhammad Ashraf, *Archeological Survey of India*, No:47, A Record of All the Quranic and Non Historical Epigraphs on the Protected Monuments in the Delhi Province, Calcutta, Government of India Publication, 1936.
4) Khan, Sir Syed Ahmad, *Asar-us-Sanadid*, Vol. I, ed. Khaliq Anjum, Delhi, Urdu Academy, Delhi, 1990.
5) Khan, Sir Syed Ahmad, *Asar-us-Sanadid*, Vol.III, ed. Khaliq Anjum, Delhi, Urdu Academy, Delhi, 1990.
6) Zafar, Hasan, *Monuments of India, Lasting Splendour of the Great Mughals* and others, Vol.II, New Delhi, Aryan Books International, 1997.
7) Zafar Hasan, *Monuments of Delhi, Lasting Splendour of the Great Mughals*,Vol.III, New Delhi, Aryan Books International, 1997.

Modern Works in Urdu:

1) Abdur Rehman, Syed Sabahuddin, *Bazm-i-Mamluqia,* Azamgarh, Matba'-i-Ma'arif, 1954.
2) Bhatti, Muhammad Ishaq, *Fuqaha-i-Hind*, Vol.I, Lahore, Idara-i-Saqafat-i-Islamia, 1974.
3) Gilani, Manazir Husain, *Hindustan Mein Musalmanon Ka Nizam Talim Wa Tarbiyat*, Delhi, Nadwat-ul-Mussanifin, 1987.
4) Nadvi, Abdul Hasanat, *Hindustan Ki Qadeem Islami Darsgahein*, Azamgarh, Darul Musaniffin, 1971.
5) Nadvi, Haji Muinuddin, *Khulafa-i-Rashidin* (being the first volume of *Siyar-us-Sahaba*), Azamgarh, Darul Musannifin, 1973.

6) Nadvi, Syed Abu Zafar, *Tarikh-i-Sindh*, Azamgarh, Matba'-i-Ma'arif, 1970.

7) Nizami, K.A., *Salatin-i-Delhi Ke Mazhabi Rujhanat*, Delhi, Nadwat-ul-Musaniffin, 1981.

8) Nizami, K.A., *Tarikh-i-Mashaikh-i-Chishti*, Vol.I, Dehi, Idara-i-Adabyat-i-Delhi, 1980.

9) Numani, Shibli, *Maqabat-i-Shibli*, Vol.3, ed. Syed Suleman Nadvi, Azamgarh, Mutba-i-Ma'arif, 1955.

10) Qazi Atahar, *Hindustan Mein Arbon Ki Hukumatein*, Delhi, Nadvat-ul-Musannifin, 1967.

11) Qazi, Atahar, *Khair-ul-Quran Ki Darsgahein Aur Unka Nizam-i-Talim Wa Tarbiyat*, Deoband, 1995.

12) Rafiq, Said Ahmad, *Islami Nizam-i-Ta'lim*, Karachi, Idarah-i- Tasnif Wa Talif, n.d.

13) Salik, Abdul Majid, *Muslim Saqafat-i-Hindustan Mein*, Lahore, Idara-i-Saqafat-i-Islamia, n.d.

14) Shaikh, M., Ikram, *Aab-i-Kauthar*, Delhi, Taj Company, 1987.

15) Syed, Abdul Hayy, *Hindustan Islami Ahd Mein*, Lucknow, Majlis-i-Tahqiqat-wa-Nashriyaat-i-Islam,1973.

16) Syed, Abdul Hayy, *Islamic Ulum wa Funun Hindustan Mein*, Azamgarh, Darul Musannifin, 1969.

Encyclopedias and Dictionary:

1) Brill, E.J., *The Encyclopedias of Islam*, Vol.IV, Leiden, The International Union of Academics, 1978.

2) Brill, E.J., *The Encyclopedias of Islam*, Vol.V, Leiden, The International Union of Academics, 1978.

3) Hughes, Thomas Patrick, *A Dictionary of Islam*, Vol.I, New Delhi, Cosmo Publication, 2004.

4) Martin, Richard-C, *Encyclopedia of Islam and the Muslim World*, Vol.II, U.S.A., Macmillan Reference, 2004.

Articles (English and Urdu):

1) Barani, Saeed Hasan, 'Imam Sughani, *Ma'arif*, Vol.24, No:1, July, 1929.
2) Hamidullah, M., 'Educational System in the time of the Prophet, *Islamic Culture*, Vol.13, No:1, Hyderabad, 1939.
3) Khan, Mohd. Abdul Mu'id, 'The Muslim Theories of Education during the middle age', *Islamic Culture*, Vol.XVIII, No:1, Hyderabad, Jan, 1944.
4) Khan, Muhammad A.R., 'A Survey of Muslim Contribution to Science and Culture', *Islamic Culture*, Vol.16, No:2, Hyderabad, 1942.
5) Khan, Muhammad Ijaz Hasan, 'Timuri Ahd Se Pehle Hindustan Mien Ilam Hadith Ka Rivaj', *Ma'arif*, Vol.24, 4 October, 1929.
6) Latif, S.A., 'Muslim Intellegensia (Danishmand) As Portrayed in the Sufic Literature of the 14th century. '
7) Maulana, Abdul Hayy, *Risalah Al Nadwah*, February, 1909.
8) Nadvi, Syed Sulayman, 'The Early Relations Between Arabia and India', *Islamic Culture*, Vol.II, No:2, Hyderabad, 1937.
9) Nadvi, Riyasat Ali, 'Kuch Fuqaha-i-Tatar Khani Ke bore Mein' *Ma'arif* 59/3, March, 1947.
10) Nizami, K.A., 'Iltutmish the mystic', *Islamic Culture*, 1946.
11) Nizami, K.A., 'The Impact of Ibn Tammiya on South Asia', in *Journal of Islamic Studies,* Oxford, Vol.I,1990.
12) Nizami, K.A., Development of the Muslim Educational System in Medieval India, *Islamic Culture*, Vol. LXX, No. 4, Hyderabad, Oct. 1996.
13) Samadi, S.B., 'Literary and scientific development and the growth of Rationalism in the time of Al Mamun' *Islamic Culture* Vol.30, No:2, Hyderabad, 1965.
14) Shirani, Mahmud, 'Adab-wa-harb-wa-Shuja'at', *Oriental College Magazine*, August, 1937.
15) Shafi Muhammad, 'Diwan-i-Mutahhar *Oriental College Magazine*, May, 1935.

16) Siddiqui, Iqtedar Husain, "Science and Scientific Instruments in the Sultanate of Delhi", *Hamdard Islamicus*, 17/3 Autumn, 1974.

17) *Urdu Magazine*, Urdu, January, 1943.

Index

'B'

'C'

'D'

'J'

'S'